×Leckie
the education publisher
for Scotland

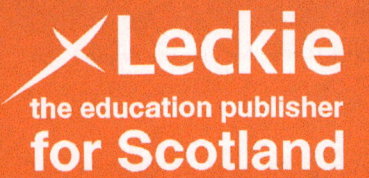

Higher
HISTORY

For SQA 2019 and beyond

Revision + Practice
2 Books in 1

© 2020 Leckie & Leckie Ltd

001/29012020

10 9 8 7 6 5 4 3 2 1

All rights reserved. No part of this publication may be reproduced, stored in a retrieval system, or transmitted in any form or by any means, electronic, mechanical, photocopying, recording or otherwise, without the prior written permission of the Publisher or a licence permitting restricted copying in the United Kingdom issued by the Copyright Licensing Agency Ltd., 90 Tottenham Court Road, London W1T 4LP.

The author asserts their moral right to be identified as the author of this work.

ISBN 9780008365318

Published by
Leckie & Leckie Ltd
An imprint of HarperCollins*Publishers*
Westerhill Road, Bishopbriggs, Glasgow, G64 2QT
T: 0844 576 8126   F: 0844 576 8131
leckiescotland@harpercollins.co.uk   www.leckiescotland.co.uk

Publisher: Sarah Mitchell
Project manager: Gillian Bowman and Lauren Murray

Special thanks to
Louise Robb (Proofread)
Sarah Duxbury (cover design)
Jouve (layout and illustration)

Printed and bound by CPI Group (UK) Ltd, Croydon CR0 4YY

A CIP Catalogue record for this book is available from the British Library.

Acknowledgements

We would like to thank the following for permission to reproduce their material:
P141 © Getty Images, P142 © Getty Images, P144 © Scottish Jewish Archive Centre, P150 © Getty Images, P151 © Popperfoto/Getty Images, P154–155 © Getty Images, P157 © Print Collector/Getty Images, P158 © UIG via Getty Images, P161a © Getty Images, P161b © IWM via Getty Images, P163 © Getty Images, P164 © Getty Images, P170–171 © Print Collector/Getty Images, P25a © Getty Images, P25b © SSPL via Getty Images, P28 © Heritage Images/Getty Images, P29 © Getty Images, P31 © Heritage Images/Getty Images, P32 © UIG via Getty Images, P35a © Getty Images, P35b © Getty Images, P38 © Popperfoto/Getty Images, P39 © SSPL via Getty Images, P40–41 © Getty Images, P42 © Getty Images, P44 © Getty Images, P47 © Getty Images, P49 © UIG via Getty Images, P51 © Print Collector/Getty Images, P58 © UIG via Getty Images, P60 © UIG via Getty Images, P62–63 © Print Collector/Getty Images, P65 © Getty Images, P66 © Getty Images, P71 © Getty Images, P72 © Getty Images, P75 © Getty Images, P76 © Getty Images, P78 © UIG via Getty Images, P80 © Getty Images, P83 © NY Daily News via Getty Images, P84 © Mondadori via Getty Images, P86–87 © AFP/Getty Images, P89 © Getty Images, P90 © Gamma-Keystone via Getty Images, P93 © Getty Images, P95 © AFP/Getty Images, P97 © Getty Images, P98 © Getty Images, P102 © Mondadori via Getty Images, P104 © Getty Images, P106 © Popperfoto/Getty Images, P107 © Popperfoto/Getty Images, P108–109 © Getty Images.

All other images © Shutterstock.com

Whilst every effort has been made to trace the copyright holders, in cases where this has been unsuccessful, or if any have inadvertently been overlooked, the Publishers would gladly receive any information enabling them to rectify any error or omission at the first opportunity.

ebook

To access the ebook version of this Revision Guide visit
www.collins.co.uk/ebooks
and follow the step-by-step instructions.

Contents

Introduction
The Higher History exam paper — 8
The History assignment — 17

PART 1: REVISION GUIDE

Question paper 1 – British, European and World History

Britain, 1851–1951
Key issue 1: An evaluation of the reasons why Britain became more democratic, 1851–1928 — 21
Key issue 2: An assessment of how democratic Britain became, 1867–1928 — 24
Key issue 3: An evaluation of the reasons why women won greater political equality by 1928 — 27
Key issue 4: An evaluation of the reasons why the Liberals introduced social welfare reforms, 1906–1914 — 31
Key issue 5: An assessment of the effectiveness of the Liberal social welfare reforms — 34
Key issue 6: An assessment of the effectiveness of the Labour social welfare reforms, 1945–1951 — 37

European and World

Germany, 1815–1939
Key issue 1: An evaluation of the reasons for the growth of nationalism in Germany, 1815–1850 — 42
Key issue 2: An assessment of the degree of growth of nationalism in Germany up to 1850 — 45
Key issue 3: An evaluation of the obstacles to German unification up to 1850 — 48
Key issue 4: An evaluation of the reasons why unification was achieved in Germany by 1871 — 52
Key issue 5: An evaluation of the reasons why the Nazis achieved power in 1933 — 55
Key issue 6: An evaluation of the reasons why the Nazis were able to stay in power, 1933–1939 — 58

USA, 1918–1968
Key issue 1: An evaluation of the reasons for changing attitudes towards immigration in the 1920s — 64
Key issue 2: An evaluation of the obstacles to the achievement of civil rights for black people up to 1941 — 68
Key issue 3: An evaluation of the reasons for the economic crisis of 1929–1933 — 71
Key issue 4: An assessment of the effectiveness of the New Deal — 74
Key issue 5: An evaluation of the reasons for the development of the Civil Rights campaign, after 1945 — 78
Key issue 6: An assessment of the effectiveness of the Civil Rights movement in meeting the needs of black Americans, up to 1968 — 82

Contents

Appeasement and the Road to War, to 1939

Key issue 1: An evaluation of the reasons for the aggressive nature of the foreign policies of Germany and Italy in the 1930s — 88

Key issue 2: An assessment of the methods used by Germany and Italy to pursue their foreign policies from 1933 — 92

Key issue 3: An evaluation of the reasons for the British policy of appeasement, 1936–1938 — 96

Key issue 4: An assessment of the success of British foreign policy in containing fascist aggression, 1935–March 1938 — 99

Key issue 5: An assessment of the Munich Agreement — 102

Key issue 6: An evaluation of the reasons for the outbreak of war in 1939 — 105

Question Paper 2 – Scottish History

The Wars of Independence, 1249–1328

Key issue 1: Alexander III and the succession problem 1286–92 — 110
Key issue 2: John Balliol and Edward I 1292–1296 — 116
Key issue 3: William Wallace and Scottish Resistance — 122
Key issue 4: The rise and triumph of Robert Bruce — 128

Migration and Empire, 1830–1939

Key issue 1: The migration of Scots — 140
Key issue 2: The experience of immigrants in Scotland — 143
Key issue 3: The impact of Scots emigrants on the Empire — 146
Key issue 4: The effects of migration and Empire on Scotland, to 1939 — 150

The Impact of the Great War, 1914–1928

Key issue 1: Scots on the Western Front — 156
Key issue 2: Domestic impact of war: society and culture — 160
Key issue 3: Domestic impact of war: industry and economy — 163
Key issue 4: Domestic impact of war: politics — 166

Answers — 172

PART 2: PRACTICE EXAM PAPERS

Introduction — 202

Paper 1 – BRITISH
The Making of Modern Britain, 1851–1951 — 210
Paper 1 – EUROPEAN AND WORLD
Germany, 1815–1939 — 212
USA, 1918–1968 — 214
Appeasement and the Road to War, to 1939 — 216
Paper 2 – SCOTTISH
The Wars of Independence, 1249–1328 — 220
Migration and Empire, 1830–1939 — 223
The Impact of the Great War, 1914–1928 — 226

ANSWERS Check your answers to the practice test papers online:
www.collins.co.uk/pages/Scottish-curriculum-free-resources

Introduction
About this book

Complete Revision and Practice

This **complete two-in-one revision and practice** book is designed to support you as a student of Higher History. It can be used either in the classroom, for regular study and homework, or for exam revision. By combining **a revision guide and one full set of practice exam papers**, this book includes everything you need to be fully familiar with the Higher History exam.

Using the revision guide

Test yourself
For every section you will be asked to 'Test yourself' and define a number of keywords. Understanding what these words mean will help you understand the issues more clearly, and ensure that you use them correctly in your assessments. You can find definitions for all of the words in the 'Answers' on page 172.

Essential knowledge
These are quick questions that you can use to make sure you know and understand the key facts for the section. The answers for these questions can be found at the back of the book.

Theme
These are questions that ask you to think a bit more deeply than the essential knowledge questions. Among other things, you will need to consider the causes of, and links between, events as well as the attitudes of people at the time in order to weigh up the relative importance of different factors. These questions will help you to develop your analysis and evaluation skills. Analysis and evaluation are worth a lot of marks in both the exam and the assignment, so it is good to get used to answering these types of questions. The answers to these questions are at the back of the book.

Using the practice exam papers

This book contains practice exam papers, which mirror the actual SQA exam as much as possible. The layout, paper colour and question level are all similar to the actual exam that you will sit, so that you are familiar with what the exam paper will look like.

The fully worked solution to each question is given online so that you can see how the right answer has been arrived at. The solutions are accompanied by a commentary that includes further explanations and advice. There is also an indication of how the marks are allocated and, where relevant, what the examiners will be looking for. Reference is made at times to the relevant sections in the revision guide.

Introduction

The topics

For Higher History you will study three topics, one British, one European/World and one Scottish. This book covers seven of the most popular topics:

British

Britain, 1851–1951

European and World

Germany, 1815–1939
USA, 1918–68
Appeasement and the Road to War, to 1939

Scottish

The Wars of Independence, 1249–1328.
Migration and Empire, 1830–1939
The Impact of the Great War, 1914–1928

In the next few pages you will find detailed information about how the exam and assignment will be set out and how they are marked. If you read this carefully you will know what the different types of question are asking you to do and exactly how you can pick up the most marks possible in your assessments.

Introduction
The Higher History exam paper

Your final exam paper will consist of TWO exam papers lasting for 1 hour and 30 minutes each. That is a total of 3 hours.

There is also an assignment, which is like a big essay. You have 1 hour and 30 minutes to write your assignment. You are allowed to choose your own title and have a written plan beside you to remind you of what you need to write. Your assignment is worth 30 marks.

What is in the exam paper?

The Higher History exam is divided into two exam papers.

The first exam paper is about British, European and world history. You write two essays, one on British history and one on European or world history. Each essay is worth 22 marks, so Higher History Paper One is worth in total 44 marks.

The second exam paper is about Scottish history. There are no essays to write but there are four different types of questions coming to a total of 36 marks.

Question paper 1: British, European and world history
Section 1

The first exam paper in Higher History is called British, European and world history and is divided between British history and European and world history.

There will be five parts in the **British history** topic. You will answer ONE question on ONE part only.

The parts are:

A: Church, State and Feudal Society, 1066–1406

B: The Century of Revolutions, 1603–1702

C: The Atlantic Slave Trade

D: Britain, 1851–1951

E: Britain and Ireland, 1900–1985

Question paper 1: British, European and world history
Section 2
European and world.

The layout of this section is very like the British section apart from the topics. There are NINE parts. You will answer ONE question on ONE part only. The parts are:

A: The Crusades, 1071–1204

B: The American Revolution, 1763–1787

C: The French Revolution, to 1799

D: Germany, 1815–1939

E: Italy, 1815–1939

F: Russia, 1881–1921

Introduction

G: USA, 1918–1968

H: Appeasement and the Road to War, to 1939

I: The Cold War, 1945–1989

Question paper 2: Scottish history

The second Higher History exam paper is called Scottish history. It is worth 36 marks out of a total of 110 for both the exam papers.

There are five parts to the Scottish section. You answer questions on ONE part only.

The parts are:

A: The Wars of Independence, 1249–1328

B: The Age of the Reformation, 1542–1603

C: The Treaty of Union, 1689–1740

D: Migration and Empire, 1830–1939

E: The Impact of the Great War, 1914–1928

Each part will be divided into four different sections called 'Key Issues'.

For example, the Key Issues for Part D: Migration and Empire, 1830–1939 are:

1. The migration of Scots.
2. The experience of immigrants in Scotland.
3. The impact of Scots emigrants on the Empire.
4. The effects of migration and empire on Scotland, to 1939.

You need to be really clear about what you have to know about each of the four sections, so check with your teacher or go to the SQA website to find out. There will be four questions based on four sources and the questions will have marks of different values. The style of the questions is based on the following question structures:

- 'How fully does Source … explain …' is worth 10 marks.
- 'Evaluate the usefulness of Source … as evidence of …' is worth 8 marks.
- 'How much do Sources X and Y reveal about differing interpretations of ...' is worth 10 marks.
- 'Explain the reasons why …' is worth 8 marks.

If the question asked "Explain the reasons why the First World War had such a significant impact on Scottish culture and society," you could write, "There were many reasons why the First World War had such a significant impact on Scottish culture and society.

The first impact was recruitment and conscription. This affected Scottish society because …

Another impact on Scottish society was the role of women. This happened because …

New laws such as DORA affected society because …

Culturally, Scottish artists and writers expressed the grief of the nation. This was important because …

and so on.

Introduction

To summarise, in your final exam:

- You have TWO final exam papers each lasting 1 hour 30 minutes, making a total time of 3 hours.
- Exam paper 1 contains questions on Britain, Europe and the world. You write one essay answer on Britain and one essay answer on Europe and the world.
- Each essay is worth 22 marks.
- Exam paper 2 contains questions on Scottish history. There are 5 parts. You answer questions on one part.
- Each part has four questions based on four sources.
- The total marks for this exam paper is 36.
- There is also a longer piece of work called the assignment, which is a longer essay based on an essay title that you choose. You have time in class to plan your assignment and you are allowed to write a plan to use when writing your assignment. It is worth 30 marks. There is more about your assignment later in this book.

How do I get as many marks as possible?

Structure

The STRUCTURE of your essay means the way you build up your essay by including various stages. Each stage of your essay has a set number of marks attached to it.

Stage 1 is an **introduction**, which is worth a maximum of 3 marks.

Stage 2 is the use of **knowledge** to show off what you know. There are 6 marks to be gained here.

Stage 3 is worth 6 marks. **Analysis** means how you explain WHY your information is important and relevant to answering the question.

Stage 4 is worth 4 marks and is for **evaluation**. That means you link the ideas you have about the main question and explain why one idea is more important than another in answering the main question.

Stage 5 is the **conclusion** and is worth 3 marks. This ends your essay by making an overall answer to the question which takes into account the factors you have written about and how you have used those factors to arrive at your overall answer.

Stage 1 – The introduction

You will get up to 3 marks for your introduction if you do 3 things:

You must include **a context**. That means you must set the scene by describing the 'back story' of the question. In a couple of sentences describe the historical situation that the question is based on. Include at least two hard facts within your description of the context.

You need to give a **line of argument**. The easiest way to do this is to use the words in the question, especially the main focus of the question. So, if a question asks, 'How important were fears over national security in causing the Liberal reforms of 1906–1914?', a simple but effective line of argument would be to write, 'Fears over national security were partly responsible for causing the Liberal reforms, but there were several other factors that pushed the Liberals towards social reform. These factors include…'

Introduction

You can use this style for almost every essay you write. To use a topic you are not likely to study, you can see how the process works. In 'The Atlantic Slave Trade' topic you could be asked 'To what extent were racist attitudes a reason for the development of the slave trade?'

Once again, a simple but effective line of argument would be to write, 'Racist attitudes were partly responsible for the development of the slave trade but there were several other factors that also led to the growth of the slave trade.'

You must also include **the main headings or factors** that you are going to explain in the main body of your essay. These can be done in a list or, more effectively, treated separately with one sentence on each. This shows that you understand the topic and are showing the marker what you are going to develop as part of your answer. An example based on the Liberal reform question mentioned earlier would be, 'The other factors that influenced the Liberals were the shock and concerns raised by the reports of Booth and Rowntree into poverty in London and York, and also worries about national efficiency. They were also aware that the growing Labour party might cause a threat and a new political idea called New Liberalism was taking hold in the party.' To show this same process working based on the Slave Trade topic mentioned before, go to the SQA website and look at Course Specifications for Higher History. Find the course descriptor for the Slave Trade topic (on page 6) and you will see that in key issue 1, which is about reasons for the development of the slave trade, there are five possible reasons listed under 'Description of content'. One of those reasons is 'racist attitudes'. In your answer you write that racist attitudes was partly the reason for the development of the slave trade, but that there were four other reasons that were also important. Write about all five reasons then make a judgement about the relative importance of each reason.

Stage 2 – Knowledge

You will get up to 6 marks for using accurate and detailed knowledge. You will not get marks for simply mentioning the facts, as they must show your relevant knowledge as you construct an answer to the main question; in other words, you will not get marks simply for including 'correct' information. For example, in an essay about votes for women, you will not get a mark for writing that the WSPU was formed by Emmeline Pankhurst in 1903. You would get a mark for writing that the WSPU formed by the Pankhursts was an important organisation in the struggle for women's rights. Always remember to make clear why you have included some information – what point are you leading up to making?

Stages 3 and 4 – Analysis and evaluation

In total there are 10 marks for this part of your answer. THAT MEANS THAT ALMOST HALF YOUR MARKS IN EACH ESSAY COMES FROM YOUR ANALYSIS AND EVALUATION.

When it comes to **analysis**, you can get up to 3 marks maximum for simply commenting on your information such as 'This was important because ...'. You would need to do that several times to get 3 marks.

To get ANOTHER three marks for developed analysis, you should weigh up your evidence by giving different points of view.

Basic analysis (3 marks max)

You will get 3 marks if you made **basic comments** about the information you have included that are relevant to the question.

Introduction

At this basic but effective level, after you have included a factual detail you could write, 'This is important because …'. That way you cannot avoid using your knowledge to make a judgement about the information.

For example, if a question asked 'To what extent was propaganda important to the Nazi control of Germany after 1933', you write a simple comment that, 'Propaganda, such as rallies at Nuremberg, was important because it was watched by thousands of Germans and they were pleased to feel proud of their country again'. That is a simple comment about propaganda. You mentioned rallies and you used the 'because' word to give a reason why they were important. By doing this you will have made a basic analysis comment.

Developed analysis giving a possible total of 6 marks for analysis.

You can get 3 more marks if you **link your comments directly to the factor** you are writing about.

To follow on from the example above about rallies and propaganda in Nazi Germany, you could continue by writing, 'By making Germans feel proud and confident again, the rallies showed that Hitler was keeping his promise of restoring German pride and destroying the hated Treaty of Versailles; these were vital steps in maintaining Nazi control over Germany.' The phrase 'were vital steps in maintaining Nazi control over Germany' is what gains you marks here because you have linked your comments to the main question.

This is a developed comment. You will get 1 mark for a developed comment and if you do it consistently throughout your essay, you can get a total possible 6 marks for analysis.

Evaluation (4 marks max)

You will get up to 4 marks for evaluating your information in terms of the question.

In other words, evaluation is the **judgements** you make about the importance of the main **FACTORS** in terms of the main question rather than just commenting on the factual details you include about each individual factor.

By referring back to the propaganda in Nazi Germany question used above, if you can suggest that, while propaganda was important, there were other more important ways the Nazis maintained control, then that is evaluation of the factors.

You could also weigh up the importance of propaganda by mentioning the negative side of propaganda that suggests it was not such an important reason for keeping control in Germany. For example, you could write, 'While propaganda was important in pleasing many Germans and keeping their support, it really only appealed to Nazi supporters. Those people who did not support the Nazis also had to be controlled and for these people the use of fear and force was more important in maintaining control.'

In this example two main factors – propaganda and force – have been matched together and an evaluation of their importance has been made.

The main thing about evaluation is to comment on the relative importance of the factors and how they help answer the main question. You should also link them to your line of argument set up in the introduction and attempt to prioritise your factors in terms of their importance to the main question.

Stage 5 – Conclusion

- The conclusion is worth up to 3 marks.
- You will get 1 mark if you just summarise the information you have included in your answer. For example, "There were several factors that combined to ...... These were ...... Overall the answer to the question is...."
- You will get 2 marks if you can make an overall judgement about the factors you have mentioned in terms of the question and if you answer the question directly. For example "My overall answer to the question in the title is ..... All the factors I have mentioned in this essay are relevant to the question because one factor did this... and another factor caused that..... Probably the most important factors were because....
- You will get 3 marks if you do all the stages above and also prioritise the factors so that it is clear which you think were most important in terms of the question and why. For example, "My overall answer to the question in the title is ..... All the factors I have mentioned in this essay are relevant but some are more important than others in terms of the overall question.

    The most important factor/factors are .... because......

    On balance, the factors that are less important than the others but which contributed to my overall decision, namely ...... are less important because ......

The essay questions are worth 22 marks each

In question paper 1 containing the British and European/World sections, you will be required to write ONE essay answer on each section. That means you write two essays and these essays can be constructed in exactly the same way.

Timing

Given that there is 90 minutes to complete Paper 1 which consists of two essays it is fairly obvious that you should spend 45 minutes on one essay and 45 minutes on the other one.

As a rough rule you should aim for about five good paragraphs between your introduction and conclusion.

Your introduction should have been well rehearsed so you could spend 5 minutes on it.

You can also rehearse good conclusions so that's another 5 minutes. Lets call the intro and conclusion together 15 minutes. That leaves 30 minutes for five paragraphs so 6 minutes for a paragraph is plenty time to do what you need to do.

But BE CAREFUL for the following reasons:

1. Do not let yourself get bogged down in detail and try to 'polish up' your first essay by stealing time from the second essay. You will not gain many more marks if any. But you will lose marks gaining time from your second essay. BE STRICT WITH YOURSELF.
2. Do not cram your essay with facts and more facts. There are only 6 fact marks in any essay. If you try to squeeze in another 10 facts you will not get any more than 6. Aim for RELEVANT facts that are important in answering the question, not just linked to the topic within the question.
3. THINK. There are 10 marks for analysis and evaluation. Allow time to make it clear why the information you are including is relevant and important to your answer and if you can , explain why some of the information is less or more important than others. In other words try to PRIORITISE your points in terms of their importance to the question.

Introduction

How do I write my answers?

The source-based questions

What follows is advice on how you might choose to answer the source-based questions. You do NOT have to copy this style but it IS effective and scores marks because you will then be in no doubt you are doing what you have to do to score marks. Try it and see.

The two-source question is worth 10 marks

You will be given two sources. Both sources will be about the same subject but will contain different points of view.

Your first task is to identify the points of view in each source and then to explain what the views are in your own words. This is not just copying the source or putting it into your own words. You must use your own knowledge to explain why the writer holds the views expressed in the source.

The next step is to do the same again with the second source and the finally to explain, using your own knowledge of any extra information, why the common issue to both sources causes such different opinions.

The 'Evaluate the evidence of Source ... as evidence of ..." question is worth 10 marks

A very important point to remember for this question is always to relate its usefulness as evidence to the Scottish context.

For example, a question about Scots in the Great War might ask about trench conditions. If you just list information about rats, lice, boredom, snipers and all the usual stuff you run the risk of gaining zero marks because you have not made it clear you are referring to Scottish soldiers. Ask for advice on how to do this and rehearse it before the exam if you do the Great War topic.

Remember to answer the question that is asked. You are not just being asked to judge how useful a source is as evidence for finding out about a specific historical event.

Below the question in the exam paper you will find this instruction:
In making a judgement you should refer to:

- *The origin and possible purpose of the source.*
- *The content of the source.*
- *Your own (recalled) knowledge.*

In reality you can get up to 4 marks for writing about **WHO** wrote it and how that makes the source more or less useful as evidence for finding out about the subject of the question. The source for this sort of question will always be from a primary source, so you can be sure the author of the source was involved in the events that the question is asking about in some way.

What type of source it is makes the source more or less useful as evidence for finding out about the subject of the question.

What was the purpose of writing the source and how does that make the source more of less useful as evidence for finding out about the subject of the question? Here is a possible plan for this part of your answer: The purpose of the source was probably to … (Inform? Persuade? Relieve boredom? Persuade someone to do something?) and

Introduction

this makes it useful because … (In other words, suggest a likely reason WHY the author of the source wrote it. Remember, even biased thoughts or propaganda are still useful because it shows how people felt at the time.)

When the source was written makes the source more of less useful as evidence for finding out about the subject of the question. The date of the source also makes the source useful because … (Was it during an important event and therefore shows how people felt at the time, or was it later, suggesting the author has had time to look back on the event and perhaps take a more balanced viewpoint?).

You can also get 2 marks for commenting on what is not in the source (from **your own knowledge**) that would, if it had been included, have made the source more useful.

You can get 2 marks for explaining why the **content** of the source is useful for judging the source's usefulness as evidence. You should select brief extracts from the source, explain what they mean in your own words and explain why your choices make the source useful as evidence in terms of the question. In other words, how does the content of the source help us to understand the events or the opinion of people involved in the event?

The **content** of the source is also useful because it contains information relevant to the topic. The source states '…' and this makes the source useful in terms of the question because '…' (In other words, how does the content of the source help us to understand the events or the opinion of people involved in the event?)

What is missing?

You can get up to 3 marks for including extra information that would have made the source more useful as evidence if the new information had been included. You need at least 3 new pieces of explained information to get the marks.

The 'How fully' question is worth 10 marks

The most important thing to remember in an answer to this question is to make a judgement in terms of the question. In other words, the questions asks 'how fully, so you **always** start your answer by writing 'the source only **partly** explains …'. That way you have made a judgement and opened up your answer so you can write about the source and extra, relevant information from your recall.

If you **do not** have a judgement, you can only get 2 of the 10 marks, no matter how much more you write.

You will be given a source that contains information relevant to the question but it will **never** give all the relevant information. There are 3 marks for this section, so to answer this part of the question you must select **four** extracts from the source that are relevant to the question asked. For each extract you select, you must make clear how it links to the question. Do that **four** times.

You must then include as much extra information from your own knowledge that would help to give a much fuller explanation or description of what the question is asking about. There are 7 marks available for this section, so you should include up to seven extra pieces of accurate and relevant information and explain in your own words **why** this extra information is relevant to the question.

This is what you write:

> The source partly explains … (*what the question is asking*). Firstly, the source states, '…' and this links to the question because …

Introduction

Do this four times for 4 marks.

Then you write:

> There are also points relevant to the question that are not mentioned in the source. Firstly … (*Include your fact knowledge and then explain how it helps to make a fuller answer to the question.*)

Do this seven times to get as many marks as possible.

The Explain question is worth 8 marks. It is not based on any sources.

The main point about this question is to be clear about what you are being asked to explain and to not just read the topic of the question.

Beware your answer does not just become a description of events linked to the question topic.

A good way to answer this question and keep it relevant is to write 'There are many reasons why …' (insert the core of the question here).

The first reason why … is because …..

The next reason why … is because … and so on until you have written at least 8 reasons.

The word 'because' is always useful because you cannot write 'because' without giving a reason and that is what the question wants you to do.

Introduction

The History assignment

Why is it important?

As part of your final exam mark you must complete an assignment. This is done earlier in the course, maybe a month or two before the exam. It is really important because it gives you a huge launch pad to success. Your final exam is out of 80 marks. The assignment can be worth 30 marks to you. The total marks for your Higher History assessment is therefore 110 and that means the History assignment is worth between one-third and one-quarter of your final mark.

What should I write about?

Your assignment can be on any topic you choose but it would be wise to write about something you know about! DO NOT try to make up your questions. Making up suitable questions is very difficult and time consuming. Don't waste your time. Choose a question from a past paper. That way you cannot be criticised for an inappropriate question.

What is the resource sheet?

When you write out your assignment under exam conditions in school or college you will have 90 minutes to do it **and** you will have your History resource sheet plan beside you to help you write your assignment.

Your History resource sheet is a sort of plan to remind you what you are going to report about and is sent to the SQA with your assignment. It must be on one side of an A4 sheet. You can bullet point information and include mind maps or other memory diagrams; however, this does **not** mean you can write out a version of your assignment then copy it across. Copying chunks of text from your resource sheet on to your assignment is **not** allowed. However, you **are** allowed to copy across source extracts you want to include in your assignment.

What are historical sources?

You can get up to 4 marks for including quotes from secondary sources written by historians, or from primary sources. These quotes **must** be fully credited in your resource sheet with the name of the author and the title of the book, article, magazine, documentary, podcast or whatever source you used. However, a mention of a vague website will not be counted as a source to gain a mark.

How should I use the source quotes?

Be careful that you do not just include a fact you find in a book, then use that as a resource. Your resources must be references: accurate and relevant. For example, do not write something like 'The First World War started in 1914 (by A. W. Riter, A History of the World)'. This has no opinion or historical argument.

A good idea here would be to use quotes from historians with different viewpoints. By doing that, you can show that events in history have different interpretations. For example, if you were writing about German nationalism in the 19th century, you could write, '"The Zollverein was the mighty lever of unification" (W. Carr, *History of Germany*)', and then you could include a different point of view suggesting that Bismarck was much more important than the Zollverein in leading to unification. Using quotes from historians can be very useful in both Paper 1 and Paper 2 as long as you remember that the quotes must express a point of view and preferably use another quote to show a different point of view.

Introduction

> In that way you can build up an argument USING your factual knowledge to show the differing opinions about a question.
>
> BUT BEWARE! Just because you name a historian does not mean your quote is useful.
>
> If you wrote "John Kerr wrote "The Second Reform Act happened in 1867" you will get no credit. It is just a statement of fact. If you wrote that John Kerr wrote that "The Second Reform Act led to a great growth in British democracy but AJP Taylor wrote that the 1867 Act did little for democracy since there was still no secret voting and power still rested with the wealthy" then there you have an argument!

How will the assignment be marked?

Your History assignment is just a big version of your essays and it is constructed in the same way. Use the advice on writing essays for sections 1 and 2 of the exam (pages 10–13) and you will be fine.

The only difference is that there are more marks for the different parts:

- You can score up to **3 marks** for your introduction.
- You can get up to **8 marks** for using accurate and relevant factual information to support your line of argument.
- You will get up to **4 marks** for using sources to support a point you are making.
- You can get up to **7 marks** for analysing and a further **5 marks** for evaluating your main points or factors to develop your line of argument. When commenting on your information in terms of the question, remember the advice on how to write analysis and evaluation for the essays (see pages 13–16).
- Finally, you can get up to **3 marks** for a conclusion that uses the style outlined for the essays in the exam (see page 13).
- Remember the words 'up to'. That means you do not get 3 marks automatically just for having a short introduction or one-sentence conclusion. The markers look to see if you have earned the marks by using your information to meet the criteria set by the SQA.

TOP TIP

Go to the SQA Higher History website and look for past papers. Open the past paper MARKING SCHEMES. Look carefully at the first few pages and you will find what is need to score marks for all the different sections of your exam.

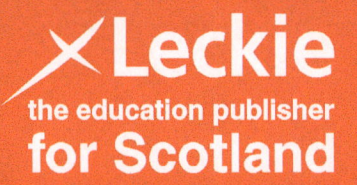

Higher HISTORY

For SQA 2019 and beyond

Leckie — the education publisher for Scotland

Revision Guide

John Kerr

Britain, 1851–1951

Key issue 1: An evaluation of the reasons why Britain became more democratic, 1851–1928

What is this section all about?

Between 1867 and 1928, many more people in Britain were given the right to vote. However, it is only in hindsight that we see an apparently linked sequence of reforms that extended the franchise in Britain. Each Parliamentary Reform Act – 1867, 1884, 1918 and 1928 – was the result of different pressures; this section is about the pressures that caused these changes.

TOP TIP
In any answer about the extension of the franchise (WHY more people gained the right to vote) you must deal with the specific reasons why each of the reforms in 1867, 1884, 1918 and 1928 were passed.

An evaluation of the reasons why Britain became more democratic, 1851–1928

- The effects of industrialisation and urbanisation
- The 1867 and 1884 Reform Acts: pressure groups changing political attitudes and gaining advantage for a political party.
- Examples of developments abroad
- Getting an advantage for a political party
- The effects of the First World War

What were the effects of industrialisation and urbanisation?

Urbanisation means the growth of towns and cities. Industrialisation means the change from home-made and locally produced items to a factory system. As more and more people came together in cramped living and working conditions, changes happened that were to have political consequences. New ideas began to spread. Working people became aware of their shared identity and that grew into an awareness of themselves as a 'working class'.

Before 1850, the old political system was based on land ownership and an unchanging society. Throughout the later 19th century, those ideas were changing as more democratic ideas spread. The 1832 Reform Act was passed to give a greater political voice to the middle classes but the years after 1850 saw the growth and expression of the working class voice. In 1867, the skilled working class (artisans), who paid a fairly high property rent in towns, were given the vote. In 1884, rural workers were given the vote on the same rules.

Question paper 1: British, European and World History

Why did the Second Reform Act of 1867 happen?

1. By the mid-19th century, political ideas of liberalism (the right of individuals to express their opinions freely) and democracy (the right of adults to choose the governments that rule them) were becoming popular in the United States and Europe. The British government policy tended to support these moves elsewhere, so how could political parties continue to block these ideas within Britain?

2. The growing respectability of urban artisans – politicians were not as concerned with the danger of revolution breaking out as they had been earlier in the century. By the 1860s, skilled working men in cities were more educated and 'respectable', so it was not such a risk giving them the vote.

3. National protest campaigns were effective – before 1867, the National Reform Act and the Reform League are examples of pressure groups. A pressure group is when people band together to demonstrate, collect petitions and in different ways apply pressure to parliament to make political changes.

4. Would there be violence if changes did not happen? Earlier in the 19th century, there was a feeling that some reform would reduce pressure for reform. After a large meeting in Hyde Park, London in 1866, riots broke out demanding reform, so perhaps it was better to grant some changes than try to hold back demands for reform?

5. Gaining political advantage – this is probably the most important reason in explaining the passing of the Second Reform Act in 1867. A new Conservative government came in to power and they knew the Liberals were thinking of making a new Reform Act. The Conservatives thought that if they got in first with their Reform Act, they would gain the votes from the new voters.

The next extension of the franchise occurred in 1884. Why did it happen?

To weaken the influence of land-owning aristocracy	The power of the land-owning aristocracy was declining by the 1880s. City-based politicians resented the power of the old land-owning class, especially now that almost half the population was living in towns. Since voting was made secret in 1872, the city MPs hoped rural working men would vote for who they wanted, not necessarily the landowners. That would weaken the power of the old land-owning families in Parliament.
Why not give the vote to rural labourers?	The different voting rules between countryside (county) and town (boroughs/burghs) seemed pointless. There now seemed little difference between urban and rural workers, so the reform act removed the distinction.
Socialism was seen as a growing threat that needed taming	If large numbers of people were denied the vote, they might be attracted to new political ideas that were more revolutionary. The political 'establishment' believed that by including more of the working classes in the political system, they might be more easily controlled and less inclined to support revolutionary ideas.

Britain, 1851–1951

Why did the First World War cause such a political change?

- In 1916, conscription was introduced for the first time in Britain and is relevant to the issue. Men were ordered to join the armed forces or do work of national importance. Was it right that the government could order men to fight and kill on its behalf and not allow these men a chance to choose the government? Franchise reform was necessary for that to happen.

- During the war, Prime Minister Herbert Asquith, who was against votes for women, was replaced by David Lloyd George, who was more willing to accept change.

- During the war, women worked for the war effort and so gained respect and balanced the negative publicity of the Suffragette campaign. By 1917/1918, there were plans to change the rules about voting as they applied to men, and as the rules were changing anyway it was suggested that some women could also be included.

- The government was worried about what Suffragettes would do when the war ended. If violent protests started up again, the government could not climb down and give women the vote, so the long dispute would continue. However, if some women were given the vote in 1918, the principle of women voting would be established and there would be no need to start up the Suffragette campaign again.

- One of the main rules about who could vote involved a residency qualification that meant that voters had to have lived at the same address for some time. Men who were away fighting had lost that qualification. It was politically unacceptable to tell those men when they returned from the war that they had lost their right to vote, so the rules had to change.

- By the end of the First World War it was clear that internationally, Britain was not living up to its title of the 'mother of democracy'. Other countries had already given the vote to men and women. Even the new Weimar Constitution of 1920 in Germany gave the vote to all men and women over 20.

Check your understanding

ESSENTIAL KNOWLEDGE

1. Choose four of the following words or phrases and explain why they are catalysts for political change in Britain between 1851 and 1951:
   - Urbanisation
   - Class consciousness
   - Industrialisation
   - War
   - Political pragmatism
   - Political pressure groups

THEME QUESTION

1. Why did industrialisation and urbanisation provoke such changes?
2. What are pressure groups?

TEST YOURSELF

Do you know the meaning of these key words?

Franchise
Electorate
Constituency
Pragmatic

Question paper 1: British, European and World History

Key issue 2: An assessment of how democratic Britain became, 1867–1928

What is this section all about?

Between 1867 and 1928, Britain became more democratic. That does not just mean more people gained the right to vote, because without a fair system of voting and a choice of who to vote for no system can be called democratic. This section is about how various important features that make a political system democratic came into being. Your task is to judge how far those changes turned Britain into a democracy.

TOP TIP
Any question based on this section will ask you how far Britain had become democratic between 1867 and a later date. It really does not matter when the end date is. Your argument should always be Britain had certainly become MORE democratic and you may want to extend your argument by explaining what had not yet happened by the time the essay end date arrived.

An assessment of how democratic Britain became, 1867–1928:
- The widening of the franchise, 1867–1928
- Changes in the distribution of seats
- Changes in laws about corruption and intimidation
- Widening membership of the House of Commons
- The role of the House of Lords

What is the definition of a democracy?

A useful way to start a 'democracy' essay is to define democracy. You should outline the rights that people should have if a country is democratic. The following sections give you ideas for what should be in an essential list for any 'democracy' answer.

The vote

The vote is a vital part of a democracy. Therefore, giving the vote to more people did make Britain

TOP TIP
Try to avoid building your essay around sweeping statements such as 'In a democracy, people have freedom of speech, freedom of religion and freedom of the press'. While these are true, very few students know enough detail to develop these points in their essays and consequently the essay loses direction.

more democratic. For this section, you need to know when the franchise was extended and who benefited.

- In 1867, most skilled working-class men in towns got the vote.
- In 1884, many more men in the countryside were given the vote.
- In 1918, men over 21 and some women over 30 gained the vote.
- Finally, in 1928 men and women over 21 were given the vote.

TOP TIP
Having the right to vote does not automatically mean that a country is democratic. There also has to be a fair voting system.

Fairness

In a democracy, people should have a fair system of voting.

1. The Ballot Act of 1872 allowed people to vote in secret for the first time. The Act affected the way the franchise was operated and ended bribery and the intimidation of voters at elections.

2. The redistribution of parliamentary seats, especially in 1867 and 1885, gave growing towns the right to send more MPs to parliament.

Voters take advantage of the full secret ballot in the British general elections of 17th April 1880.

3. Another move towards fairness at elections was the Corrupt and Illegal Practices Act, which made election fraud or bribery criminal offences.

Choice

A country is not democratic if voters have no choice, even if they can vote in secret! Until the end of the 19th century, British politics was dominated by two political parties – the Conservatives and the Liberals. In 1900, the Labour Representation Committee, soon known as the Labour Party, was created. As a result of the creation of the Labour Party, the electorate (people with the right to vote) now had a genuine choice between parties with different policies and ideas.

Access to information

Voters need information about their candidates, which is why access to information is a vital part of a democracy. As the size of the electorate grew, individual political parties had to make sure that voters could be reached and persuaded to vote for them. The spread of railways across Britain also allowed news and information to spread quickly and for politicians to tour their constituencies explaining their policies. Sources of information could be accessed at the new public libraries being built across cities, the spread of cheap daily newspapers, and increasingly popular public meetings where speakers explained the big issues of the time.

Railways had helped the circulation of newspapers, distributing them quickly so that they were available all over Britain on the day they were published.

Question paper 1: British, European and World History

The power of the Lords

By 1900 there were many more voters and the power of landowners seemed to have been reduced. Elections were still infrequent and the unelected House of Lords had the power to veto, or scrap, any of the proposals for new laws that came from the House of Commons. The Parliament Act of 1911 reduced the power of the House of Lords and replaced their veto with the ability to delay bills from the House of Commons for two years. It meant that the House of Lords, which was not elected by anyone, could no longer stop the work of the House of Commons.

Participation

For most of the 19th century, MPs were not paid and had to own land. Working class men who had to work for fairly low wages could not afford to give up their day jobs. In 1858, the Property Qualification was abolished. That meant MPs no longer had to own land. Although this is before 1867, it would be a perfectly valid thing to write about. More importantly, as part of the Parliament Act 1911, MPs started to be paid, thereby allowing ordinary people to stand for election.

Check your understanding

ESSENTIAL KNOWLEDGE

1. Which was the more important House before 1911 in terms of law making?
2. Which is the more important House in terms of democracy?
3. Why could Britain not be called fully democratic in 1928?
4. Choose two of the following headings and in no more than two sentences explain why they are relevant points to make in an answer about the growth of democracy:
   - The right to vote
   - A fair system of voting
   - Choice
   - Information

THEME QUESTION

1. Which is more democratic – House of Commons or House of Lords?

TEST YOURSELF

Do you know the meaning of these key words?

Veto

Participation

'The Commons'

Redistribution of seats

Britain, 1851–1951

Key issue 3: An evaluation of the reasons why women won greater political equality by 1928

What is this section all about?

You must know about reasons why some women gained the right to vote in the early 20th century. You must also be able to describe the most important reasons and then be able to explain which of those reasons you think were the most significant for women gaining the right to vote.

An evaluation of the reasons why women won greater political equality by 1928:
- Changing attitudes to women in society
- The women's suffrage campaigns
- The militant Suffragette campaign up to 1914
- The part played by women in the war effort, 1914–18
- The example of other countries

The changing status of women in society

By 1900, women, especially middle-class women, were better educated, often at universities, and could even vote in local politics. New professions were opening to women, while they were also increasingly important in trade unions. Changes in the law had also improved women's social position and by the end of the 19th century, married women were no longer the possessions of their husbands. Married women could own their own property and could gain custody of their own children after divorce, something that was not possible in 1850.

TOP TIP

Avoid making generalised comments such as, 'women were seen as second-class citizens'. That attitude was more common in 1850 but had changed by 1900.

27

Question paper 1: British, European and World History

However – BEWARE!! For many women, especially working-class women, their lives changed little. The majority of women still suffered from low pay, bad working conditions, abuse, poverty and sexist prejudice. It was those difficulties faced by the majority of women that caused Emmeline Pankhurst to start the Women's Social and Political Union (WSPU) to help women's **social** position by gaining a **political** voice. Not all attitudes did change and many women were against votes for women.

The WSPU shop in Reading, Berkshire, July 1910.

> ### Think point
> An issue that is often ignored in the story of votes for women is that many MEN did not have the vote before 1914 and it was hardly likely that women would gain the vote before men. Even after the reform of 1884, almost 40% of men did not have the right to vote.

How important were the women's suffrage campaigns?

In 1897, a number of local women's suffrage societies formed the National Union of Women's Suffrage Societies (NUWSS). Clearly, the separate suffrage societies had not had much success before forming the NUWSS so one answer is that the early suffrage societies did not achieve very much. The NUWSS was nicknamed the Suffragists and they believed in peaceful tactics to win the vote.

> ### Think point
> Recent historians suggest that the NUWSS was more important than previously thought. Membership of the NUWSS remained high – 53,000 members in 1914, and when the Suffragettes became more violent, membership of the NUWSS rose as women left the WSPU!

How important was the militant Suffragette campaign?

In 1903, the Women's Social and Political Union (WSPU) was formed. It was members of the WSPU that became known as Suffragettes. Their motto was 'deeds not words' and from 1912 onwards the Suffragettes became more militant, which means they used more violent protest methods.

There is great debate among historians regarding the importance of the Suffragettes. It could be argued that they kept the issue of women's suffrage in the news as violent

> **TOP TIP**
> Do not spend a long time just describing what the Suffragettes did. Use some examples to help answer the question set but also explain why your description is relevant to answering the question.

Suffragette methods (such as firebombs and attacking politicians, hunger strikes and the resulting Cat and Mouse Act) made big headlines. However, as the Suffragettes adopted more militant tactics between 1912 and 1914, it could be argued that they alienated the public. Furthermore, it can be argued that their tactics made the government determined not to give in to what would today be called terrorism. The suspension of the Suffragette campaign during the war meant that the government could grant the vote to women without appearing to give in to violence.

On the other hand, it can be argued that one reason the government gave the vote to some women in 1918 was to prevent the Suffragettes from restarting their campaign after the war. So, indirectly, it could be argued that the influence of the Suffragettes continued until 1918.

How important was the women's war effort?

It will always be relevant to argue that the war work done by women during the Great War influenced the political decision to give some women the right to vote. However, there are two ways of doing this. The first way is the rather easy, simplistic way. Many candidates argue that because women replaced men on the home front during the war, they were granted the vote as a 'thank you' in 1918. Women's war work **did** gain women respectability and support. The sight of women doing war work acted as a balance to counter the negative images of women during Suffragette 'outrages'.

A woman munitions worker operating a machine in an armaments factory during the First World War.

However, the women who worked hard and risked their lives in munitions factories were mostly single and in their late teens or early 20s. The women who were given the vote were 'respectable' ladies who were 30 or over and who were property owners or married to property owners. So can the argument about a 'thank you' for war effort really be the whole answer?

By 1917/1918 there were plans to change the rules about voting as they applied to men. With such changes happening anyway, it was suggested that some 'respectable' women should be added to the list of new voters in part to stop the Suffragettes from starting action again.

Question paper 1: British, European and World History

Did changes around the world have an effect?

Throughout the later 19th century, some European countries, US states and British Empire colonies gave women the right to vote on certain conditions. By 1918 it would be fair to say that the issue of votes for women had spread around the world. Britain was certainly not leading the way in democratic reform. The Representation of the People Act (1918) gave the vote to 8 million women over the age of 30 who met at least one of the following requirements: were either a householder or the wife of a householder; or lived in property with an annual rent of at least £5; or were a graduate of a British university.

However, women under 30 and many poor women over 30 still did not have the vote and had to wait another 10 years until they did. Following the passing of the 1918 Act, the NUWSS and WSPU were both disbanded and replaced by a new organisation called the National Union of Societies for Equal Citizenship. This group campaigned for equal voting rights, equal pay and an end to discrimination at work. In 1928, the Equal Franchise Act gave women and men equal rights to vote. It had ceased to be a big issue.

Check your understanding

ESSENTIAL KNOWLEDGE

1. What were the main differences between the 'gists' (NUWSS) and the 'gettes' (WSPU)?
2. In what ways would it be wrong to say all women were second-class citizens in 1900?
3. Why could it be argued that the introduction of the Cat and Mouse Act marked the failure of the tactics of both sides in the struggle for women's votes up to that point?

THEME QUESTION

1. Why does this section ask about 'greater **political** equality' for women?

TEST YOURSELF

Do you know the meaning of these key words?

Militant

Suffrage

Representation of People Act

Equal franchise

Britain, 1851–1951

Key issue 4: An evaluation of the reasons why the Liberals introduced social welfare reforms, 1906–1914

What is this section all about?

Before 1906, governments took very little responsibility for helping the poor. Laissez-faire was a phrase that described government attitudes to the welfare of its people in the 19th century. It meant do little, leave alone. However, between 1906 and 1914 the Liberal government passed a series of reforms aimed at helping ease the problem of poverty. This section is about the reasons why those changes happened. You should then be able to judge which reasons you think were most important.

An evaluation of the reasons why the Liberals introduced social welfare reforms, 1906–1914:
- Concerns over poverty – the social surveys of Booth and Rowntree
- The example of municipal socialism
- Reforms done by foreign examples
- Fears about national efficiency
- Fears over national security
- Competition from the new Labour Party
- The ideas of the New Liberalism
- Hopes to gain advantage for the Liberals

The social surveys

The Booth (London) and Rowntree (York) reports showed that poverty had very specific causes well beyond the ability of an individual to 'help themselves'. What could any individual do about low pay, unemployment, sickness and old age? The report by Charles Booth in London presented its findings as hard, statistical facts – not opinions. Booth showed that poverty had causes often beyond the control of the poor themselves. Many politicians realised that a laissez-faire social policy was no longer acceptable. The Rowntree report showed that 28% of the York population lived in extreme poverty. If York had such problems then so would other British cities and so the problem of poverty was therefore a national problem.

A group of children gathered by an alley in a York slum, 1901.

Question paper 1: British, European and World History

Municipal socialism

Municipal socialism meant local authorities using money raised from local taxation for the public's benefit. For example, Glasgow town council took control of the city water supply and provided street lighting along with many other municipal services, all paid for by local taxation. The example of local authorities trying to deal with the problem of poverty was used as a model to persuade national government that political intervention was both possible and desirable on a national scale.

Worries about national security

When the Boer War (in South Africa) started in 1899, volunteers rushed to join up but almost 25% of them were rejected because they were not fit enough. If men of military age were so unfit for service, would that affect Britain's ability to protect its Empire? The government was well aware of the growth of large European armies, especially Germany. What would happen if Britain faced a strong modern army in the near future?

Worries about national efficiency

By the end of the 19th century, Britain was no longer the world's strongest industrial nation and was facing serious competition from new industrial nations such as Germany. However, in Germany a system of welfare benefits and old-age pensions had already been set up. If a main competitor could afford to do it, why could Britain not do likewise?

The challenge of the Labour Party

Since 1884, many working-class men had the vote yet could only vote for middle-class political parties. In 1900, the Labour Representation Committee was formed, which quickly became known as the Labour Party. This new working-class party would take votes away from the Liberals unless the Liberals paid attention to the shocking living conditions of many working-class voters.

The first Parliamentary Labour Party gathered on the terrace of the House of Commons, London, 1906.

Britain, 1851–1951

New Liberal ideas

A new generation of Liberal politicians genuinely believed that the government had a responsibility to help the poor. When the old Liberal Prime Minister died, a younger man with new Liberal ideas became Prime Minister. He was Asquith and he brought into government several new politicians who shared his ideas. The other reasons are important influences but without Liberal politicians ready to do something to ease poverty, would anything really have happened? Therefore, you could argue that it was the existence of Liberal politicians in positions of government power that meant the issue of poverty could be ignored no longer.

Check your understanding

ESSENTIAL KNOWLEDGE

1. Why was the evidence presented in the Charles Booth report on London life and poverty different from earlier investigations and therefore very persuasive?
2. Why did the Rowntree report raise concerns on a national scale, more so than the Booth report?

THEME QUESTION

1. How did the reports on poverty from Booth and Rowntree play a big part in undermining laissez-faire ideas?

TEST YOURSELF

Do you know the meaning of these key words?

Laissez-faire

Intervention

Municipal

Socialism

Question paper 1: British, European and World History

Key issue 5: An assessment of the effectiveness of the Liberal social welfare reforms

What is this section all about?

Between 1906 and 1914, the Liberal reforms tried to deal with the problem of poverty and focused on four groups: the old, the young, the sick and the unemployed. In your answer you must decide how successful the reforms were in dealing with the problem of poverty as it affected each of these four groups.

An assessment of the effectiveness of the Liberal social welfare reforms
- The aims of the Liberal reforms
- Liberal reforms and the needs of the old
- Liberal reforms and the needs of the young
- Liberal reforms and the needs of the sick
- Liberal reforms and the needs of the unemployed

Reforms affecting the old

In 1908, the government started paying up to 5 shillings (25 pence) a week to people over 70 who had an income of up to £21 a year. A married couple got 37·5 pence each week but anyone with an income of over £31·50 a year got no pension. Neither did those who had avoided work, had criminal records or were habitually drunk. Many elderly people needed help long before they reached 70, and most died before receiving a pension. Also, old-age pensions were below the poverty line calculated by Rowntree in York.

Reforms affecting the young

In 1906, the government permitted local authorities to provide free school meals for poor children. In 1907, school medical inspections started, although it was not until 1912 that free medical treatment was available. In 1908, juvenile courts and borstals – young people's prisons – were started. All these reforms, including restricting the sale of cigarettes and alcohol to children, were together called the Children's Charter. Researchers found that during school holidays the growth of poor children slowed and body weight often declined. This suggested that school meals were an important part of the health of poor children. Medical inspections did little to solve any problems they discovered, so it was not until free medical treatment for school children was started that problems could be dealt with. Early attempts to protect children from 'social evils' such as smoking and alcohol by setting minimum ages at which these things could be bought only had limited success.

School children in the East End of London being served with free meals.

TOP TIP

Any question about the success of the Liberal reforms will require you to:
1. Explain what social problems faced Britain in the early 20th century.
2. Link the problems to detailed knowledge of the reforms passed by the Liberals.
3. Decide whether or not the reforms helped to solve the problems.

Reforms affecting the sick

The National Insurance Act of 1911 (Part 1) gave some medical benefits to workers who paid into a national insurance scheme. There was no free National Health Service at that time so any help was better than none. Everyone on low wages – up to £160 a year – was insured. An insured worker got ten shillings a week (50 pence) when off sick but the benefits only lasted for 26 weeks. Contributions were seen by some workers as a wage cut, because their contribution was deducted from the wages they received. Only the insured worker got free medical treatment from a doctor. Other family members did not benefit from the scheme, no matter how sick they were.

Reforms affecting the unemployed

The National Insurance Act Part 2 was aimed at helping the unemployed. The Act of 1911 was only meant to cover temporary unemployment and only applied to seven trades, most of which suffered seasonal unemployment. Labour exchanges were started so that workers could find out easily what jobs were available in their area. Most insured workers got seven shillings (35 pence) a week for a maximum of 15 weeks. By 1913, over 2.3 million workers were insured against unemployment and 15 million were insured against sickness. When long-term unemployment increased after World War I, the system started to fail because the payments of those in work did not provide enough income for the government to pay out money to the unemployed.

Men queuing up at the new Labour Exchange at Camberwell Green, London.

Question paper 1: British, European and World History

Reforms to help the employed

The Liberals also recognised that workers faced problems even when in work. A series of reforms helped improve working conditions.

- Trade unions (organisations of workers that struggled to get higher wages and shorter working hours for members) were under threat of being financially broken as a result of previous laws. The Trades Disputes Act of 1906 protected unions from being forced to pay for all losses by employers during strikes.
- If workers were injured at work as a result of employers not taking necessary safety precautions, then the injured worker could gain compensation as a result of the Workmen's Compensation Act of 1906.
- In 1908, miners finally gained an 8-hour working day. They had campaigned for this for a very long time.
- More leisure time was given to shop workers when they were given a half day on a Saturday.

What were the aims of the reforms?

You must be aware of what the **aims** of the reforms were, otherwise you cannot judge how effective they were. A useful argument to use is that the Liberals aimed to provide help to groups who were poor through no fault of their own. The Liberal reforms were a transition point – a half-way house – between the laissez-faire ideology of the 19th century and the Welfare State ideas of the 1950s. A transition point, in this case, means the moment of change between one set of ideas and another. The National Insurance Act is a good illustration of the transition in government policy. The government was prepared to intervene to help the poor, but as part of the deal the poor also had to help themselves by paying contributions towards their benefits. Winston Churchill, who at the time was a Liberal MP, neatly summed up the aim of the Liberal reforms. He said, 'if we see a drowning man we do not drag him to the shore. Instead we provide help to allow him to swim ashore'. In other words, the Liberals tried to help some of the poorer sections of society to help themselves.

Check your understanding

ESSENTIAL KNOWLEDGE

1. What did Churchill mean when he said he would not pull a drowning man to shore but he would provide a lifebelt?
2. What did Churchill's comment above have to do with the Liberal reforms?

THEME QUESTION

1. Is it fair to say the Liberal reforms were passed for political self-interest rather than a desire to help the poor?
2. Did the Liberals lay the foundations of the Welfare State?

TEST YOURSELF

Do you know the meaning of these key words?

Contributory   Borstals
Interventionist   Labour exchange
Transition

Britain, 1851–1951

Key issue 6: An assessment of the effectiveness of the Labour social welfare reforms, 1945–1951

What is this section all about?

Some historians argue that Labour's reforms were the start of a Welfare State in Britain in which the government looked after all its citizens from 'the cradle to the grave'. In 1945, Labour became the new government and between 1945 and 1951 they launched a series of social reforms aimed to improve five 'giant problems' identified a few years earlier by the Beveridge Report.

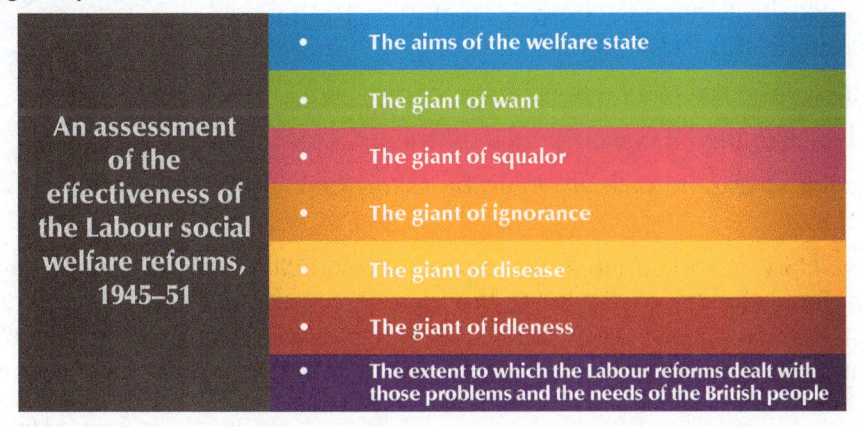

An assessment of the effectiveness of the Labour social welfare reforms, 1945–51
- The aims of the welfare state
- The giant of want
- The giant of squalor
- The giant of ignorance
- The giant of disease
- The giant of idleness
- The extent to which the Labour reforms dealt with those problems and the needs of the British people

What does the Second World War have to do with Labour's reforms?

The phrase 'post-war must be better than pre-war' sums up public attitudes during the war; it meant that people wanted a better Britain after the war. In 1942, the Beveridge Report identified five key social problems that faced Britain. They were called the Five Giants. In 1945, a new Labour government introduced a series of reforms that aimed to deal with each of the five giant problems identified by Beveridge. These giants were:

1. Want (poverty)
2. Disease (bad health)
3. Squalor (bad housing)
4. Ignorance (poor education)
5. Idleness (unemployment)

TOP TIP
An easy way to learn what Labour did is to know a bit about the Beveridge Report.

Question paper 1: British, European and World History

What was done to ease the problem of 'want'?

The Family Allowance Act (started by the wartime government) paid a small amount of money to all mothers of two or more children. The Industrial Injuries Act paid compensation for all injuries caused at work, and all workers were covered. The National Insurance Act of 1946 improved the old Liberal Act – all people in work were included in this insurance. The National Assistance Act helped people who were not in work or the old who had not paid enough contributions into the new National Insurance scheme. It was a safety net to ensure that nobody fell into poverty. By including all workers and families in the benefits scheme, it seemed this would be very helpful.

What was done to ease the problem of 'disease'?

The National Health Service (NHS) was created in 1948. The NHS was based on three main aims:

1. Universal access: the NHS was for everybody.
2. Comprehensive: the NHS would treat all medical problems.
3. Free at point of use: no patient would be asked to pay for any treatment.

Overall, the NHS was welcomed and did provide medical help from 'the cradle to the grave'. By 1950, the idea of 'free for all treatment' was damaged when charges were introduced for spectacles and dental treatment.

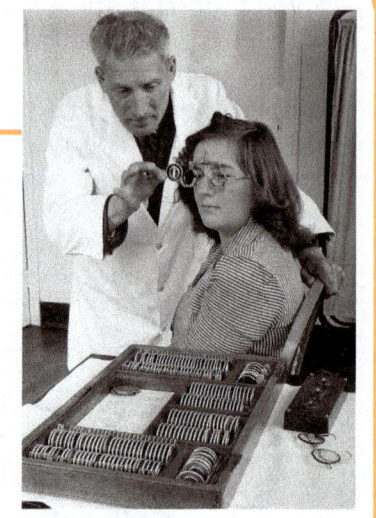

Under the new National Health Service system, spectacles could be provided free of charge on a doctor's prescription.

What was done to ease the problem of 'squalor'?

Most of Britain's cities still had slum areas and overcrowding was still a serious problem made worse by bomb damage during the war. The government aimed to build 200,000 houses each year; most were council houses for rent and many were 'prefabricated, factory made houses' or 'prefabs' for short. These were quickly assembled on site.

The New Towns Act in 1946 laid the plans for 14 New Towns to be built. These were to be 'people-friendly' towns to relieve the housing problems in older cities. However, Labour did not build as many houses as it promised and by 1951 there was still overcrowding and long waiting lists for council housing. New town areas often became places where workers lived but they still commuted into the older towns for work. There were some complaints that new estates and new towns were 'soulless', while old communities were uprooted.

Britain, 1851–1951

What was done to ease the problem of 'ignorance' (bad education)?

Many children received no education past primary stage and poorer parents could not afford the fees that some secondary schools charged. Labour put the Education Act of 1944 into operation. It raised the school leaving age to 15. All children were to get free secondary education. An 11+ exam placed children either in senior secondary schools or junior secondary. Children who passed went to senior secondary where they would stay beyond 15 years old and were expected to go to university, get jobs in management and the professions. Children who failed the exam were not expected to stay at school after 15. These children were expected to get unskilled jobs.

For those who passed the 11+ exam, the system worked well. However, those children who failed the exam seemed to be stuck in a trap of low expectations and inferior education. Many people opposed the idea of deciding a child's future at 11 or 12.

What was done to ease the problem of 'idleness' (unemployment)?

The government agreed to aim for 'full employment'. Labour also nationalised some industries. Nationalisation means the government took over the running of certain industries and used tax money to keep an industry going. Nationalisation was one way of keeping full employment. However, it was costly and at times led to bad management.

A nationalisation poster, giving notice of the passing of control of the railways to the British Transport Commission.

Check your understanding

ESSENTIAL KNOWLEDGE

1. Why was post war a good time for Labour to start its reforms?
2. What is the link between the Beveridge Report of 1942 and the Labour social reforms?
3. In what sense can all the reforms be attempts to attack poverty?

TEST YOURSELF

Do you know the meaning of these key words?

Post war   The 5 giants
Cradle to grave   Welfare State

THEME QUESTION

1. Why was a Welfare State easier to establish after the Second World War?
2. Explain why the Labour government of 1945–1951 is often thought of as the founder of the Welfare State.

Britain 1851–1951

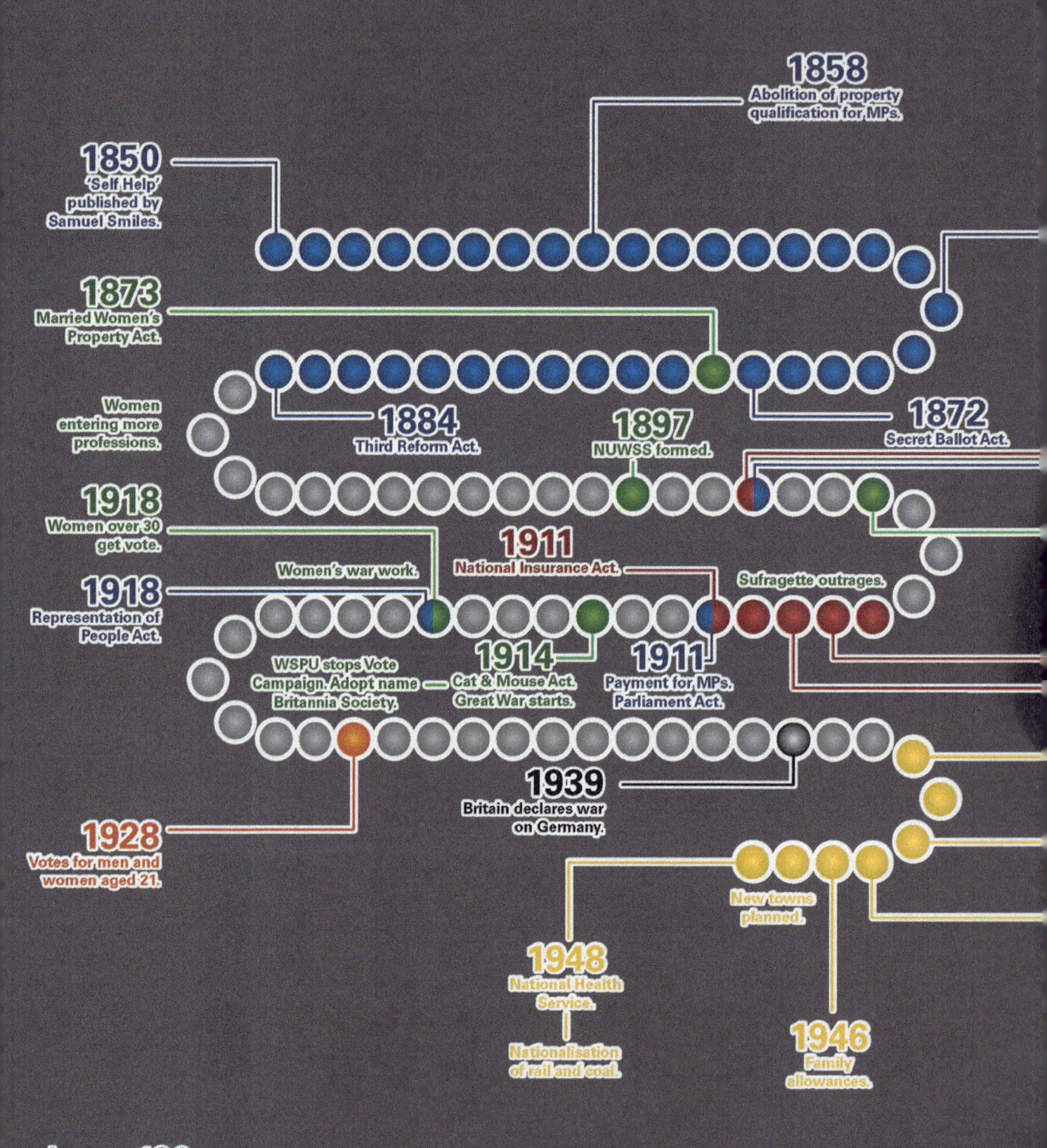

1858 Abolition of property qualification for MPs.

1850 'Self Help' published by Samuel Smiles.

1873 Married Women's Property Act.

Women entering more professions.

1884 Third Reform Act.

1897 NUWSS formed.

1872 Secret Ballot Act.

1918 Women over 30 get vote.

1918 Representation of People Act.

Women's war work.

1911 National Insurance Act.

Suffragette outrages.

WSPU stops Vote Campaign. Adopt name Britannia Society.

1914 Cat & Mouse Act. Great War starts.

1911 Payment for MPs. Parliament Act.

1939 Britain declares war on Germany.

1928 Votes for men and women aged 21.

New towns planned.

1948 National Health Service.

Nationalisation of rail and coal.

1946 Family allowances.

Issues 1 & 2
Issue 3
Issues 4–5
Issue 6
Issue 1–2 & 3

1867
Second Reform Act.

1900
Booth and Rowntree reports on poverty.

1900
Labour representation committee (Labour party born)

1903
WSPU formed.

1907-8
Children's Charter. Medical inspection.

1909
Old age pensions.

1942
Beveridge Report.

1944
Education Act.

1945
Labour wins General Election.

Question paper 1: British, European and World History

Key issue 1: An evaluation of the reasons for the growth of nationalism in Germany, 1815–1850

What is this section all about?

Nationalism in this section means the belief that people who share a common identity and language should be part of a single united country. Although Germany did not become a single united country until 1871, in the first half of the 19th century changes were happening that took the German states some way towards thinking about nationalism.

Why did nationalism grow in Germany between 1815 and 1850?

- Economic factors
- The Zollverein
- Cultural factors
- Military weakness
- Effects of French Revolution and Napoleonic Wars
- Role of the Liberals

Cultural factors

During the Napoleonic Wars the French invaded and occupied German states. Many Germans began to identify with things that made them feel more 'German'. A sort of patriotic pride swept across the land. This was summed up by Head of the University of Berlin, Fichte, who described 'Germany' as 'the fatherland' where all people spoke the same language and sang the same songs. German poets and authors, such as the Grimm brothers, and composers such as Beethoven, encouraged feelings of national pride in the German states. The growing popularity of German musicians and writers gave people a sense of belonging – in other words, a national identity was growing.

The Grimm brothers were German authors of fairy tales, folk songs and folk tales based on pre-Christian Germanic mythology.

Germany, 1815–1939

The relative importance of cultural nationalism

Cultural nationalism is a reason for the growing sense of German identity but there is some doubt over how important an influence it was in uniting Germany. Very few Germans could read and even fewer could afford to go to musical concerts to hear the music of Beethoven. Historian Golo Mann doubted whether those Germans would really claim that 'cultural nationalism' was a vital factor in their lives. He wrote that most Germans 'seldom looked up from the plough'; in other words, most Germans either did not know about big national issues or were more concerned with surviving day-to-day. Cultural nationalism is a factor in the growth of German nationalism but perhaps not the most important factor.

Economic factors and the Zollverein

Prussia was the centre of an industrial revolution in Germany with resources of iron and coal. To encourage trade, Prussia formed a customs union in 1818 that grew into a customs union called Zollverein by 1830. The Zollverein included 25 German states with a population of 26 million people. Austria chose not to be part of it. At the same time, a new railway network, centred in Prussia, linked German states. With increasing trade and an industrial revolution that caused people to move between the German states, new ideas spread more easily.

Why was the Zollverein so important in the growth of nationalism?

- The Zollverein didn't just help trade; it also helped nationalism to spread.
- Without the Zollverein, Prussia would not have had the muscle to defeat the power of Austria.
- Historian William Carr has called the Zollverein, 'the mighty lever of German unification'.
- The Zollverein can be thought of as a prototype (or early version) of a Germany that excluded Austrian influence, known as Kleindeutschland.
- The Zollverein was very important because Prussia became a challenger to Austria for influence over the German states.

Effects of the French Revolution and Napoleonic Wars

Before 1800, Germany was split into more than 400 separate states. Between 1800 and 1815 the German states had been conquered by the French and merged into 38 larger states called the Confederation of the Rhine. It is easy to see the Confederation of the Rhine as a first step towards unification, especially when, after Napoleon was defeated in 1815, the Confederation was used as the model for a new German Assembly. However, the Assembly of the German Confederation – also called the Diet – represented the rulers of the German states, not the people. It did not aim at German national unity. Rule 2 of the Confederation said 'the aim of the German Confederation is to ... guard the independence of the separate German states'.

In 1815, the German states were divided and Austrian power was too strong. The individual princes who ruled the separate German states within the German Assembly did not support liberalism or nationalism. Neither did Austria, which dominated the German Assembly.

Question paper 1: British, European and World History

GOT IT? ☐ ☐ ☐

Role of the Liberals

Nationalism was the desire of people with a common national identity to have their own country, whereas liberalism was the desire to have a parliament where the people of the country elected rulers. Many German students were attracted by the idea of a stronger and more united Germany. As part of their studies, German students travelled between universities in different German states and they took with them new ideas about liberalism and nationalism. Student societies called Burschenshaften also promoted nationalist ideas. However, emotional and intellectual support for the ideas of nationalism and liberalism were not strong enough to challenge those who were against German nationalism.

The 1848 revolutions

The German Confederation was created to stop moves towards unity by placing the interests of the separate state rulers first. This was shown by the revolutions of 1848. Both liberals and nationalists supported those revolutions. The 1848 revolutions suggest there was growing support for nationalism in Germany, but the failure of the revolutions to bring about big changes by 1850 suggests that support for nationalism was not yet strong enough to challenge the political and military power of Austria. Austria was not yet ready to lose its grip on the German states.

A meeting of Revolutionaries in a cellar in Berlin, the plotters are of all ages and classes.

TOP TIP

Remember that issues 1, 2 and 3 of this topic (Germany 1815–1939) all cover very similar ground. Be careful to keep your answer and your use of facts very focused on the question being asked.

Check Your Understanding

TEST YOURSELF

Do you know the meaning of these key words?

Liberalism Zollverein
Nationalism Napoleonic Wars
Identity Confederation

ESSENTIAL KNOWLEDGE

1. Why did the German princes oppose nationalism?
2. Why was 1848 an important year for Nationalist hopes?

THEME QUESTION

1. Why did nationalism become such a political force in Germany?
2. In what ways did the German states make most progress towards uniting before 1848?

Germany, 1815–1939

Key issue 2: An assessment of the degree of growth of nationalism in Germany up to 1850

What is this section all about?

In Section 1 you found out about the reasons why nationalism was growing in Germany between 1815 and 1848. This section covers similar information but in this section you must be able to judge just how much growth nationalism had made up to 1850. The end date is important because very important changes took place in the story of German nationalism between 1848 and 1851.

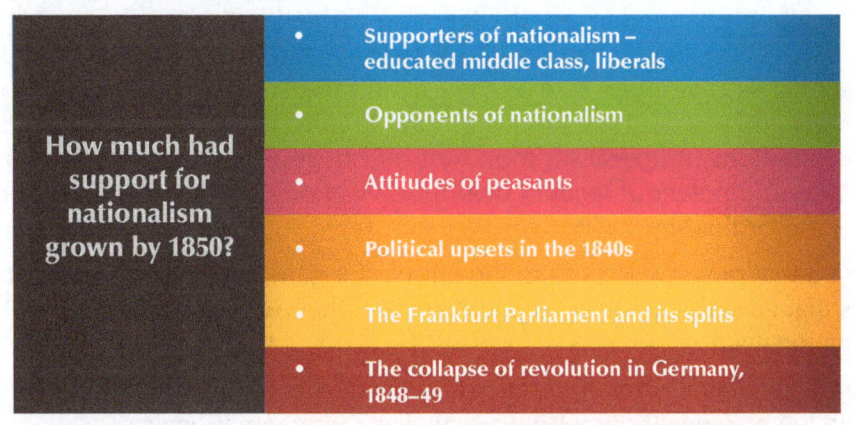

How much had support for nationalism grown by 1850?
- Supporters of nationalism – educated middle class, liberals
- Opponents of nationalism
- Attitudes of peasants
- Political upsets in the 1840s
- The Frankfurt Parliament and its splits
- The collapse of revolution in Germany, 1848–49

The supporters of nationalism – the educated middle class and liberals

Fichte, the head of the University of Berlin, declared that freedom is the right to be German and sort out one's own problems without interference from foreigners. Both middle-class businessmen and the educated middle classes saw advantages in economic unity. On the other hand, businessmen were interested in making money and that is what economic unity delivered through the Zollverein. Political unity was not a priority for them. Students had a more idealistic view and supported the idea of a Germany united in culture and identity by music, art and language. However, Austria worried that such ideas might lead to political unity so stamped on the ideas in the Karlsbad Decrees of 1819. It seemed as if moves towards political nationalism were dead. As a result, intellectual and student ideas had a limited effect on the growth of nationalism.

Political nationalism would require a major shift in the power balance between those who wanted change and those who did not. For most of the period 1815–1859 those who did not want change were much stronger than those who did. Political moves towards

45

nationalism are easy to see and therefore do something about. Associations, clubs and gatherings can all be stopped and because all ideas were spread as books, newspapers or by word of mouth, they were easy to censor or ban.

The opponents of nationalism

The princes

The German princes wanted to turn the clock back to a time when their power and authority was unchallenged and the pressures of nationalism and especially liberalism did not threaten their existence. The princes opposed nationalism because they feared Prussianisation – absorption into the Prussian state – and the loss of their influence and identity in an enlarged 'Germany'.

Prince Metternich

The person who represented most opposition to nationalism was the Austrian Chancellor Prince Metternich who hoped to use the German Confederation to block any political change that would threaten the power of the old rulers. Metternich also hoped to stop the spread of nationalism and liberalism as they would threaten his power. If nationalism took root in the Austrian Empire, the states within the Empire would want to break away to form their own nations. If liberalism took root in the Empire, then Metternich's power and the power of the old powerful leaders would be weakened by parliaments representing the wishes of the ordinary people.

It has been said that power comes from the barrel of a gun. The princes and Metternich had the guns that gave them power so could enforce their wishes – and their wishes were opposed to nationalism.

Emotional and intellectual support for the ideas of nationalism and liberalism were not yet strong enough to challenge those who were against German nationalism.

The attitudes of peasants

As mentioned before, most Germans either did not know about big national issues or were more concerned with surviving day-to-day. Peasants (poor farmers) are always concerned with stability and land ownership. Major political changes are a concern to them because political changes could lead to conflict and that could mean the difference between life and death to them. The aims and ideas of the Nationalists and Liberals seemed to offer no practical help to the bulk of the population who were peasants working the land.

Germany, 1815–1939

Political upset in the 1840s and the revolutions of 1848

Across Europe, the late 1840s had seen a series of bad harvests and potato famines. People were hungry and wanted changes to improve their lives. A rising middle class wanted more political influence, while nationalists and liberals wanted political change. In March 1848, giant demonstrations rocked Berlin, capital of Prussia, and eventually the King, Frederick William IV, agreed that a new German parliament called a National Assembly would meet in the city of Frankfurt in May 1848. By the summer of 1848 it seemed as if the revolutions had succeeded – but they failed.

The Frankfurt Parliament (German National Assembly) gathered between 1848 and 1849 during the period of widespread revolution in Frankfurt.

There were four main reasons why the revolutions of 1848 failed:

- The first reason involved suspicions between the poorer working classes and the more wealthy middle classes.
- A second reason was the argument over the future shape of Germany. Should a united Germany be Grossdeutsch (including Austria) or Kleindeutsch (excluding Austria)?
- The third and vital reason for the failure of the 1848 revolution was the recovery of Austria and its allies in the German states. By 1849 the Austrian army was ready to crush opposition, bring back the old rulers and restore the Austrian-controlled German Confederation.
- The fourth and final reason for the failure of the revolution was the lack of strong leadership. In the spring of 1848, King Frederick William IV of Prussia said he would lead a united Germany. However, in March 1849 he refused the Crown of Germany.

Is the changing attitude of Frederick William really surprising? If Frederick William had tried to resist Austria he would have risked losing power again. In other words, King Frederick William IV was looking out for himself. The early revolutions seemed successful only because Austria – the power most against the new ideas – was militarily distracted and weak.

Check Your Understanding

ESSENTIAL KNOWLEDGE

1. What was Prussianisation?
2. Who was Frederick William IV and why was he important in the story of the 1848 revolutions?

THEME QUESTION

1. How can the words Austria, Metternich and Karlsbad Decrees be linked together?
2. Were the 1848 revolutions in Germany doomed to failure?

TEST YOURSELF

Do you know the meaning of these key words?

Metternich
Grossdeutschland
Kleindeutschland

Question paper 1: British, European and World History

Key issue 3: An evaluation of the obstacles to German unification up to 1850

What is this section all about?

As a historian, you must always be aware of the dangers of hindsight. Everyone can be wise after an event happens and think that what happened was always inevitable. However, just because Germany was united as one country in 1871 it does not mean that German unification was inevitable. There were many obstacles or problems on the way to unification and this section is about you being able to describe what those obstacles were and to judge how important they were.

An evaluation of the obstacles to German unification, 1815–50:
- Divisions among the nationalists
- Austrian strength
- The German princes
- Religious differences
- Economic differences
- Indifference of the masses
- Resentment towards Prussia

The German princes

Historian David Thomson wrote that Napoleon brought 'liberalism by intention but nationalism by inadvertence'. What he meant was that when Napoleon invaded the German states, the people in those states resented the invaders. The princes also disliked the French because Napoleon took away their power, so to get their power back and force the French out, the princes and the people were united. While Napoleon and the French forces occupied the German states, all of the German princes had promised their peoples a genuine constitutional government. Once the French had gone, however, only six states kept their promise.

In 1851, Eduard Burckhardt published a booklet entitled 'Proclamations and Promises Made by German Princes from 1813–1849'. The booklet was a complete collection of the meaningless promises made by the German princes. They wanted to turn the clock back to a time when the power and authority of the princes were unchallenged and the pressures of nationalism and especially liberalism did not threaten their existence. After the Karlsbad Decrees were sanctioned, the German princes felt safe from change.

When the revolutions of 1848 swept over Germany, once again the princes offered change and once again when the power of Austria reasserted itself the princes forgot their promises and returned to their old ways. Change would not happen until either it was in the princes' best interests to support change, or it was forced upon them.

Germany, 1815–1939

Religious differences

The different German states identified with and supported either Protestant beliefs or Catholic beliefs. Roman Catholicism was strongest in the southern and western German states, while Protestantism was firmly established in the north-eastern and central regions. Religion also marked a main difference between the two strongest powers. Prussia in the north-east was Protestant, while Catholic Austria supported and was supported by the Catholic German states. As the 19th century progressed, the Catholic states were increasingly worried about Prussia's growing influence. On the other hand, Protestant states were equally protective of their religious identity and were wary of closer links with Catholic states. Religious divisions between the German states meant they were unlikely to choose unity as it would mean losing their separate religious identity.

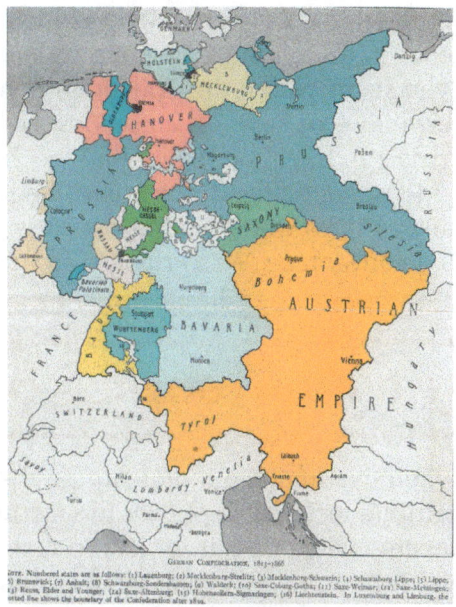

A map of the German Confederation 1815–1866. The dominant states are Austria (yellow) and Prussia (blue).

Economic differences

The industrial revolution and the growth of the railway network in Germany led to easier access to different resources across the German Confederation. This helped to stimulate economic growth and that led to the introduction of the Zollverein customs union. The exclusion of Austria from the Zollverein was a concern to many states. Southern states did not benefit from the economic growth of northern Germany. States more closely linked to Austria were mainly agricultural and much poorer. Those southern states looked to Austria for leadership.

Although Prussia had invited Austria to join the Zollverein, it was obvious to all that if Austria were to join it would be putting itself at a disadvantage. The differences between Prussia and Austria were further illustrated when Austria proposed its own customs union. However, given Austria's geographical position and limited natural resources, a separate customs union based around Austria was never really an option. The main river in Austria is the Danube but that river flows into the Black Sea, the furthest point in Europe away from the growth areas of north-eastern Europe. There was still no real economic unity in Germany and suspicions between the northern, more industrial, trading areas and the southern, more agricultural, areas were yet more obstacles to unification.

Resentment towards Prussia

Although the Zollverein helped increase prosperity and trade within member states, other states felt the Zollverein was mainly designed to increase the power of Prussia. Even states within the Zollverein benefiting from Prussian economic growth remained suspicious of Prussian ambitions. For example, some states claimed economic union with Prussia masked the reality that the Zollverein was based on the Prussian taxation system and Prussia made all the controlling decisions. All trade seemed centred on Prussia, all railway lines were focused on Prussia and Prussia's access to the river Rhine gave it a huge advantage. Was Prussia's aim to unite Germany or just increase its own power?

The indifference of the masses

When the French put pressure on the French–German border in the 1830s, a wave of patriotic feeling swept over the German states. A song called 'The Watch on the Rhine' became very popular for its pro-German and anti-French feelings but apart from that there was little to really excite the German population about nationalism or liberalism – or even unification. As long as businesses made money and farms produced food, why should people want change that might cause disruption and conflict? The ideas of nationalism, liberalism and unification were not widely supported. In short, the German people were largely indifferent until 1848.

Divisions between the nationalists

The 1848 revolutions suggest there was growing support for nationalism in Germany but the failure of the revolutions to bring about big changes by 1850 suggests that support for nationalism was not yet strong enough to challenge the power of Austria. One of the biggest problems facing the nationalists, and therefore the difficulty of attracting support, was the argument over the future shape of Germany. Those who supported a Germany including Austria supported Grossdeutchland. They argued that Austria shared a common language with Germany and it would make no sense to exclude Austria from Germany.

On the other side of the argument were those who supported Kleindeutschland. That means 'smaller Germany' – a Germany without Austria. Supporters of Kleindeutschland argued that Austria was a huge state that would swamp the other German states and, as a Catholic power, would always attract the southern German states and alienate the northern, Protestant states.

Germany, 1815–1939

GOT IT?

A united Germany?

The argument was left unsolved when the 1848/9 revolutions collapsed and Austria reasserted its power using its armies. Nevertheless, Frederick William was still ambitious. He liked the idea of leading a united Germany, so he tried to create a different form of united assembly under his authority called the Erfurt Union. It was to be an assembly of German princes under Frederick William's control. However, the princes did not want to join, worried that they were being 'bullied' by Frederick William into joining the union.

Meanwhile, Austria was determined to destroy the Prussian challenge to its power, and Schwarzenberg, the new chancellor of Austria, said, 'we shall not let ourselves be thrown out of Germany'. When the Prussian and Austrian politicians met at Olmutz, it looked as if Prussia's chance to lead a united Germany was over forever because:

- Prussia had to agree to the cancellation of the Erfurt Union.
- Prussia had to promise never again to challenge Austria's power.
- The old German Confederation was put back in place.

His Majesty Friedrich Wilhelm IV, King of Prussia announces the unity of the German nation to Berliners in 1848.

Check Your Understanding

TEST YOURSELF

Do you know the meaning of these key words?
German princes
Constitutional government

ESSENTIAL KNOWLEDGE

1. Why was religion a factor in unification?
2. How did the Erfurt Union and 'the humiliation of Olmutz' illustrate both the ambitions of Prussia and its weaknesses?

THEME QUESTION

1. In hindsight, how was the power of Austria in Germany doomed after 1815?
2. How could you argue that disputes over Kleindeutschland and Grossdeutschland lay at the heart of the problems of unification?

51

Question paper 1: British, European and World History

Key issue 4: An evaluation of the reasons why unification was achieved in Germany by 1871

What is this section all about?

TOP TIP
Learn to spell Bismarck's name correctly – a small point but it irritates markers.

By 1871 Germany was united. Historians debate how important a Prussian politician called Otto von Bismarck was to unification. Some say he was the architect of unification while others argue that he had the talent to make best use of circumstances over which he had little personal control. Your task is to examine all the relevant factors and reach a decision about why Germany was united in 1871.

An evaluation of the reasons why unification was achieved in Germany by 1871:
- Prussian military strength
- Prussian economic strength
- The decline of Austria
- The role of Bismarck
- The attitude of other states
- Actions of Napoleon III

Prussian military strength

In 1860, the Prussian Minister of War presented to the Landtag a plan that would restructure the Prussian army and increase its size. After a long argument about who would pay for the reforms, Bismarck cut through the red tape and ordered local people to pay increased taxes. The plans to reform the army were the work of Prussian Generals von Roon and von Moltke. The reforms made the Prussian army the most efficient in Europe, in contrast to the Austrian army that was recovering from its disastrous war against Italy just a few months before. The army was equipped with modern weapons and trained in the latest tactics. All that was needed was to find a way of gaining battle experience.

Prussian economic strength and influence

In 1859, a group of nationalist lawyers, teachers and businessmen formed a group called the Nationalverein. They said that the German Confederation should be replaced and it was the duty of every German to support Prussia in order to achieve firm, strong government. The Zollverein, the network of railways and Prussia's industrial revolution were all increasing Prussian influence

Germany, 1815–1939

in Europe. In the 1850s, Prussia was developing the ability to challenge Austria. Economically, industrially, diplomatically and militarily, Prussia was recovering its strength at a time when Austria was in decline. Clearly, hopes for unification under Prussian leadership were still alive in 1859, nine years after the Olmutz 'humiliation'. The hopes of nationalists were not dead.

The decline of Austria

Austria was facing serious problems in the 1850s as its power decreased. Austria knew it would have to break up the Zollverein if Prussian economic strength was to be weakened but Austria was simply not in a position to offer other states strong reasons to join their alternative customs union.

In 1854, Russia was at war with Britain and France. When Russia asked for help, Austria refused. Russia was furious. Austria had lost an ally. The Austrian army was described as 'weak and disorganised' in a war against France in 1859. When Austria was defeated it was exposed as weak, poorly equipped and out of touch with modern military tactics.

The role of Bismarck

Bismarck became **the** vital figure in the unification of Germany. Much of what he did was to increase the power and influence of Prussia. Prussia was victorious in three wars, against Denmark in 1864, Austria in 1866 and France between 1870 and 1871. The result of the wars was an increase in the power of Prussia and the unification of Germany. Bismarck knew that if Prussia was to be the most powerful state in Germany, Austrian power would have to be weakened – but not yet. The newly reformed Prussian army needed to be tested in battle.

Bismarck's first step in weakening Austria's power was a war with Denmark. An argument over the territories of Schleswig and Holstein led to war. At the Convention of Gastein (August 1865), it was agreed that Holstein would be run by Austria and Schleswig would be run by Prussia. Austria was politically and militarily cornered by Bismarck, who could now provoke war with Austria when it suited him.

War with Austria 1866

TOP TIP
When writing about Bismarck try to use the words opportunist, pragmatic and realpolitik. If you don't know what they mean, find out!

Bismarck wanted to ensure that when Prussia fought Austria, Russia and France would not support Austria. In 1865, Bismarck arranged a meeting with the French leader Napoleon III. Without making any promises, Bismarck hinted very strongly that France would get extra territory, possibly in the Rhineland, if France stayed out of a war between Prussia and Austria. In 1866, Bismarck was ready to fight. After a crushing victory over Austria, the Treaty of Prague ended the war. Bismarck never wanted to destroy Austria, only Austria's influence over the German states. Bismarck did what was necessary to achieve his aim – and nothing more. By the end of 1866, a North German Confederation was created after the German Confederation was ended. A Kleindeutsch had been created – a North German state without Austrian influence – and it seemed as if Germany was close to unity.

Question paper 1: British, European and World History

Got it? ☐ ☐ ☐

War with France

In 1868, a revolution in Spain led to a search for a new ruler. A distant relative of the Spanish royal family was found called Leopold of Hohenzollern but Leopold was a Prussian. France was worried because in a future conflict France might be trapped between a strong Prussia to the north of France and a Prussian 'puppet' government in Spain to the south. The French protested strongly and even insisted that the Hohenzollern family should give up its claim to the Spanish throne forever. King William of Prussia politely refused the French demand but Bismarck saw his chance and altered the telegram slightly so that it appeared the King had insulted the French ambassador. The edited version of the telegram had the effect that Bismarck intended. The French public demanded war because of the 'Prussian insult'. Bismarck had got what he wanted.

Bismarck's master plan?

Did Bismarck have a master plan? The safest answer, and the nearest to the truth, is that Bismarck had the political skill to take advantage of circumstances as they arose and over which he often had no direct control. Supporters of this view believe Bismarck was an opportunist – taking advantage of situations as they happened.

Historians use the war with France as an example of Bismarck deliberately using a situation that arose and manipulating it to his advantage. Another view is that Bismarck acted as a catalyst that speeded up change that would have happened anyway. Changes such as the Zollverein, the spread of railways and growing nationalism would have united Germany eventually. The fact is that Bismarck did fight three wars, which resulted ultimately in unification. Bismarck, in the words of one historian, was like a card player who, although he did not deal the cards, played his hand very well.

Check Your Understanding

ESSENTIAL KNOWLEDGE

1. Why did Bismarck fight the war with Denmark?
2. Why did he fight a war against Austria?
3. Why did he fight a war with France?

THEME QUESTION

1. Was Bismarck the man who united Germany or just the catalyst?

TEST YOURSELF

Do you know the meaning of these key words?

Landtag
Nationalverein
Schleswig Holstein
Opportunist

Germany, 1815–1939

Key issue 5: An evaluation of the reasons why the Nazis achieved power in 1933

What is this section about?

The new Germany that emerged at the end of the Great War was a democratic republic described as 'the world's most perfect democracy – on paper'. By 1933, Weimar democracy was destroyed by the Nazis. Your task is to explain why the Nazis came to power – was it because of the weaknesses of the Weimar Republic, the attractiveness of the Nazis or because of other reasons that helped the Nazis?

An evaluation of the reasons why the Nazis achieved power in 1933:
- Weaknesses of Weimar Republic
- Resentment towards the Treaty of Versailles
- Economic difficulties
- Social and economic divisions
- The appeal of the Nazis after 1928
- The role of Hitler
- Weaknesses and mistakes of opponents

The Weimar Republic's weaknesses

The new democratic system had flaws that could be exploited by groups that wanted to destroy Weimar. Many Germans blamed the Weimar government for their problems.

The new government was blamed for the Treaty of Versailles

On 28th June 1919, the victorious allies made Germany sign the Treaty of Versailles, which many Germans called a Diktat (i.e., a dictated treaty that was forced on them). Germany was forced to accept blame for causing the war and also all the deaths and destruction that resulted from the war. Although they were powerless to change it, the Weimar government was blamed for accepting such a humiliating peace treaty.

The Weimar Republic was weakened by several political groups opposed to its democratic ideas

In 1919, the Spartacists, who later became known as the Communist Party or KPD tried to start a revolution to create a new communist Germany. The Spartacist rising was defeated with great brutality by an alliance between the new socialist government or SPD and gangs of ex-soldiers called Freikorps. Ten years later when Hitler was rising to power, the hatred felt by the Communists towards the SPD for destroying the Spartacist rising prevented the left wing from uniting against Hitler in elections.

The Weimar Republic was equally hated by the right wing

When the Weimar government tried to carry out the military cuts imposed by the Versailles Treaty, German officers supported the Kapp Putsch – an attempt to overthrow the government and bring the Kaiser back. The right also included many professionals whose early careers had been spent within the Imperial Germany of the Kaiser. All these people still identified with 'old' Germany while working within new Germany. They were unlikely to support the new democracy when a crisis arose in the early 1930s.

The Weimar Republic was blamed for economic difficulties, especially the hyperinflation of 1923 and the depression of 1929

In 1923, France, with Belgian help, invaded the Ruhr, Germany's industrial heartland to enforce the payment of reparations. In response, workers in the Ruhr went on strike and the German government printed more and more paper money to pay the strikers. The German currency collapsed and by November 1923, German money was worthless. This was the time of hyperinflation.

You cannot overstate the impact hyperinflation had on the German people, especially the middle classes. It was described as 'the scar that never healed'. The German economic crisis of the early 1920s only ended when American money was pumped into the German economy and a time of relative political and economic stability followed. When the American economy collapsed in 1929 and US money was withdrawn from Germany, unemployment began to rise fast. Many Germans blamed the government.

The Weimar Republic was blamed for weakening German politics

The new Weimar Constitution was meant to be fair to all. Instead, the new voting system, based on proportional representation, produced a series of short-lived, indecisive governments and gave representation in the Reichstag to minority parties such as the Nazis whose main aim was to destroy the new Republic.

The Weimar Republic was blamed for confusion within the new democratic system

Although the constitution was written to make a fair and democratic system, confusion about the voting system and the power of the President increased discontent. The voting system was based on proportional representation. Deals had to be done between parties and coalition governments set up. These coalition governments were unlikely to put into action strong, decisive policies. The system also allowed small, extremist parties such as the Nazis and the Communists to gain some representation in the Reichstag. Article 48 of the Constitution gave the President (elected every 7 years) the power to rule in an emergency without needing approval from the Reichstag. But what might happen if an extreme politician – such as Hitler – gained control over the President?

The Weimar Republic was unable to deal with the rising appeal of the Nazis after 1928

In 1928, the Nazis had 12 seats in the Reichstag, but by 1930 they had 108. The economic crash was the catalyst that transformed the appeal of the Nazis. As the historian AJP Taylor said, 'it was the Great Depression that put the wind in Hitler's sails'. As American banks collapsed after the Wall Street Crash, they demanded the return of the loans they had made to Germany. With the end of the US loans, unemployment in Germany rocketed and economic chaos followed. Although hyperinflation did not return, by 1930 the German people were desperate for a saviour to help them out of the mess.

In 1923, the Nazis had tried to grab power in Munich but they failed, Hitler was arrested and sentenced to a short term in prison. While in prison, Hitler reached a decision about

Germany, 1815–1939

how he would try to gain power – he is reported as saying, 'we must hold our noses and enter the Reichstag'. In other words, Hitler would campaign for power legally and destroy the system he despised from within. The Nazi use of propaganda also convinced many Germans that their best hopes for the future lay with the Nazis. Many Germans approved of the SA (a Nazi paramilitary group) attacking communists and it appeared to many that the Nazis were a strong positive force in Germany, especially when compared to the weak and divided political parties of the Weimar Republic.

By 1930, nationalist groups led by Alfred Hugenberg saw the Nazis as a possible route to power. Hitler was happy to use Hugenberg, who owned most of Germany's new cinema industry and hundreds of local newspapers. Hitler saw a way of becoming a nationally-known figure very quickly in a pre-television age. All Hitler needed was the opportunity to spread his message of a new Germany under Nazism. As unemployment rose towards 6 million, Nazi posters claimed 'Hitler – Our Last Hope'. Hitler offered simplistic answers to complex problems and the removal of difficult decisions.

Can Weimar politicians be blamed for Hitler's rise and the collapse of Weimar?

As Hitler and the Nazis rose in popularity, some Weimar politicians made the mistake of believing that they could use Hitler to achieve their own anti-democratic ambitions. President Hindenburg and other Weimar politicians had been acting in an undemocratic way since 1930. The two politicians most closely associated with this attempt to 'use' Hitler were von Papen and General von Schleicher. In January 1933, Hitler was invited to become Chancellor of Germany legally, within the Weimar Republic's Constitution.

TOP TIP

Some people get confused by left and right wing. For this topic 'the left' or 'left wing' means people who wanted to overthrow the old system and give more power to the workers. They also wanted to share wealth more equally; for example, communists. The term 'right wing' means people who put the good of the nation first and believed in a strong authority figure at the head of government.

TEST YOURSELF

Do you know the meaning of these key words?

Weimar
Spartacists
Hindenburg
Hugenberg
Hyperinflation

Check Your Understanding

ESSENTIAL KNOWLEDGE

1. Why was the Weimar Constitution described as the most perfect democracy – on paper?
2. Why was Hitler called 'the Legal Dictator'?

THEME QUESTION

1. Did the Weimar Republic collapse because of weaknesses within its own system or because it was attacked by enemies who wanted its destruction?

Question paper 1: British, European and World History

Key issue 6: An evaluation of the reasons why the Nazis were able to stay in power, 1933–1939

What is this section all about?

Between January 1933 and August 1934, Hitler took steps to move from being legal Chancellor in a democratic government to dictator of a totalitarian state. Democracy was destroyed, opposition was crushed and Hitler established a police state controlling the daily lives of German citizens by means of 'carrot and stick' methods. Your task is to consider all the ways Hitler maintained power in Germany up until 1939 and decide which were the most effective methods.

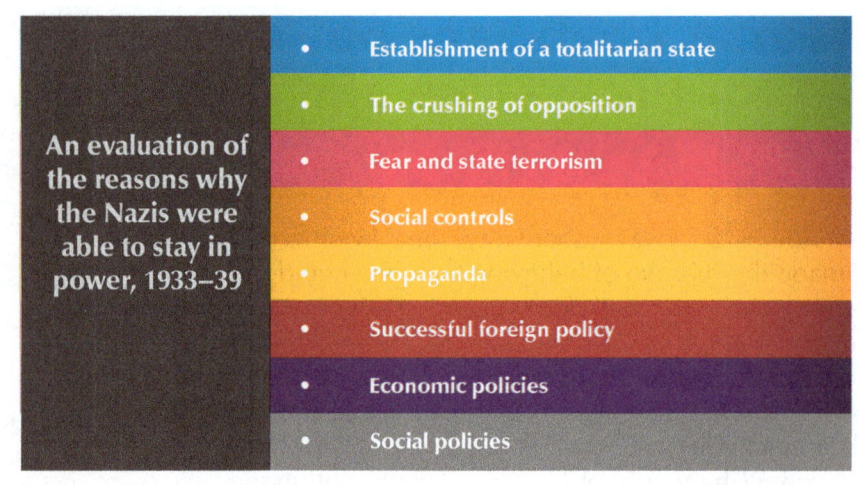

An evaluation of the reasons why the Nazis were able to stay in power, 1933–39
- Establishment of a totalitarian state
- The crushing of opposition
- Fear and state terrorism
- Social controls
- Propaganda
- Successful foreign policy
- Economic policies
- Social policies

Establishing a totalitarian state

Hitler knew that the power of the Reichstag and the Weimar Constitution would have to be destroyed. In February 1933, the Reichstag caught fire. Hitler immediately put the blame on the Communists who were Hitler's main opposition. Hitler could claim that the Communists had shown their anti-democratic ideas by burning the Reichstag. Hitler claimed that Germany was under threat of a communist revolution and issued a decree 'for the protection of the People and State'. It banned many freedoms and allowed imprisonment without trial. Following the 'protection of the People and State', the Enabling Act authorised the Nazi-influenced government to issue laws that the Reichstag could not change. The Enabling Act effectively killed Weimar democracy. The Nazis had established a legal dictatorship.

Germany, 1815–1939

The crushing of opposition

An authoritarian state can tolerate no challenge to its power. Very quickly Hitler made sure all German states were ruled directly from Berlin and the individual states had no separate political voice. On 14th July 1933, the Nazi government declared the Nazi party to be the only legal political party in Germany. Without political choice there was no democracy. Behind the scenes, Hitler needed the support of important groups of people – especially the army – but by 1934 the Nazi's private army, the SA, seemed to threaten Hitler's relationship with the army officers.

'The Night of the Long Knives'

The SA had caused much of the violence that disturbed Germany through the later 1920s and by 1934 Hitler saw them as, at best, an embarrassment and, at worst, a threat to his security.

The leader of the SA was Ernst Rohm. He planned to merge the regular army with the poorly trained SA to make a people's army. Hitler knew he had to choose between his old friends in the SA or the regular army officer class. Hitler's elimination of the SA leadership happened on 30th June 1934. It was called 'The Night of the Long Knives'. Hitler's private bodyguard, the SS, was used to kill many of Hitler's enemies, including Rohm. The ruthless murder of suspected enemies made Hitler more secure and it pleased the regular army.

The Oath of Loyalty and the death of Hindenburg

Hindenburg's death signalled the final end of the Weimar Constitution. When he died, Hitler merged the role of President and Chancellor to become Fuhrer. Earlier, every individual member of the armed forces had to take an Oath of Loyalty to Hitler personally. The result was that, by August 1934, Hitler had complete power.

The Nazi police state

Nazi Germany was a totalitarian police state that aimed at total control of all aspects of life in Germany. Hitler had the power to make laws, to enforce the laws and to control the law courts.

In Nazi Germany, opposition was not tolerated. Most non-Nazis in Germany believed that resistance was hopeless.

Hitler deliberately unleashed a reign of terror with the intention of destroying all opposition and conditioning the rest of the population to obey. People were kept in prison with no idea why they were there or when they would be released. The Nazis destroyed the system of justice, civil rights and individual freedoms. Hitler also gained support, or at least no resistance, from the bulk of the German population with policies that were popular.

Hitler's policies

Most Germans were not active Nazis, but Nazism gave many Germans what they wanted. They were prepared to acquiesce (go along with) the Nazi dictatorship. For most Germans, life seemed better and more secure than in the 1920s.

Work, leisure and the economy

When Hitler became Chancellor in 1933, unemployment stood at 25·9 %. By 1939, it stood at less than 1%. Hitler had delivered his promise of providing work and bread for the German people. It's hardly surprising that many Germans saw Hitler as their saviour and willingly supported him. The German Labour Front allowed workers to campaign for improved working conditions and gave workers access to the popular 'Strength Through Joy' movement, which provided leisure activities for thousands of German workers.

Education and German youth

The purpose of youth organisations such as the Hitler Youth and the League of German Maidens was to prepare the boys for military service and the girls for motherhood. In schools, the German youth was indoctrinated with Nazi ideas.

Religion

Hitler believed that control of the churches was important to the maintenance of Nazi authority. As early as 1933 a Concordat, or agreement, was reached with the Catholic Church. Protestant churches were put under the control of the Reichbishop who only allowed church ministers who supported the Nazis to continue working.

The use of propaganda

Propaganda was vitally important for the Nazis to maintain control, spread its system of beliefs and to persuade the population to support the new regime.

Got it? ☐ ☐ ☐   **Germany, 1815–1939**

Anti-Semitism

In Nazi Germany, Jews were visible targets who could be blamed for all of Germany's problems. The removal of thousands of Jews from their jobs also created vacancies in the labour market that could be filled by non-Jewish members of the 'master race'.

TOP TIP
Anti-Semitism is the hatred of Jews.

Foreign policy

In 1919, the Treaty of Versailles humiliated Germany. One of the attractions of the Nazi party was its promise to destroy the Treaty of Versailles and make Germany a strong and respected nation again. By 1935, Germany was rearming and in 1936, German troops moved into the demilitarised Rhineland. Germany could now reinforce its western border in preparation for changing the map of east central Europe. In 1938, Anschluss with Austria (the incorporation of Austria into Germany) saw German power increasing and later the same year Britain and France gave in to all of Hitler's demands over Czechoslovakia in a desperate attempt to appease him and so avoid the risk of war. In 1939, when German forces invaded Poland, Hitler had no reason to suspect that there would be any serious consequences. Between 1933 and 1939, Hitler had restored the international power and status of Germany and the German public celebrated Nazi success.

TEST YOURSELF

Do you know the meaning of these key words?

Totalitarian
Dictatorship
Anti-Semitism
Oath
Appease
Acquiesce

Check Your Understanding

ESSENTIAL KNOWLEDGE

1. Why was the Reichstag fire important to Hitler's rise to power?
2. Why was the Night of the Long Knives necessary for Hitler?
3. Why did Hitler and Nazism appeal to many Germans in the early 1930s?

THEME QUESTION

1. Is it true to say that the Nazis kept control in Germany by carrot and stick methods?
2. When did Hitler really have complete power in Germany?
3. Would you have supported Hitler if you had been alive in 1930s Germany?

Germany 1800–1939

Issues 1–3
Issue 4
Issues 1–3 and 4 overlap
Issue 5
Issue 6

1800
Napoleon has abolished over 400 German States and created Confederation of the Rhine.

1834
Zollverein starts. 'German' economic growth boosted by customs union and spread of railways.

1848/9
Revolutions fail. Frankfurt parliament collapses.

1866
War with Austria.

1871
War with France. Germany united.

1918
Germany defeated.

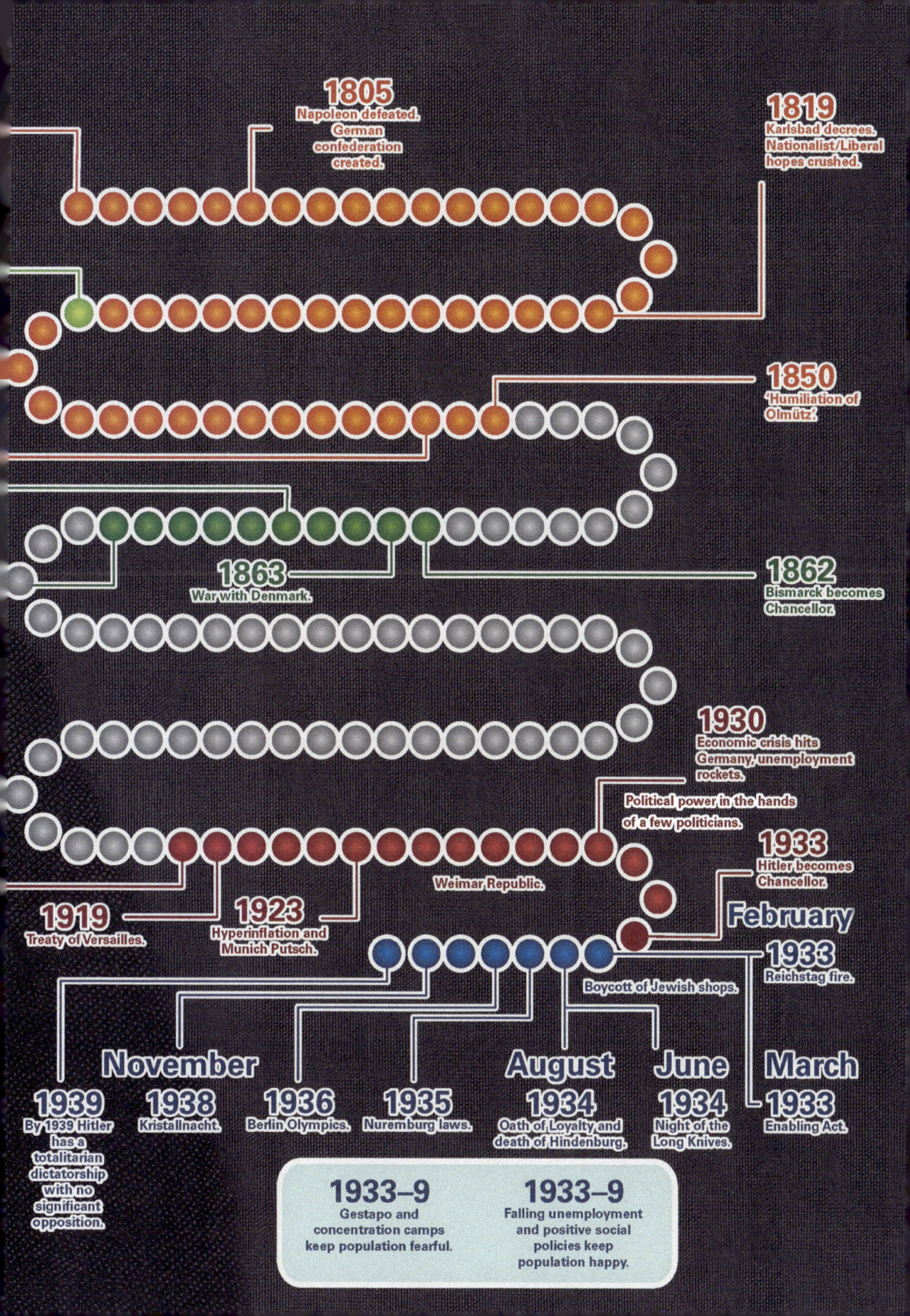

1805 Napoleon defeated. German confederation created.

1819 Karlsbad decrees. Nationalist/Liberal hopes crushed.

1850 'Humiliation of Olmütz'.

1863 War with Denmark.

1862 Bismarck becomes Chancellor.

1930 Economic crisis hits Germany, unemployment rockets.

Political power in the hands of a few politicians.

1933 Hitler becomes Chancellor.

Weimar Republic.

1919 Treaty of Versailles.

1923 Hyperinflation and Munich Putsch.

Boycott of Jewish shops.

February 1933 Reichstag fire.

November 1938 Kristallnacht.

1936 Berlin Olympics.

1935 Nuremburg laws.

August 1934 Oath of Loyalty and death of Hindenburg.

June 1934 Night of the Long Knives.

March 1933 Enabling Act.

1939 By 1939 Hitler has a totalitarian dictatorship with no significant opposition.

1933–9 Gestapo and concentration camps keep population fearful.

1933–9 Falling unemployment and positive social policies keep population happy.

Question paper 1: British, European and World History

Key issue 1: An evaluation of the reasons for changing attitudes towards immigration in the 1920s

What is this section all about?

The USA had an open door policy towards immigration that meant people from all over the world were free to go to America to start new lives. By 1918, the USA was a multi-ethnic society. In the years that followed it became less easy for immigrants to enter the USA. This section is about why attitudes hardened against immigrants and what was done to restrict immigration.

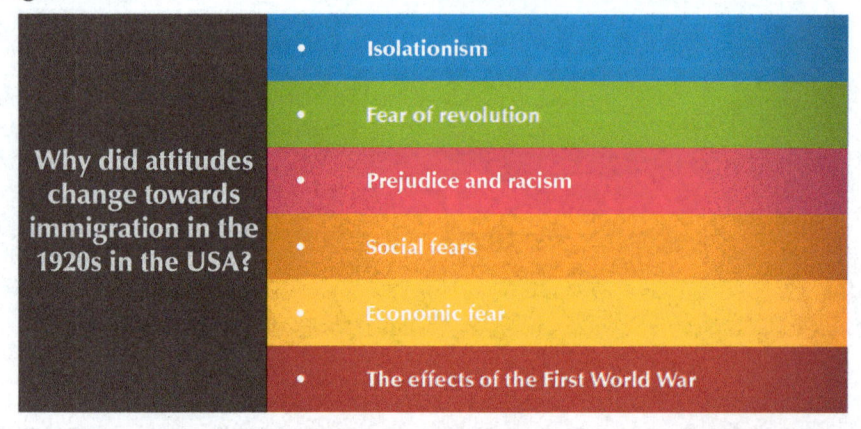

Why did attitudes change towards immigration in the 1920s in the USA?
- Isolationism
- Fear of revolution
- Prejudice and racism
- Social fears
- Economic fear
- The effects of the First World War

Fear-driven attitudes

Prejudice and racism

Up until the 1880s, most migrants to the USA came from northern and western Europe – places such as Britain, Germany and Scandinavia. After 1880, the majority of migrants came from southern and eastern Europe – places such as Russia, Poland and Italy. The older, more established sons and daughters of immigrants were eventually described as WASPs, which stood for White, Anglo-Saxon Protestants. These WASPs disliked the thousands of 'new' immigrants from southern and eastern Europe who flooded into American after 1900. When the First World War ended in 1918 there was a concern that America would be flooded by millions more of these new immigrants.

Many white Americans were afraid that the arrival of new immigrants from southern and eastern Europe threatened their way of life and their Protestant religion. Consequently a wave of 'nativism' spread through the country. 'Nativists' claimed to have scientific evidence to support their belief that 'new' immigrants were physically and mentally inferior to WASPs. This was the 'science' of Eugenics. In 1916, Madison Grant published a book called 'The Passing of the Great Race'. Grant argued that the 'new immigrants' were inferior to the older type of immigrant and that immigrants should be stopped from entering the country. Around the same time, the Ku Klux Klan (KKK) was reinvented in 1915 with a new slogan – 'America for Americans'. Americans blamed many of their problems on the new immigrants. The answer to America's problems seemed to be to stop immigration, especially those from 'undesirable' parts of the world.

Social fears

Anti-immigration groups in the USA claimed immigrants made houses and jobs harder to get for Americans. The great majority of new immigrants settled in cities in the north-east of the USA, in and around New York. Landlords knew that high demand for housing meant they could raise rents. As a result, the white, working-class residents also saw their rents being forced up and housing harder to find as a result of competition from immigrants.

Meanwhile, outside the big cities – in small-town America and rural communities – Americans felt they were being invaded and that America was no longer the country they once knew. These nativists feared that the 'invasion' of Jews and Catholics from eastern and southern Europe would undermine their way of life, and that the stories they heard of crime, immorality and sin were all the fault of these 'new' types of immigrants.

Economic fears

In the early 1900s, new ways of working in factories were being introduced that speeded up the production of many things. Factory owners realised they could make huge profits while at the same time employing immigrants and paying them rock-bottom wages. Suddenly, skilled workers in factories saw their jobs threatened by competition from new immigrants.

New immigrants were also used as 'strike breakers'. Immigrants were usually prepared to work longer hours for lower wages than their American fellow workers simply because long hours and low wages in the USA were much better than they were used to. As the resentment towards immigrant strike breakers and rising rents increased, so did the desire to stop immigrants coming into the country.

Fear of crime

Americans feared that immigrants brought more crime. In the early 1920s, organised crime was increasing. One of the most famous names to link immigrants to crime was Alphonse Gabriel 'Al' Capone. Capone was born in New York City but his parents were Italian immigrants. Capone represented the fear and dislike that many Americans had of organised crime and reinforced the stereotype that all Italian immigrants were in some way linked to crime.

Question paper 1: British, European and World History

After World War I, the US banned the sale of all alcohol. This was called Prohibition. Organised crime gangs stepped in to supply the 'booze'. In the minds of the public, a strong connection was made between crime and the organised crime gangs of Italian immigrants, especially the Mafia with its roots in Sicily. Sacco and Vanzetti were two Italian immigrant anarchists who were convicted of robbery and murder, and their trial linked crime, immigrants and political revolutionary ideas in the minds of Americans. Many Americans felt that the two men should be found guilty not because they were guilty of robbery and murder, but because they were immigrants and had strong, radical ideas about changing the US system.

Fear of revolution

In 1917, the Russian Revolution turned Russia into a communist state. As many thousands of immigrants to the USA came from Russia and eastern Europe, the American authorities began to fear that the immigrants would bring communist ideas with them and perhaps start a revolution. This was called the 'red scare'.

In 1919, there was a huge wave of strikes in the USA. The strikers were often unskilled and semi-skilled workers, many of whom were recent immigrants from southern and eastern Europe. People against the unions wasted no time in linking the union strikes with the spread of communism. The red scare was made worse by the terrorist activities of small revolutionary groups inside America who sent letter bombs to government officials. Public fears of violent red revolution seemed to be confirmed. When it became clear that there was no risk of revolution in America, the 'red scare' faded away – but not before it increased suspicion of immigrants.

The First World War

A large part of the US immigrant population was of German or Austrian origin, but during the war the American public were persuaded that Germany was an enemy of America. Propaganda stories reporting German atrocities increased dislike of immigrants from Germany and the old Austrian Empire. A second anti-German connection was made by people wanting to stop immigration. Many Germans were involved in the brewing industry and if alcohol was a threat to the American way of life, then it stood to reason Germans were a bad influence too! Anti-immigration groups had found another way to stir up feeling against immigrants. After the First World War, the USA adopted an isolationist policy. That meant that the USA wanted nothing to do with Europe or its problems. Most of the US population had chosen to leave Europe behind and by 1918 many in America wanted to stop immigrants from Europe bringing their problems into the USA.

Got it? ☐ ☐ ☐   USA, 1918–1968

Restrictions on immigration

The USA had already been trying to stop immigrants from Asia since the 1880s; the Chinese Exclusion Act tried to stop and even remove Chinese immigrants who had settled in the Californian area since the 1870s. In the early 1900s other laws tried to restrict the immigration of people judged to be unsuitable or unable to read English. By 1921, the US government took its first steps towards closing the open door for European immigrants. Both the 1921 and the 1924 Immigration Acts made it harder for people from southern, central and eastern Europe to emigrate to America. By 1929, it became even harder to gain entry to the USA and by 1930, immigration from southern and eastern Europe and Asia had almost stopped.

Check Your Understanding

ESSENTIAL KNOWLEDGE

1. What was the 'open door' policy towards immigration to the USA?
2. Was USA policy towards immigration in the 1920s racist?
3. Why was the Sacco Vanzetti case so important in the increased dislike of immigrants?

THEME QUESTION

1. How could any American descended from an immigrant justify his or her position towards immigrants in the 1920s?

TEST YOURSELF

Do you know the meaning of these key words?

Multi-ethnic
Prohibition
Nativism
Immigration
Red
Isolationism
Mafia

Question paper 1: British, European and World History

Key issue 2: An evaluation of the obstacles to the achievement of civil rights for black people up to 1941

What is this section all about?

Although slavery ended in 1865, the black population of the USA was still not 'free at last'. Under slavery, most black Americans were controlled. After slavery, new ways of control were introduced. Jim Crow laws restricted freedom while the Ku Klux Klan controlled black Americans by fear. By the 1920s and 30s little had changed, with racism restricting black progress and weaknesses within the black community creating yet another obstacle to the achievement of civil rights.

What were the main problems that faced black Americans in achieving civil rights before 1941

- Difficulties created by the Jim Crow laws
- The 'separate but equal' decision of the Supreme Court
- Popular prejudice
- Activities of the Ku Klux Klan; lack of political influence; divisions in the black community

Racism

In the southern states, an economy had developed based on slavery. Slaves were used in the tobacco, cotton and sugar plantations. Slaves far outnumbered the white population but slaves were easily controlled. They had no freedom and were property to be bought and sold. However, after 1865 when slavery was ended, the white population was worried. How could they control people who they had grown up believing were inferior and even a threat to the white way of life? The answer lay in new laws and the use of violence.

Legal problems

The southern states used 'Jim Crow' laws to maintain a segregated society in which white authority kept control over the black population. The name Jim Crow is just a nickname for all sorts of laws that treated black Americans unfairly, made sure black and white people were kept separate and that black Americans were denied their legal rights. The situation was made even worse by a decision of the Supreme Court in 1896.

The Supreme Court is the most important legal court in America. It decides if any law takes away or limits the basic rights of people that are guaranteed in the American Constitution. In 1896, the Supreme Court decided it was acceptable for black and white Americans to be segregated as long as equal facilities were provided for each race. This decision was called the 'Separate but Equal' decision. It accepted that Jim Crow laws were legal and acceptable across the USA. Mainly as a result of this ruling, segregation was strengthened and did not start to break down until 1954, another 60 years away.

The activities of the Ku Klux Klan

In 1915, the Ku Klux Klan was reborn, claiming to be a patriotic organisation protecting 'the American way of life' devoted to '100% Americanism'. In the South, the KKK used fear to stop black Americans registering to vote. The KKK was against any attempt to improve civil rights and believed that black Americans were inferior human beings. One estimate of Klan membership made in the 1920s was as high as three million. By the end of the 1930s, the Klan was not as important as it had been but terror, fear and the difficulty of winning any justice or fair treatment still dominated the minds of black Americans, especially in the South.

Lack of political influence

Many southern states created new voting rules that made it very difficult for black Americans to register to vote and as a result, by 1900 very few black people in the South were able to vote. With no vote, black Americans could not elect politicians to fight against Jim Crow laws. Politicians in the South relied on white voters. Because many of the white voters were also racist, it made no political sense for any politician to campaign to help black people in the South.

TOP TIP
This section will only require you to focus on the years **before** 1941. Be careful that you do not get confused and write about events in the 1950s and 60s. You will get no marks for doing so in this question.

In the northern cities, the power of a united black vote could be seen when many black politicians at local and national level were elected. Since the First World War there had been a flood of black migration north to the industrial cities where much better pay could be found. It was called the Great Migration. However, in the north, thousands of poor white Americans were also looking for work and housing and saw black Americans as unwelcome competition. In 1919, there were several race riots in northern cities such as Washington and Chicago. The riots were sparked off by racial tensions made worse by a lack of adequate housing. Black Americans consequently found themselves segregated into communities and areas of cities known as ghettos. Although there were many social problems in the ghetto, those places did create a united black electorate.

However, across the USA as a whole there was little black political influence. The 1930s was a time of economic depression in America and President Roosevelt needed the support of his Democratic Party to put his economic reforms called 'the New Deal' into operation. However, many Democrats in Congress came from southern states and were opposed to any move towards civil rights. As a result, President Roosevelt refused to tackle any of the long-standing social problems, such as racism and segregation, that afflicted American society.

Question paper 1: British, European and World History

Divisions in the black community

In the years following the Supreme Court decision of 1896, several organisations were formed to help improve the lives of black Americans and fight segregation. There were three main arguments about how to win civil rights and these can be seen in the ideologies of three civil rights leaders:

- Booker T. Washington argued that black people could only achieve an equal place in mixed society if they were educated first.
- In 1909, W.E.B. Du Bois became the first leader of the National Association for the Advancement of Colored People (NAACP). That organisation worked within the legal system in its struggle to improve employment, housing, voting rights and education for black Americans. Du Bois placed the responsibility for racial inequality squarely on whites and refused to accept that blacks were in any way inferior. He proposed complete racial equality.
- Marcus Garvey introduced his Universal Negro Improvement Association (UNIA) to New York City in 1916 and by 1922, the UNIA claimed a membership of 6 million. Garvey argued that white racism would not change and so Garvey urged blacks to be proud of their black identity. However, Garvey was found guilty of fraud in 1925 and his appeal faded away until his ideas became popular again in the 1960s.

These three leaders demonstrate that many black Americans were challenging 'white power' long before 1945. However, the fact that there were three different organisations with different aims and methods weakened the overall campaign for civil rights. Before 1941, black Americans had made little progress towards civil rights. The reasons for the lack of progress could be summed up as social, economic and political with quite a lot of terror tactics and bullying by the KKK on top of that. All that was about to change after the Second World War.

Check Your Understanding

ESSENTIAL KNOWLEDGE

1. What was the 'Separate but Equal' decision?
2. Why did that decision cause such problems for black progress towards civil rights?

THEME QUESTION

1. Why did the Jim Crow laws and the KKK all grow in popularity in the years AFTER slavery was abolished in the 1860s?
2. How would you summarise the main ideas of the three different black organisations?
3. Why would many white Americans dislike those black organisations?

TEST YOURSELF

Do you know the meaning of these key words?

Jim Crow laws

Segregation

Civil rights

USA, 1918–1968

Key issue 3: An evaluation of the reasons for the economic crisis of 1929–1933

What is this section all about?

In 1929, the Wall Street Crash marked the beginning of a US economic crisis that created a worldwide Depression. A phrase now used to describe the events of 1929 is that the Wall Street Crash was the symptom, not the disease. In other words, the economic crash did not cause the crisis, the Crash of 1929 was the product of much longer-term causes of the Depression that lasted in America from 1929 until 1933.

An evaluation of the reasons for the economic crisis of 1929–33
- Republican government policies in the 1920s
- Overproduction of goods
- Underconsumption – the saturation of the US market
- Weaknesses of the US banking system
- International economic problems
- The Wall Street Crash

Republican government policies and the boom of the 1920s

In the 1920s, industrial production in America doubled and the economy boomed. The First World War made most of Europe poorer but made America rich. New, more efficient methods of production were introduced during the war to increase production. The new industry of advertising persuaded Americans those consumer goods such as radios, refrigerators and vacuum cleaners were now affordable necessities. Hire purchase became common as a way to pay for these new consumer goods. Confident Americans were happy to buy goods on credit, so long as they knew they would have good wages and plenty of work, for as long as they wanted them.

Women soldering radio chassis at Belmont Radio, 1922.

TOP TIP
Remember this section is about why the economic crash happened and is not about why there was a boom in 1920s America. Beware you don't find yourself writing too much description about 'the boom'.

Factors that contributed to the economic crisis

Overproduction and underconsumption

Put simply, this means that too much was being made and too little was being bought. Only a wealthy minority of the US population could afford the new consumer goods that rolled off factory production lines. If factories could not sell what they made, they would have to stop, and pay off their workers, thus creating unemployment. Mass production was only successful when there was mass consumption. By the end of the 1920s it was clear the market for the new consumer goods was saturated. Those who wanted the goods now had them. The rest of America was too poor to afford them. The economic boom of the 1920s was only a good time for some. In 1929, President Hoover said, 'we in America today are nearer to the final triumph over poverty than ever before in the history of any land'. But one year earlier, in 1928, it was estimated that 42% of Americans did not earn enough to buy adequate food, clothing or shelter.

International problems

New laws such as the Fordney McCumber law created a system of economic protection. Protection meant raising taxes on imports to America in order to make them more expensive to buy than American products so that Americans would choose to buy American-made products. In theory, consumption of American goods would rise and that would solve the problem of overproduction. In reality, protectionism made the US economy worse. Foreign countries were angered by America's raising of tariff barriers so they raised taxes on American goods arriving in their country.

The weak banking system

In the 1920s there was no control over banks. Anyone could open a bank and in hundreds of small communities local people put their money into the banks for safe-keeping and a small amount of interest. The banks then used that money to make investments that made some money for the banks. The problem was that as the economic boom grew, banks began to invest savers' money in stocks and shares, hoping to make a large profit by selling the same stocks and shares when prices rose.

The boom was encouraged by the Republican Party, who governed America throughout the 1920s. The Republicans believed that they should not interfere in business matters. This policy was called laissez-faire and was summed up by President Coolidge when he said that 'the chief business of the American people is business'.

The Wall Street Crash

By the late 1920s, ordinary people, banks and even big businesses were buying shares 'on the margin'. This meant that the buyers did not have the money to pay for the shares they bought. They intended to pay off their debt by selling their shares for a big profit when share prices rose. After all, that was what had been happening year after year in the late 1920s. But what would happen if share prices started to fall? What would happen if savers suddenly wanted their savings back from banks that had been gambling on share prices rising?

Got it? ☐ ☐ ☐   USA, 1918–1968

During the late 1920s, the economic boom started to slow down. As factory production started to fall, shareholders realised that the boom was slowing down and suddenly everyone was selling and no one was buying shares. On 29th October 1929, share values collapsed completely and thousands of Americans were financially ruined as the Wall Street Crash revealed how fragile and unstable the boom of the 1920s really was.

The Depression

When the Crash happened, savers wanted their money back. Banks could not cope with the demand. The normal banking system almost ceased to exist and without a stable and efficient banking system, the economy could not function properly. Between 1929 and 1932, over 100,000 businesses collapsed and 15 million people became unemployed – millions of whom lost not only their jobs, but their savings and homes as well. However, very few politicians realised the seriousness of the crisis and believed that the economy would eventually recover by itself without the need for federal intervention.

What did the government do to help?

The Crash and the Depression were the result of long-term problems and Republican policies were not entirely to blame. However, while President Hoover's representative said that prosperity was 'just around the corner', the Republicans did too little to help the economy recover. Although Hoover forced the federal government to do far more than would have been thought possible, in the early 1920s federal spending on job creation was far outweighed by cutbacks at state and local level. Overall, Republican attempts to bring America out of the Depression were described as 'too little, too late'.

Check Your Understanding

ESSENTIAL KNOWLEDGE

1. What do boom and crash mean in economic terms?
2. What is a saturated market?
3. Why were the Republicans criticised for providing 'too little, too late' to help the economy out of the Depression?

THEME QUESTION

1. Why is the Wall Street Crash described as 'the symptom, not the disease'?
2. Do you think that Republican laissez-faire policies were the main reason for the Depression?

TEST YOURSELF

Do you know the meaning of these key words?

Hire purchase
Underconsumption
Overproduction
Protection
Tariffs

Question paper 1: British, European and World History

Key issue 4: An assessment of the effectiveness of the New Deal

What is this section all about?

By the end of 1932, the USA was deep in Depression. In November, there was a Presidential election and the Democratic candidate, Franklin Delano Roosevelt (FDR), won it. Immediately FDR launched into economic changes aimed at helping America to recover. You will need to know what the New Deal did to help the US economy and be able to judge how successful it was in bringing America out of the Depression.

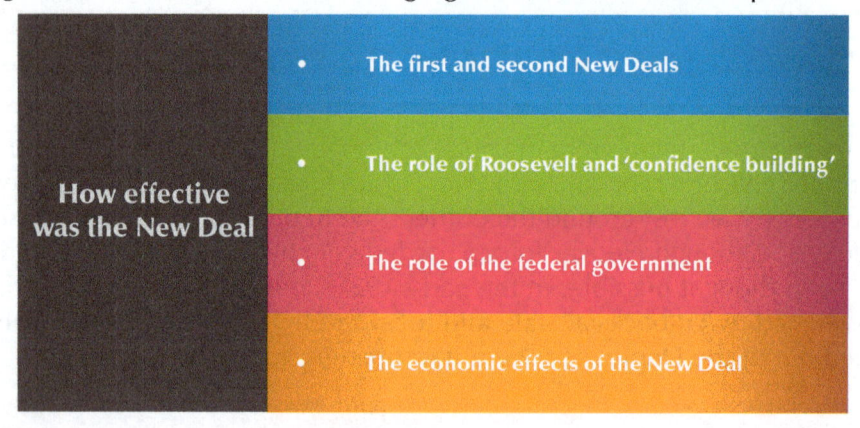

How effective was the New Deal
- The first and second New Deals
- The role of Roosevelt and 'confidence building'
- The role of the federal government
- The economic effects of the New Deal

FDR

In March 1933, at the height of the Depression, Franklin Delano Roosevelt (popularly known as FDR) became President of the United States. He told Americans that the only thing they had 'to fear was fear itself' and offered a 'New Deal for the American people'. Roosevelt gave people confidence that something could be done to get America out of the Depression. He believed only large-scale government action could help. FDR's ideas were completely different from the laissez-faire approach of the Republicans and the idea of 'rugged individualism'.

There were three main aims to Roosevelt's New Deal, called the Three Rs:
- Relief – the federal government took action to help the millions of unemployed.
- Recovery – the federal government took action to rebuild the shattered economy.
- Reform – the federal government made new laws to create a fairer society.

If you start with these points and fit your detailed information around them, you will have a structure for your answer. In the information on the New Deal that follows, decide which of the actions of the New Deal are best filed under Relief, Recovery or Reform.

USA, 1918–1968

The Alphabet Agencies

To achieve relief and recovery, new government departments were set up. They were known by their initials and were soon nicknamed the 'Alphabet Agencies'.

The main agencies and acts were:

- The Agricultural Adjustment Act (AAA) helped farmers by keeping prices steady and limiting overproduction.
- The Civilian Conservation Corps (CCC) created work for single men aged between 18 and 25. It gave them three meals a day and a small wage.
- The Farm Credit Act (FCA) helped farmers by giving them low interest loans to get them over the hard times.
- The Federal Emergency Relief Administration (FERA) helped the very poor by providing more soup kitchens and money to cover clothing and schooling costs.
- The Home Owners Loan Corporation (HOLC) loaned money to people who faced eviction from their homes because they could not keep up repayments on their mortgage.
- The National Recovery Administration (NRA) aimed to increase workers' wages and improve working conditions.
- The Public Works Administration (PWA) provided work building hospitals, dams, bridges and schools.
- The Tennessee Valley Authority (TVA) aimed to build dams and power plants that would bring electric power to rural areas along the Tennessee River in seven states. In addition, the TVA gave work to thousands of unemployed construction workers in many southern states.

TOP TIP

In any answer on the New Deal, you must be able to name several agencies, what they tried to do and how they tried to do it.

Alphabet agencies depicted in a cartoon parody of President Roosevelt's New Deal using alphabet cards of the sort used to teach children to read.

There were several more things that Roosevelt did to help the economy:

Action	Reason
Banks were closed for 3 days in March 1933. Inspectors checked the accounts and ensured that the banks were being properly run.	To restore public confidence in the banks, to encourage more savings in the banks and also stop people from withdrawing their savings.
The Economy Act cut the wages of all state employees by 15%.	The federal government saved $1 billion, which it was able to spend on relief programmes.

Question paper 1: British, European and World History

Action	Reason
The Beer-Wine Revenue Act (22nd March 1933) made the sale of alcoholic drinks containing up to 3·2% alcohol legal and ended Prohibition.	Prohibition had increased gangster crime and was very unpopular because it banned the sale of alcoholic drinks. Many people were happy with the more free attitude to drinking and the government increased its income through taxation of alcohol.

Was the New Deal doing too much?

Opponents of Roosevelt's New Deal believed that Roosevelt was taking America towards socialism or even communism! The people who thought this were usually rich Republicans who either disliked Roosevelt's plans to tax the rich or believed the New Deal was 'not the American way'. They thought that Roosevelt was acting like a dictator and that federal power was becoming too strong and was taking away individual states' rights to run their own affairs. States, especially in the South, did not like federal government telling them what to do. They thought that the government was wasting money on job creation schemes that were not necessary and on providing help to people who should have relied on 'rugged individualism'.

The Second New Deal

Between 1935 and 1937, more reforms were passed that tried to improve living and working conditions for ordinary Americans, including:

- The National Labor Relations Act (1935) – often called the 'Wagner Act' – gave workers the right to join trade unions and stopped employers from punishing workers who joined those unions.
- The Social Security Act (1935) provided the foundation for a new state pension scheme for old people and widows. Help was also provided for disabled people and poor children.
- The Soil Conservation and Domestic Allotment Act (1936) made it possible for farmers to receive financial aid from the federal government if they conserved and improved the soil on their farms.
- The Works Progress Administration (WPA) gave work to about 2 million people, building roads, schools, tunnels and even a windbreak of trees to protect the Dust Bowl from more erosion.
- The Resettlement Administration and the Farm Security Administration tried to help the sharecroppers and tenant farmers who had not been helped by the AAA.

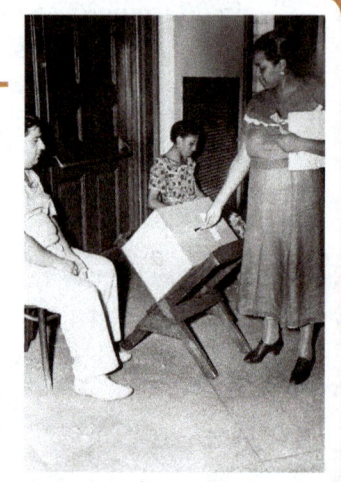

A worker placing her vote into a ballot box, voting in the first consent election held in DC under the Wagner Act.

Got it? ☐ ☐ ☐   USA, 1918–1968

The New Deal did achieve its objective of providing relief for many Americans but the help was very basic. However, the long-term effects of the relief were more important; the idea of granting relief to people who fell on hard times was accepted as 'normal' as opposed to the previously widespread belief in 'rugged individualism'.

TOP TIP

You are likely to be asked to assess the importance or success of the New Deal. To answer that question fully you must be able to explain:
- why the New Deal was started
- what the aims of the New Deal were
- what the New Deal did
- whether or not the New Deal pulled America out of the Depression.

Recovery

The economy hit rock bottom in the winter of 1932–3. After Roosevelt launched the New Deal, the American economy improved every year between 1933 and 1937. However, unemployment was still a big problem and at no time in the 1930s were as many people employed as there had been in 1919. World War II was more important to American recovery than the New Deal – the war guaranteed American recovery and growth by increasing the demand for American manufactured goods. Unemployment fell rapidly as businesses and factories swung into war production.

Check Your Understanding

TEST YOURSELF

Do you know the meaning of these key words?

FDR

Federal

Rugged individualism

ESSENTIAL KNOWLEDGE

1. What were the Three Rs?
2. What were the Alphabet Agencies?
3. In what ways was the New Deal the opposite of the laissez-faire ideas of previous governments?
4. Why did some states dislike the New Deal?

THEME QUESTION

1. In brief, how did the New Deal policies differ from those of the Republican party of the 1920s?

Question paper 1: British, European and World History

Key issue 5: An evaluation of the reasons for the development of the Civil Rights campaign, after 1945

What is this section all about?

Until the Second World War, little had changed to improve the lives of black Americans since the 'Separate but Equal' Supreme Court decision of 1896. However, between the 1950s and 1960s huge changes took place in the lives of all black Americans and this section is about why and how the Civil Rights movement developed at this time.

TOP TIP

The main point of any question on this section will focus on **why** the Civil Rights movement grew after 1945. It is okay to write about the time between 1945 and the early 1960s.

Why did the Civil Rights campaign grow after 1945

- The continuation of prejudice and discrimination
- The experience of black servicemen in the Second World War
- The formation of effective black organizations
- The emergence of effective black leaders
- The role of Martin Luther King

Black servicemen in the Second World War

When black American soldiers returned from the Second World War they wanted a change. They wanted civil rights. They said, 'No more Jim Crow'. During the war, the US army was segregated but black servicemen in Europe found they had freedoms they had never experienced in America. Even in prisoner of war camps, black airmen were treated as officers regardless of their colour. As a result, many black soldiers, sailors and airmen supported the Double V campaign. 'Double V' meant two victories: victory against the enemy abroad, and victory against the enemy at home. The first targets of the Civil Rights movement of the 1950s were segregation and 'Jim Crow' laws.

Black American soldiers with Czechoslovakian women and children in liberated Plzen, Czechoslovakia, in May 1945.

USA, 1918–1968

Continuing discrimination and prejudice

Crow laws still controlled every aspect of a black person's life, especially in the South. The Ku Klux Klan still got away, quite literally, with murder. The continuing problem of prejudice and discrimination was shown most clearly when Emmett Till was murdered. Till was a 14-year-old black boy from Chicago on holiday in the South and his murder shocked America, especially when his mother showed the brutalised body of her son to the nation in an open-topped coffin. The Emmett Till case had a motivating effect on the Civil Rights movement. The North became aware of the full horror of segregation and persecution of black Americans in the South.

The 1954 Supreme Court ruling

In 1954, the Supreme Court ruled that segregation had no place in modern American education. For the first time, the highest court in the USA had decided that segregation was wrong. That decision overturned the 'Separate but Equal' decision of 1896 that had justified and made respectable Jim Crow discrimination for the previous 60 years. The Supreme Court decision of 1954 showed that segregation could be changed and it opened the doors to demands to end segregation everywhere.

Development and formation of effective black organisations

NAACP and MIA

The bus boycott in Montgomery, Alabama had important results for the Civil Rights movement. Remember the date – it was 1955, just one year after the Supreme Court of the USA had declared that segregation was wrong in schools. The NAACP wanted to argue that if segregation was wrong in schools, was it not also wrong in everyday life, such as on buses?

The NAACP used the arrest of Rosa Parks – who refused to give up her seat on a segregated bus – to challenge Alabama's segregation laws. What was even more important was that the black community in Montgomery began a boycott of the city's buses in support of Rosa Parks. The bus boycott had huge consequences for the Civil Rights movement. It showed the economic and political power of the black community when it united. A new organisation was formed – the Montgomery Improvement Association (MIA). The bus boycott showed what could be achieved by organised, peaceful, non-violent protest. Another big result of the bus boycott was the emergence of a new Civil Rights leader – Martin Luther King.

The NAACP continued to campaign for civil rights by working through the law courts. Their next target was schools. In September 1957, the NAACP decided to test the willingness of states in the South to desegregate their schools with a campaign centred on Little Rock High School, Arkansas. What was more important, once again, was the way that mass media, especially TV, was helping the Civil Rights movement. The sight of screaming white crowds stopping American students going to school made national news headlines. For the first time, people across the USA and the world could see what was happening in places such as Little Rock.

Question paper 1: British, European and World History

Emergence of new organisations and new leadership

SCLC, SNCC and CORE

Organisations such as the NAACP were thought to be too slow and too 'old'. The pictures of soldiers protecting children going to school in Little Rock along with the success of direct action in the Montgomery Bus Boycott caused people to rethink their protest methods.

In 1957, Martin Luther King, the Reverend Ralph Abernathy and others formed the Southern Christian Leadership Conference (SCLC). The campaigns of the 1950s and early 1960s were influenced by protest methods preached by Martin Luther King. King believed that non-violent, peaceful civil disobedience was the best weapon in the fight for civil rights. King argued that it was the responsibility and right of the citizens of a country to protest against a law that was wrong. Two such protest methods that used non-violent civil disobedience tactics were the sit-ins and the freedom rides.

How successful were sit-ins?

Black students had created SNCC in April 1960 to help coordinate, support and publicise the sit-in campaign. SNCC stood for Student Nonviolent Coordinating Committee and their first target was segregated lunch counters across the South. National television coverage highlighted the violent racist reaction of many Southerners against non-violent demonstrators. The use of non-violent protest in the face of extreme provocation gained the Civil Rights demonstrators support across the country. However, the sit-ins did not end all segregation in the South and their impact was only really felt at a local level.

How successful were freedom rides?

Martin Luther King poses with members of the Student Nonviolent Coordinating Committee (SNCC).

In 1961, a group of black and white members of a non-violent protest group called CORE – the Congress of Racial Equality – wanted to test if segregation on interstate highways really had ended. The CORE Freedom Riders were met with heavy resistance from Southern whites. Once again the TV news coverage of the attacks on the Freedom Riders deeply shocked the American public.

Got it? ☐ ☐ ☐   USA, 1918–1968

Important points to make
- The actions of black and white students breathed new life into the Civil Rights movement. Sit-ins and freedom rides challenged segregation in the South and pushed the federal government into taking action to enforce federal law and change the racist attitudes in the South.
- The actions of new, effective Civil Rights organisations such as CORE, SNCC, SCLC and the MIA demonstrated that anyone who opposed segregation could take direct action themselves to campaign for civil rights.

TOP TIP
There are lots of interesting and memorable events and people in this section. Beware that you do not have long descriptive sections in your answer that are not focused on the essay question. Always ask yourself when writing a narrative section, what point am I trying to make? How does it link to the main question?

Check Your Understanding

TEST YOURSELF

Do you know the meaning of these key words?

Double V
Boycott
Desegregate
Integration
Civil disobedience
The South

ESSENTIAL KNOWLEDGE

1. Why was the development of TV such an important factor in the Civil Rights campaign?
2. Why were non-violent civil disobedience tactics so effective?
3. Can you think of four examples of such tactics?

THEME QUESTION

1. Why was the Supreme Court decision of 1954 such an important turning point?
2. After so many years of segregation and discrimination, why did Civil Rights protests erupt in the 1950s?

81

Question paper 1: British, European and World History

Key issue 6: An assessment of the effectiveness of the Civil Rights movement in meeting the needs of black Americans, up to 1968

What is this section all about?

By 1965, it looked as if the Civil Rights movement had been very effective in meeting the needs of black Americans. In 1964, a Civil Rights Act was passed and in 1965, a Voting Rights Act allowed black Americans to register to vote easily and fairly. It seemed to most of white America that the Civil Rights demonstrators of the 1950s and early 60s had got what they wanted. What puzzled and angered the government and also most of white America were the riots that broke out in US cities between 1964 and 1968 and also the rise of black radical groups that seemed to reject integration and adopted a much more violent, threatening image. Race relations in the USA seemed very different by 1968 than it had in 1964.

How effective was the Civil Rights movement in meeting the needs of black Americans, up to 1968
- Aims of the Civil Rights movement
- Roles of NAACP, CORE, SCLC and Martin Luther King in desegregation
- Methods and tactics of Civil Rights campaigns
- Changes in federal policy
- Social, economic and political changes
- The resultant rise of black radical movements

Growing support for Civil Rights

Through the 50s and early 60s the Civil Rights movement was mostly united behind one aim – the removal of Jim Crow laws and segregation. By early 1962, Martin Luther King staged the biggest demonstration yet at Birmingham, Alabama. King used school children and students in his demonstrations and his tactics were risky but they worked. White authority seemed unable to understand how smart young black organisers would use film of white racist reaction to gain worldwide support for their cause. American people watched their televisions in shock and disbelief as white police officers savagely attacked school children as young as eight, first with powerful fire hoses and then with tear gas, dogs and even electric cattle prods. Finally, President Kennedy appeared on television and promised action based on the principle that 'race has no place in American society'.

Federal support and the wining of civil rights, 1964/65

A few months after the demonstrations in Birmingham, Alabama, Martin Luther King delivered his 'I Have a Dream' speech, which made clear to the world exactly why the Civil Rights movement existed. In 1964 it looked as if all the aims of the Civil Rights movement had been achieved when the US government passed the Civil Rights Act.

The force of police fire hoses on demonstrators in Birmingham, Alabama.

The last big Civil Rights issue in the South was the right to vote freely. In March 1965, a march from Selma to Birmingham, Alabama, was to publicise the way authorities in the South made it difficult for black Americans to vote easily. Sunday 7th March 1965, 'Bloody Sunday', as the day became known, was a turning point in the campaign for fair voting. All across America people were horrified as they watched on TV police on horseback charge and beat the peaceful demonstrators before releasing tear gas.

In August 1965, Congress passed the Voting Rights Act. The 1965 Act helped improve the living and working conditions of many black Americans because white politicians now realised they needed black voters' support if they wanted to stay in power. The Voting Rights Act marked the end of the Civil Rights campaigns in the South.

Why did Black Radical groups rise up in the mid-1960s?

For many young black Americans in the cities, the Civil Rights movement of the 1950s and early 1960s was an irrelevance. By 1965, half of all black Americans lived in the cities of the north and west, most of them in slum areas that were known as ghettos. They had to live with bad housing, high rents, unemployment, poverty and hunger.

The new groups who used violent direct action in their protests were called collectively Black Radicals. The anger and frustration of those Black Radical groups was the **result** of feeling their issues had been ignored by the Civil Rights campaigns in the South and a Civil Rights Act that did nothing to help the problems of the ghettos.

The long hot summers 1964–1968

The social and economic problems of the cities led directly to the riots that erupted in 1965. The importance of the Watts Riot, and others that followed, was to show that poverty, hunger, bad housing and unemployment were far more important to black people in the cities than the 'older' civil rights issues of desegregation and voting rights in the South.

Who were the Black Radical groups?

Faced with these problems, many black Americans in the cities were attracted to the ideas of the Nation of Islam. The Nation of Islam completely rejected the integration ideas of people such as Martin Luther King. While the Nation of Islam was strong in New York and the north-eastern cities of the USA, another Black Radical group was growing on the West Coast. The Black Panther Party represented the complete opposite of Martin Luther King's ideas and supported the anti-white, black separatist ideas of Stokely Carmichael and Malcolm X.

How did federal authority react to the Black Radical groups?

By the mid-1960s, federal authority became worried about the protest groups – was there some sort of plot to take over the USA? Federal government represented the views of most of white America. Attention was drifting away from civil rights towards the Vietnam War. Surely the civil rights issue had been sorted by the Civil Rights Act and the Voting Rights Act? There was increasing white resentment with the black urban protestors who seemed 'ungrateful' for previous legislation.

The importance of the Kerner Commission

More riots followed during the long, hot summers of the next few years. One of the most destructive riots was in Detroit. After the Detroit riot, President Johnson asked Otto Kerner, governor of the state of Illinois, to investigate thoroughly the causes of the urban riots.

The Kerner Commission shocked the American public. It ended by saying that 'our nation is moving towards two societies, one black, one white – separate and unequal'. White society created the ghettos, white society kept them going and white society did nothing to improve them. The Kerner Commission reminded America that it was still a long way from being a free and equal society.

Houses burning during the Detroit race riots, July 1967.

Got it? ☐ ☐ ☐   USA, 1918–1968

1968: free at last?

On 4th April 1968, Martin Luther King was shot and killed as he stood on his motel balcony in Memphis, Tennessee. It seemed that the non-violent Civil Rights movement had died with King. Martin Luther King was a charismatic leader; even Stokely Carmichael said that Martin Luther King was the one man who the masses of black Americans would listen to. Nearly every black American, and most whites, agree that Martin Luther King was one of the most important leaders of any colour in the 20th century. King remains an icon, representing dignified protest against unjust conditions and unfair treatment of human beings. However, at the 1968 Mexico Olympics, when two US athletes won medals, they refused to look at the USA flag as the national anthem played and instead raised their black gloved fists in a Black Power salute. The world was left in no doubt that the problem of race relations in the USA was far from being solved.

Check Your Understanding

ESSENTIAL KNOWLEDGE

1. What links Black Power, Black Panthers and Nation of Islam?
2. How would you have felt about the Black Radical groups if you were white in 1967?
3. How would you have felt if you were a black urban youth living in a ghetto?
4. Why was the Kerner Report so shocking?

THEME QUESTION

1. Why was white America so angered by the Black Radical protests of the later 1960s?
2. In what ways were the Black Radical protests different from the earlier campaigns of the Civil Rights movement?
3. Why is the Kerner Report so important to a course about US civil rights that ends in 1968?

TEST YOURSELF

Do you know the meaning of these key words?

Black Radical
Civil Rights Act
Voting Rights Act
Ghetto
Kerner

USA 1896–1968

Issue 1
Issue 2
Issue 3
Issue 4
Issues 5–6
Issues 1&3

1896
Supreme court decision – 'separate but equal'.

1919
Chicago race riots.

1919-20
Palmer raids.

1920s
A series of laws to restrict immigration.
Sacco/Vanzetti trial.

1929
Wall Street crash.
Depression.

1954
Supreme Court decision – segregation wrong in education.

1909 NAACP formed.

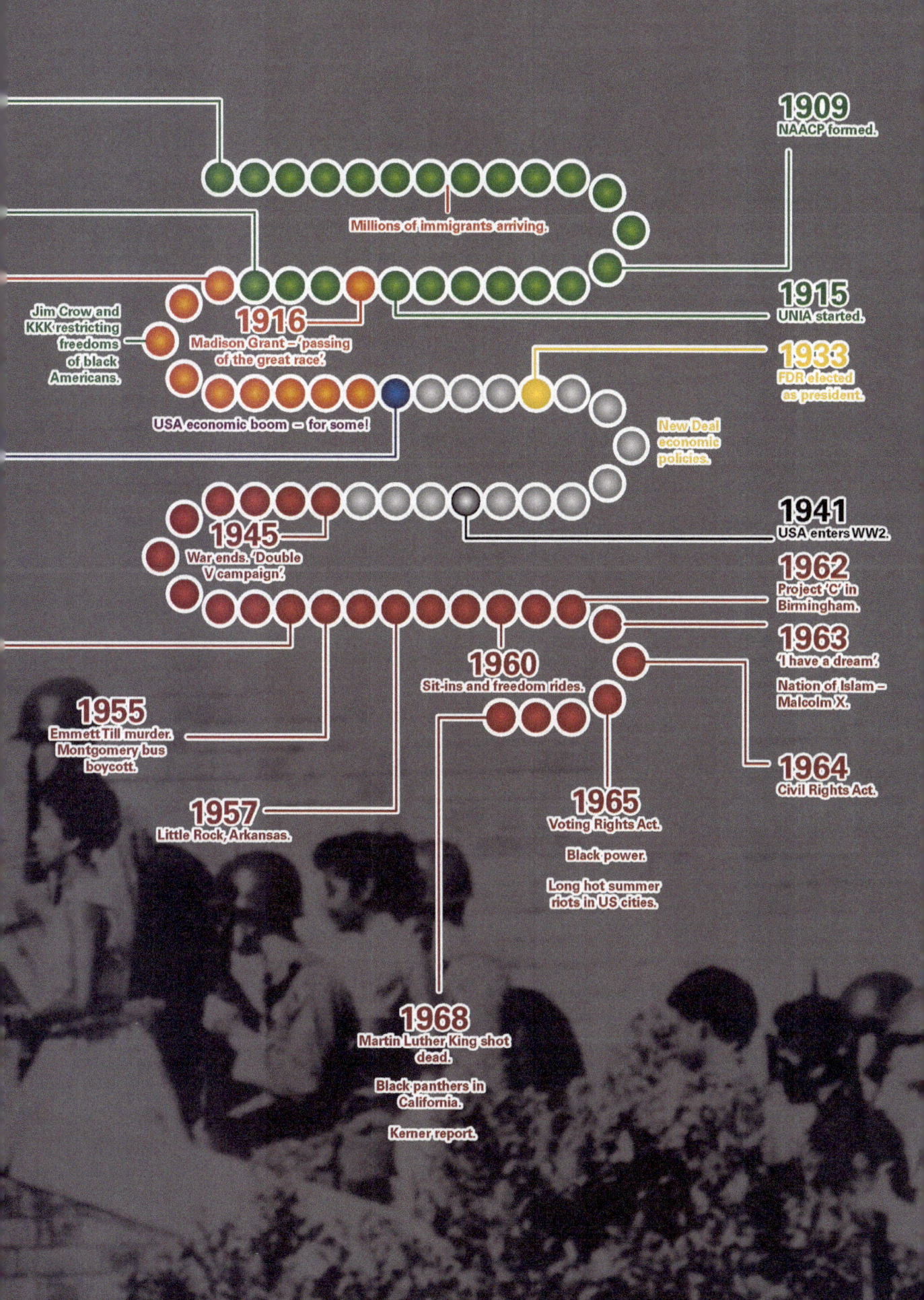

Millions of immigrants arriving.

1915 UNIA started.

Jim Crow and KKK restricting freedoms of black Americans.

1916 Madison Grant – 'passing of the great race'.

1933 FDR elected as president.

USA economic boom – for some!

New Deal economic policies.

1941 USA enters WW2.

1945 War ends. 'Double V campaign'.

1962 Project 'C' in Birmingham.

1963 'I have a dream'. Nation of Islam – Malcolm X.

1960 Sit-ins and freedom rides.

1964 Civil Rights Act.

1955 Emmett Till murder. Montgomery bus boycott.

1957 Little Rock, Arkansas.

1965 Voting Rights Act.

Black power.

Long hot summer riots in US cities.

1968 Martin Luther King shot dead.

Black panthers in California.

Kerner report.

Question paper 1: British, European and World History

Key issue 1: An evaluation of the reasons for the aggressive nature of the foreign policies of Germany and Italy in the 1930s

What is this section all about?

TOP TIP
You must mention both Germany and Italy in this answer.

The Great War was meant to be the war to end all wars. After the war, certain assumptions were made by the victors. These assumptions were that all countries would be democracies, no country would want to go to war again, and if any problems did arise then the League of Nations would maintain world peace. By the 1930s, Germany and Italy were fascist states prepared to use aggression to get what they wanted. This section is about why the fascist states were so prepared to use war to get what they wanted.

Why were the foreign policies of Germany and Italy in the 1930s so aggressive?
- The results of the Peace Settlement of 1919
- Fascist ideology
- Economic difficulties after 1929
- Weakness of the League of Nations
- The British policy of appeasement

The Peace Settlement of 1919

The Paris Peace Settlement was meant to guarantee that there would never again be a war in Europe. However the treaties pleased no one. In 1919 the victorious allies made Germany sign the Treaty of Versailles. Germany was forced to accept blame for causing the war and all the death and destruction that resulted from it. They called the treaty a Diktat – a dictated treaty that was forced on them. Hitler claimed his actions in the 1930s were merely demands for 'fair treatment' to balance the unfair treaty.

Italy hoped to gain land from Austria-Hungary, but when the peace treaties were signed, Italy got almost nothing. When Mussolini came to power in 1922 he promised to make Italy great again and wipe out the embarrassment of the peace treaties.

Appeasement and the Road to War, to 1939

Weakness of the League of Nations

The purpose of the League of Nations was to ensure world peace through a combination of disarmament and collective security. Both those methods failed.

Disarmament means countries giving up their weapons and would only work if the countries trusted each other, but France refused to disarm. By 1934, the Disarmament Conferences failed to reach any agreement.

What was collective security?

Collective security meant member states agreeing to work together to guarantee peace and security in the world. In the 1930s collective security failed because members of the League of Nations were not prepared to get involved in issues beyond their own national interest. By the mid-1930s, the League had failed and the failure of the League is linked closely to the adoption of the policy of appeasement by Britain.

An international conference of the League of Nations, which was formed after the end of the Great War to solve international disputes.

Fascist ideology and foreign policy

A fascist dictatorship is a country controlled by one person at the head of the only political party in that country. Germany under Hitler and Italy under Mussolini were examples of fascist dictatorships. Hitler had a planned and detailed foreign policy that was also linked to his fascist ideology. Hitler's foreign policy was expansionist and potentially aggressive.

The Treaty of Versailles had to be destroyed

The treaty symbolised Germany's humiliation. Most of what happened later can be directly linked to Hitler's aim of destroying the Treaty of Versailles.

All German-speaking people must live in one enlarged Germany

He said that all Germans had the right to live in Germany and if that meant the borders of Germany had to spread to take in extra Germans, then he was prepared to make that happen. That would also mean that conflict with neighbouring countries was likely.

Question paper 1: British, European and World History

Germans were the master race
Hitler believed Aryans, or Germans, were the master race. Hitler talked about 'inferior' races such as Jews and Slavs or Poles as sub-humans – not even real people. Hitler believed 'inferior races' had one purpose in life: to serve the master race.

Germany must have Lebensraum
Hitler believed that Germany was defeated in the Great War partly because it ran out of food and oil. Hitler knew that the resources he wanted could be found in Russia. Most of Hitler's foreign policy was powered by his need for eastwards expansion towards and into Russia. This policy aim was called Lebensraum.

In summary, fascist ideology wanted to change the Paris Peace Settlement, restore national pride, develop national empires and military strength, build up economic power and take resources as required from whoever had them.

Economic difficulties after 1929

In 1929, the US economy crashed. The recession that followed spread around the world. In Germany, unemployment reached 6 million and Hitler claimed he was Germany's last hope and that he could solve the economic problems.

In Italy, Mussolini's economic policies were already showing signs of failure by 1929. In the 1930s he relied on foreign policy adventures to distract the Italian people from the failures of his government. An example of Mussolini's aggressive foreign policy is the Italian attack on Abyssinia, a free nation in Africa where Mussolini hoped he could steal land and resources.

A portrait of Mussolini set up by colonist soldiers beside a road in Abyssinia (now known as Ethiopia).

Got it? ☐ ☐ ☐   **Appeasement and the Road to War, to 1939**

The British policy of appeasement

The aim of appeasement was to remove the possibility of conflict. In the 1930s, most of the British government and the public seemed to support the policy – but perhaps what they really supported was anything that would avoid war. Appeasement was meant to avoid war, but Britain declared war on Germany on 3rd September 1939. Appeasement failed.

Most historians accept that the Second World War was caused by German aggression, but some argue that Neville Chamberlain, British Prime Minister from 1937 to 1940, and other supporters of appeasement, were responsible for encouraging fascist aggression, which eventually led to the Second World War.

TEST YOURSELF

Do you know the meaning of these key words?

Fascism
League of Nations
Disarmament
Lebensraum

Check Your Understanding

ESSENTIAL KNOWLEDGE

1. How could the League of Nations try to ensure peace?
2. Why did the League fail to keep peace?
3. What was the purpose of appeasement?
4. Why was appeasement adopted as a British policy?

THEME QUESTION

1. Why was fascist aggression such a surprise in the 1930s?
2. Why was aggression inevitable for fascist states to realise their ambitions?

Question paper 1: British, European and World History

Key issue 2: An assessment of the methods used by Germany and Italy to pursue their foreign policies from 1933

What is this section all about?

Between 1933 and 1939, the fascist powers of Germany and Italy used a combination of aggression and diplomacy to get what they wanted. Faced with a combination of excuses, justifications and all-out threats on one hand, and the desire for self-interest on the other, Britain found it hard to deal with fascist aggression.

How did Germany and Italy develop their foreign policies from 1933 onwards?
- Rearmament by Germany
- Military agreements and pacts
- Political alliances
- Fascist strategies employed in the crises between 1933 and 1939

Broken treaties

Abyssinia
Italy, a League of Nations member, attacked Abyssinia, another League member. Italy simply ignored the rules of the League of Nations when it attacked Abyssinia. Britain's military leaders believed that Britain could not defeat Italy quickly and so tried to do a deal with Italy. In effect, Italy gained Abyssinia by using force and although Abyssinia was a League of Nations member, Britain did nothing to protect Abyssinia against the first clear example of fascist aggression.

Rearming and conscription
In 1935, Hitler announced he would rearm Germany and bring back conscription. Both of these were necessary before Hitler could use military force. Both of these actions also broke the Treaty of Versailles. Hitler also used France's refusal to disarm as an excuse to claim he needed to defend himself against a strong neighbour.

Appeasement and the Road to War, to 1939

The Anglo-German Naval Treaty

This treaty was signed in 1935. The German navy was severely reduced by the Versailles Treaty. Germany was not allowed any submarines, yet Britain accepted the expansion of the German navy, including submarines, when it agreed the Naval Treaty with Germany. Britain was now directly involved in an agreement that broke the Treaty of Versailles.

Think point

As appeasement continued, was Hitler encouraged in his use of threat and bluff by the weakness of Britain? Put simply, did Hitler simply 'play' Britain with a combination of excuses and justifications? How could Britain justify war to defend a treaty that Hitler broke in 1936 or 1938 when Britain had already been prepared to break Versailles by accepting the naval treaty in 1935?

Remilitarisation of the Rhineland

On 7th March 1936, Hitler remilitarised the Rhineland. Hitler claimed he was justified as France refused to disarm and had made a potentially threatening alliance with Russia. There was no doubt that the remilitarisation of the Rhineland broke the Versailles Treaty, but what was Britain to do? It had already accepted the Anglo-German Naval Treaty that broke the Versailles Treaty. Hitler used diplomacy; in exchange for being allowed to remilitarise the Rhineland, Hitler promised Germany would return to the League of Nations, start discussing disarmament, and make a 25-year peace promise with Britain! Could Britain really turn down these peaceful promises and use force against Hitler?

German troops marching over the Rhine in Cologne 1936, into the demilitarised zone of the Rhineland, breaking the terms of the Treaty of Versailles.

The Spanish Civil War

This war lasted from 1936 until 1939. It was fought between two opposing groups in Spain – the Nationalists and the Republicans. The Republicans were the elected government and should have received help from democratic countries such as Britain and France. The rebels were the Nationalists – and they got military help from Hitler and Mussolini. The Nationalists won the war and Spain became a fascist country.

Question paper 1: British, European and World History

The Spanish Civil War made the fascist states stronger. Hitler used the Spanish Civil War as a testing ground for his air force, codenamed the Condor Legion. The tactics developed in the Spanish Civil War were vital to develop 'Blitzkrieg' or 'lightning war attack' into Western Europe in 1940. Italy used the war to show off Italian strength and to gain naval bases in Majorca, Ibiza and Minorca. Meanwhile, Britain and France followed a policy of non-intervention that meant they did nothing to help the elected government. It seemed that appeasement just meant giving in and doing nothing to stop the spread of fascism.

Eastern Europe

Austria, March 1938

In March 1938, German troops marched into Austria, against the rules of the Treaty of Versailles. That event was called 'Anschluss', which means the joining together of Austria and Germany. Hitler wanted to create a 'Greater Germany' and start spreading east as part of his Lebensraum plan. When German troops marched into Austria, Hitler claimed they were only moving in to help stabilise the country from communist troubles. He also pointed to the cheering crowds who welcomed the Germans. Once again, Hitler was using excuses and justifications to confuse international reaction.

Czechoslovakia

Czechoslovakia was a new country created after the Great War. It contained many different nationalities of which there were 3 million German speakers who lived in an area called the Sudetenland. Hitler claimed the German-speaking population of the Sudetenland was being persecuted, so he would then have his excuse to invade, claiming he was protecting the Sudeten Germans from Czech persecution.

Poland

By the summer of 1939, Hitler used his tried and tested methods of creating excuses for Germany to take action against Poland. Poland was created at the end of the Great War, partly from land taken from Germany and Russia. Part of Poland – The Polish Corridor – contained mostly German-speaking people. Naturally, Hitler complained about the treatment of Germans in the Polish Corridor and this became Hitler's excuse for pressurising Poland in 1939.

Military agreements, pacts and alliances

The German–Polish Non-Aggression Pact

This pact between Nazi Germany and Poland was signed on 26th January 1934 and promised peace for 10 years. Germany gained respectability and calmed international fears. Hitler had no doubts about breaking the agreement five years later when it suited him to do so.

Got it? ☐ ☐ ☐   **Appeasement and the Road to War, to 1939**

The Rome-Berlin Axis
The fascist powers did not join forces until the Rome-Berlin axis in 1936. It was made stronger by the Pact of Steel, which was an agreement between Italy and Germany signed on 22nd May 1939 for immediate aid and military support in the event of war.

The Anti-Comintern Pact
This pact between Nazi Germany and Japan in 1936 was aimed against Communist Russia. Japan could pressurise Russia's far eastern frontier while Germany pressurised the west. Italy joined in 1937.

The Munich Agreement
These negotiations led to Hitler gaining the Sudetenland and weakening Czechoslovakia.

The Nazi–Soviet Non-Aggression Pact, August 1939
Both Hitler and Stalin bought time for themselves. For Hitler it seemed he could now fight a short, easy war against Poland with no threat of Russia getting involved.

Adolf Hitler and Italian Foreign Minister Galeazzo Ciano, smiling from a balcony with the Italian Kingdom's flag in the background after the signature of the 'Pact of Steel' in Berlin, 1939.

TOP TIP
Comintern was an abbreviation of Communist International. So an anti-Comintern agreement would be an alliance against the spread of communism.

Check Your Understanding

TEST YOURSELF

Do you know the meaning of these key words?

Anglo, as in Anglo-German Treaty

Remilitarisation

Diplomacy

Pact

Justification

ESSENTIAL KNOWLEDGE

1. Summarise the methods used by Hitler to promote his foreign policies and give examples.
2. Which of all the deals made was most likely to lead to war and why?

THEME QUESTION

1. Can you see any pattern in the way Hitler developed his foreign policy power through the 1930s?
2. Why was his strategy of threats and promises more effective than just threats?

Question paper 1: British, European and World History

Key issue 3: An evaluation of the reasons for the British policy of appeasement, 1936–1938

What is this section all about?

This section asks the simple question – why did Britain adopt a policy of appeasement? In the 1950s and 1960s the policy of appeasement was condemned as a policy of cowardice and foolishness that simply encouraged Hitler to demand more and more. Recent research, however, shows that there were very many sensible reasons to explain why Britain adopted a policy of appeasement in the 1930s.

Why did Britain adopt a policy of appeasement?
- Economic difficulties
- Attitudes to the Paris Peace Settlement
- Public opinion
- Pacifism
- Concern over the Empire
- Lack of reliable allies
- Military weakness
- Fear of spread of Communism
- Beliefs of Chamberlain

What were the reasons for appeasement?

Economic concerns

As early as 1934, the Committee of Imperial (Empire) Defence warned that Hitler was 'the ultimate potential enemy'. In the mid-1930s Britain was in a depression. That meant many people were unemployed and the government had little money to spend. Should the available money be used to build more weapons or should the government invest in 'better' things such as new homes, new hospitals and better roads? The British public was opposed to more spending on weapons. By 1937, Hitler was growing stronger while Britain's economy was still relatively weak. Without military resources, was there an alternative to appeasement?

Attitudes to the Paris Peace Settlement

By the 1930s, most of the British public felt the Treaty of Versailles was too harsh on Germany. In hindsight we know Hitler was heading towards war, but between 1936 and 1938 Hitler attacked no one. In 1935, Britain even negotiated a change in the treaty with the Anglo–German Naval Agreement. In 1936, he remilitarised the Rhineland but that was still part of Germany and people said he was only moving soldiers in his own back garden. In March 1938, German troops were welcomed into Austria. What was there to fight about?

Appeasement and the Road to War, to 1939

Public opinion

In 1918, the public were told they had fought 'the war to end all wars'. It was impossible for any politician to suggest a policy that would result in the children of the Great War soldiers, now in their late teens and early 20s, to follow in their fathers' footsteps to relive the horrors of the that war.

The British public was anti-war for two main reasons. One reason looked to the past. The horrors of the Great War were still fresh in the minds of the public. The other looked to the future. By the mid-1930s the government and public were terrified of gas bombs falling from the air. For the first time British cities would be in the front line of enemy attack. That must not be allowed to happen.

Crowds in Salzburg, Austria celebrate the arrival of the German troops during the Anschluss, 13th March 1938.

Pacifism

Pacifism means fear of war and the desire to avoid conflict at any cost. By 1936, support for pacifism was at its height. Public opinion polls found that the most favoured foreign policy in the late 1930s was not appeasement but support for the League of Nations. The public still hoped that if nations stood together then fascist aggression could be stopped. Clearly the public was concerned about the danger of war – but be careful not to assume that meant support for appeasement.

Concern over the Empire

The British Empire was huge and defence of the Empire was Britain's number one concern. Already by 1934 the Committee of Imperial Defence had warned the government that Britain was not strong enough to fight a war against Germany, Italy and Japan together. In other words, Britain was unable to defend its Empire from attack.

Another concern was Empire unity. South Africa at that time was a part of the British Empire and at an Empire conference in 1937, the South African leader had said that if Britain became involved in a war with Germany, South Africa might not help Britain. Would the rest of the Empire follow South Africa and refuse to help if Britain got involved in a war?

Britain had no reliable allies

By the late 1930s, Britain had no allies apart from the Empire – and that was causing concern. Chamberlain knew he could expect no help from the USA, Britain also felt that France would be no help because of political arguments between French politicians. Some of them were terrified of Hitler and wanted to do a deal with him.

Fear of communism

Many people in Britain thought Hitler had brought strong, sensible government to Germany. The big political fear for Europe in the 1930s was communism. A common saying at the time was 'better Hitlerism than communism'. British politicians thought that if Hitler was overthrown, communism might grow in Germany and then spread across Europe.

Question paper 1: British, European and World History

Military weakness
The heads of Britain's armed forces – the Chiefs of Staff – had consistently warned Chamberlain that Britain was too weak to fight. At the same time, Hitler's propaganda encouraged Britain and France to believe that Nazi forces were stronger than they really were. The fighter planes and radar that saved Britain from defeat in 1940 were still at the development stage in the late 1930s. Britain needed time to rearm.

Chamberlain's own beliefs
Chamberlain was a man who thought he could maintain peace in Europe. Some critics say Chamberlain was fooled by Hitler. But was he? At the Munich meeting, Chamberlain made it clear to his assistants that there was no choice but to deal with Hitler, whether or not he was pushing Europe to war. Hitler could not be wished away, so Britain had to get the best deal it could. What choice did Chamberlain have but to appease?

Chamberlain, Ribbentrop and Hitler in Munich, 1938.

Check Your Understanding

ESSENTIAL KNOWLEDGE

1. Why was the Empire a vital British interest?
2. Why was appeasement adopted as a British policy?
3. Why did the idea of bombing worry people so much?

THEME QUESTION

1. Was appeasement a policy of cowardice?

TEST YOURSELF

Do you know the meaning of these key words?

League of Nations
Disarmament
Lebensraum
Imperial
Pacifism
Isolationist
Hitlerism

Appeasement and the Road to War, to 1939

Key issue 4: An assessment of the success of British foreign policy in containing fascist aggression, 1935–March 1938

What is this section all about?

Between 1933 and 1938, Britain did avoid becoming involved in the big European war that was threatened at this time. On the other hand, critics of British policy have argued that all Britain did was to encourage Hitler to demand more and more. When fascist powers became involved with Abyssinia, the Rhineland, Spain and Austria, realists argued: what could Britain have done? This section is about how Britain responded to the actions of Germany and Italy between 1933 and 1938. It also covers thinking about how successful Britain was in containing the spread of fascist influence and power across Europe up to and including the Anschluss with Austria in March 1938.

TOP TIP

The secret of a successful answer here is to look closely at the question. You are **not** asked to decide if British foreign policy, known as appeasement, was a failure or not. What you should do is think about 'containing fascist aggression'. Containing does **not** mean stopping or defeating fascism. What it does mean is, did Britain prevent fascism from spreading and avoid small conflicts from becoming large wars?

How successful was British foreign policy in containing fascist aggression between 1935 and March 1938?

- The aims of appeasement
- Abyssinia, 1935
- The remilitarisation of the Rhineland
- The Anglo–German Naval Agreement, 1935
- Non-intervention in the Spanish Civil War
- The Anschluss of March 1938

Appeasement's main aims between 1935 and 1938

The first aim was to solve genuine grievances arising from the peace treaties after World War I and thereby prevent any conflict spreading to involve Britain. The second was to protect Britain's interests, especially the Empire. Both of these aims can be seen running through British actions between 1935 and 1938. The first example of containing fascist aggression came with Italy's attack on Abyssinia.

Question paper 1: British, European and World History

Crisis 1 – Abyssinia

When Mussolini launched his invasion of Abyssinia, Britain was faced with a problem. Mussolini had broken the rules of the League, so Italy should be punished. Britain and France were in a difficult position. Britain's military leaders believed that Britain could not defeat Italy quickly. Their solution was the Hoare–Laval Plan, but when details of the plan were leaked, Britain and France were accused of 'selling out' League principles and putting self-interest before supporting the League.

> **TOP TIP**
> Make the point that the Hoare–Laval plan was an attempt to stop the war and so contain fascist aggression and avoid alienating Italy. However, collective security was abandoned, fascist aggression seemed to be accepted and a League member was not supported – all because of self-interest.

Crisis 2 – Hitler's naval treaty

Hitler was building up his navy against the Versailles rules, so in June 1935 Britain signed a naval treaty with Germany. The Treaty of Versailles had cut the size of the German navy but the new treaty accepted that Germany should have a navy up to one-third the size of the British navy **and** Germany was allowed to build submarines!

Because Germany was determined to rearm and build up its navy anyway, Britain could argue that it would be more sensible to allow a limited growth in the German navy and at least know the problem that Britain was about to face; in other words, try to contain, or limit, the growth of the navy.

Crisis 3 – the Rhineland crisis

On 7th March 1936, Hitler remilitarised the Rhineland. The Rhineland was part of Germany but no German soldiers were allowed there. That was one of the rules in the Treaty of Versailles but could any politician justify sending British troops to attack Germany when Germany had attacked no other country? Any action against Hitler would escalate the problem, the opposite of containment. Many people in Britain believed that Germany had been too severely treated at Versailles. As Lord Lothian said, the Germans are 'only moving troops into their own back garden'. The British government saw a chance to secure future peace and 'contain' any future aggression. In exchange for a German return to the League of Nations, acceptance of arms limitations, and giving up claims for more land in Europe, Germany would be allowed to remilitarise the Rhineland. Britain also wanted talks on an 'air agreement' to outlawing bombing.

Crisis 4 – The Spanish Civil War

The Spanish Civil War lasted from 1936 until 1939 and Britain was determined not to let it grow into a big European war. The official policy of Britain was non-intervention but neither Britain nor France, who had organised the Non-Intervention Committee, stood up against the interventionist policies of the dictators. In one way, non-intervention could be called a success because a major European war was not sparked off by the Spanish war. Selfishly, most of the British public were quite happy that wars could be fought elsewhere

Got it? ☐ ☐ ☐   **Appeasement and the Road to War, to 1939**

and not involve Britain. Newsreels showing the bombing of Madrid and Guernica, a Spanish town, by German aircraft, code-named 'the Condor Legion', came to symbolise the fear that in a future war, bombing of cities would cause massive loss of life.

Crisis 5 – Anschluss, March 1938

In March 1938, German troops marched into Austria, against the rules of the Treaty of Versailles. Britain and France appeased Hitler and did nothing to help Austria. In February 1938, Hitler tried to put pressure on Schuschnigg, the Austrian Chancellor. At a meeting in February 1938, Hitler told Schuschnigg that Austria could expect no help from Britain and France and that Germany was now allied to Italy, the former protector of Austria.

On 12th March 1938, German troops marched unopposed into Austria. Opinion in Britain was divided about what to do. Many Britons felt that Versailles had been too harsh and, as Austria shared a common culture and language with Germany, Anschluss was inevitable. On the other hand, anti-appeasers felt that Hitler was a bully who would keep coming back for more unless he was stopped and that appeasement just encouraged Hitler's aggression.

Britain had for a long time been aware of Hitler's ambitions in Eastern Europe. Austria was the first stage in his move eastwards towards Russia. It was clear to see where Hitler's next move would be. The western part of Czechoslovakia had German troops to its north, west and south. Although Britain could do little to stop Anschluss, the policy of appeasement was making it very easy for Hitler to move eastwards and seize more land in his move towards Lebensraum. Finally, as a result of British inaction, no small European country had any belief that Britain or France could or would really help them. Appeasement was seen as a policy to benefit Britain only and help no one else.

Check Your Understanding

ESSENTIAL KNOWLEDGE

1. In what way does containment apply to the Rhineland 1936, Spain 1936–1939 and Anschluss, March 1938?
2. Why was the existence of the Condor Legion another problem for Britain in dealing with Hitler?

THEME QUESTION

1. Does containment mean to stop something?
2. Why does the answer to that question affect your judgement on the main title of this section?

TEST YOURSELF

Do you know the meaning of these key words?

Containment
Anschluss
Schuschnigg
Condor Legion
Non-intervention

Question paper 1: British, European and World History

Key issue 5: An assessment of the Munich Agreement

What is this section all about?

By the summer of 1938 another international crisis was brewing. Czechoslovakia, and in particular an area of the country called the Sudetenland, was at the heart of the crisis. Czechoslovakia was a new country created after the Great War. It contained many different nationalities of which there were 3 million German speakers who lived in the Sudetenland. In 1938, Europe was close to war because of a crisis over the Sudetenland.

An assessment of the Munich Agreement:
- The context – why did Munich happen?
- Arguments in support of the Munich Settlement
- Arguments against the Munich Settlement
- Contemporary points of view in favour of the Munich Settlement
- Contemporary points of view against the Munich Settlement

The Czech crisis

Hitler's ambition of Lebensraum meant eastwards expansion towards Russia, but Czechoslovakia, with its strong defences, was a barrier to his plans. The crisis seemed to be solved by an agreement at Munich at the end of September 1938. Hitler was given immediate access to the Sudetenland and Czechoslovakia was broken up and left defenceless. The Munich Agreement is still controversial. Some historians believe the agreement was a practical solution given the circumstances of the time. Others believe Munich was a cowardly sell-out of an ally.

German troops cross the border between Ebersbach (Germany) and Georgswalde (Czechoslovakia), thus occupying the Sudetenland, 1st October 1938.

Appeasement and the Road to War, to 1939

Why was Britain involved in the Czech crisis?

France had an alliance with Czechoslovakia and might therefore fight to help its ally. In March 1936, Britain had described French security as a vital British interest but Britain had no intention of becoming involved in a war because of France's alliance with Czechoslovakia.

On 12th September 1938 the Czech crisis got worse. War was looking dangerously close. In the space of two weeks, between 15th and 29th September, the British Prime Minister, Neville Chamberlain flew three times to meet Hitler.

> ### Think point
> Back in May 1938, Hitler had secretly ordered his army to be ready to attack Czechoslovakia by 1st October 1938. Britain knew about the plan. That deadline provides the reason why there was such desperate activity in September 1938 to avoid the German attack on Czechoslovakia that would have dragged France, and soon afterwards Britain, into war.

The first meeting

Hitler demanded the Sudetenland at some point in the future. Chamberlain returned to Britain and gained the agreement of France and Czechoslovakia. Chamberlain was pleased because he seemed to have solved the crisis.

The second meeting

Hitler was determined to provoke a war and said he wanted the Sudetenland immediately or there would be war. Chamberlain was horrified by Hitler's change of demands. War was likely. Hitler had demanded a reply from Britain by 2pm on 28th September. The offer of a new meeting – at Munich – came just before 2pm.

The third meeting

On 29th September 1938 – the Munich conference – Britain, France, Germany and Italy (which was Germany's ally) met to discuss the future of the Sudetenland. It was agreed that Germany was to get the Sudetenland almost immediately. Czechoslovakia's leaders were not invited to the conference and their territory was given away without their agreement. At a private meeting between Hitler and Chamberlain, Hitler promised he had no more territorial demands to make in Europe and that there would be no war between Britain and Germany.

The Munich agreement – realism or sell out?

The Munich settlement broke up Czechoslovakia without any member of the Czech government present at the meetings. It seemed to be the ultimate betrayal of a friend. Churchill described the Munich settlement as 'an unmitigated defeat'. He said, 'we have eaten dirt in vain'. The letters columns of newspapers were full of criticisms of Chamberlain and of the Munich agreement. A letter to *The Scotsman* describes the Munich settlement as being like 'throwing Czechoslovakia to the wolves'. Czechoslovakia played no part at the Munich conference and that was wrong according to the anti-appeasers in Britain.

On the other hand, the British public seemed to like the Munich settlement but that was mainly because war had been avoided. There are others who argue that Chamberlain had little choice and Munich delayed the war that seemed likely to start in October 1938.

Question paper 1: British, European and World History

GOT IT? ☐ ☐ ☐

Think point
Britain had no link with Czechoslovakia, nor was it a vital British interest. Also, Britain was too weak to win a war, so why get involved in a war with no hope of winning.

The policy of appeasement was not meant to defeat Hitler. It was meant to maintain the peace in Europe and that is what the Munich agreement did … at least for a short time. Hitler was given the Sudetenland as the price of avoiding war. As Hitler said, 'I have no more territorial demands to make in Europe' and Chamberlain's private talk with Hitler at Munich resulted in the famous 'piece of paper' that promised 'peace in our time'.

Although it is hard to see Munich as 'peace with honour', as Chamberlain claimed, perhaps it can be seen as a realistic response to the situation at the time. As a historian, AJP Taylor, pointed out in the 1960s, 'the settlement at Munich was a triumph for British policy … Appeasement had not been created as a policy to save Austria or Czechoslovakia. It was created to keep peace and avoid war by negotiation. With that definition how can people criticise Chamberlain at Munich?'

Chamberlain holding the paper containing the resolution to commit to peaceful methods signed by both Hitler and himself.

In Britain, most people were greatly relieved that war had been avoided. Few looked to the future implications of such a settlement. The fear of war, especially gas bombing, was enough to make the public glad that peace had been purchased, even temporarily, at some other country's cost. A cartoon at the time showed Chamberlain outside the 'World Theatre' promising 'Catastrophe' as its next production. Chamberlain is shown sticking a new poster across 'Catastrophe', the new poster simply says, 'Postponed'. Most of the British population hoped for peace but realised the Munich settlement had only just delayed the inevitable. Events in March 1939 were to prove their suspicions correct.

Check Your Understanding

ESSENTIAL KNOWLEDGE

1. Why did Anschluss make pressure on Sudentenland both easy and inevitable?
2. How did the Munich settlement leave the door to Eastern Europe and Lebensraum wide open for Hitler?
3. As a summary, how could the Munich settlement be seen as both a disaster and a success for British foreign policy in September 1938?
4. War postponed or war prevented. Which phrase could more easily be used in a description of the Munich settlement?

TEST YOURSELF
Do you know the meaning of these key words?
Czechoslovakia
Sudetenland
Lebensraum

THEME QUESTION

1. Was the Munich agreement a pragmatic triumph for British foreign policy?

Appeasement and the Road to War, to 1939

Key issue 6: An evaluation of the reasons for the outbreak of war in 1939

What is this section all about?

In brief, it is about why Britain stopped appeasing and why Britain declared war on Germany in September 1939. In March 1939, Hitler ignored the Munich agreement and invaded western Czechoslovakia. In response, Britain and France promised their support to Hitler's likely next targets – Romania and Poland. But why should Hitler think those promises meant any more than the others that had been broken?

Why was appeasement abandoned and why did war break out in 1939?

- Changing British attitudes towards appeasement
- Occupation of Bohemia and the collapse of Czechoslovakia
- The developing crisis over Poland
- British diplomacy and relations with the Soviet Union
- The position of France
- The Nazi–Soviet Pact
- The invasion of Poland

Why was the policy of appeasement abandoned?

In any essay about the outbreak of war, you will need to make clear why the policy of appeasement – British foreign policy for the previous 4 years – was suddenly abandoned. The following points will help make it clear.

- In March 1939, Hitler tore up the promises made at Munich and invaded the western parts of Czechoslovakia, called Bohemia and Moravia. Appeasement was discredited and Hitler's actions effectively destroyed any hopes that appeasement might prevent war.
- Public opinion in Britain and France moved towards an acceptance that Hitler could only be stopped by force.

Question paper 1: British, European and World History

- The Polish Corridor issue became Hitler's next excuse for pressurising Poland in 1939. Poland was created at the end of the Great War, partly from land taken from Germany and Russia. The Polish Corridor was a strip of land taken from Germany and contained mostly German-speaking people. Naturally, Hitler complained about the treatment of Germans in the Polish Corridor.
- On 1st April 1939, Chamberlain announced that Britain and France would help Poland 'in the event of any action by Germany which clearly threatened Polish independence'.

A Nazi propaganda postcard shows Adolf Hitler's 'thorn in the flesh' problem of the Polish corridor, asking the question of whether the other European countries would allow the same situation to continue.

- Hitler took no notice. After Britain's failure to take action to stop Hitler on many previous occasions, why should Hitler worry now?
- Britain hoped that Hitler would not risk a war next door to Russia. Britain thought that Russia would help Britain if Britain did stand up to Hitler.

The Russian situation

Unfortunately, Russia was more concerned with its own problems than with helping Britain.
- Stalin, the Russian leader, was also already annoyed and suspicious of Britain and France.
- Stalin had not been invited to the Munich conference and he was convinced that Britain was encouraging Hitler to move eastwards against Russia. Stalin knew that Russia was not ready to fight and he knew that he needed either strong allies or more time to build up Russian defences.
- Stalin knew he had to do something to buy time. What happened next was a disaster for British diplomacy and for hopes of future peace.

GOT IT? ☐ ☐ ☐ **Appeasement and the Road to War, to 1939**

The Nazi–Soviet non-aggression agreement

The agreement signed between Hitler and Stalin on 23rd August 1939 shocked the world. The agreement stated that Germany and Russia would not fight each other. There was also a secret part to the agreement: in private, Stalin and Hitler had agreed to divide up Poland between them! The immediate consequence of the agreement was that Stalin had bought time, Hitler could have a short limited war with Poland – and Poland was doomed.

German tanks drive over a bridge to cross the river during the Nazi invasion and occupation of Poland at the start of the Second World War.

One week after the Nazi–Soviet agreement was signed, Nazi tanks rolled into Poland on 1st September 1939.

When Nazi troops invaded Poland on 1st September, Chamberlain warned Hitler to retreat by 11am on Sunday 3rd September or face the consequences. Hitler was sure that Britain would back down but this time there was no appeasement. On the morning of 3rd September 1939, Chamberlain spoke on radio to the British people to tell them that, 'this country is at war with Germany'. Britain's declaration of war on Germany was followed by similar declarations from Australia, New Zealand, France, South Africa and Canada. The Second World War had started. Appeasement had ended.

TOP TIP
Between the 1920s and the 1980s the words Russian, USSR, Soviet Union and Soviet were interchangeable. They all meant the same thing.

Check Your Understanding

TEST YOURSELF
Do you know the meaning of these key words?
Polish corridor
Bohemia and Moravia
Stalin

ESSENTIAL KNOWLEDGE

1. Why did Britain promise help to both Poland and Romania?
2. Why did the Nazi–Soviet agreement shock the world?

THEME QUESTION

1. When did appeasement really end?
2. How had the aims of and reasons for appeasement changed between 1935 and September 1938?
3. To what extent did the actions and inactions of Britain contribute to the outbreak of war in September 1939?

107

1918
Great War, ends.

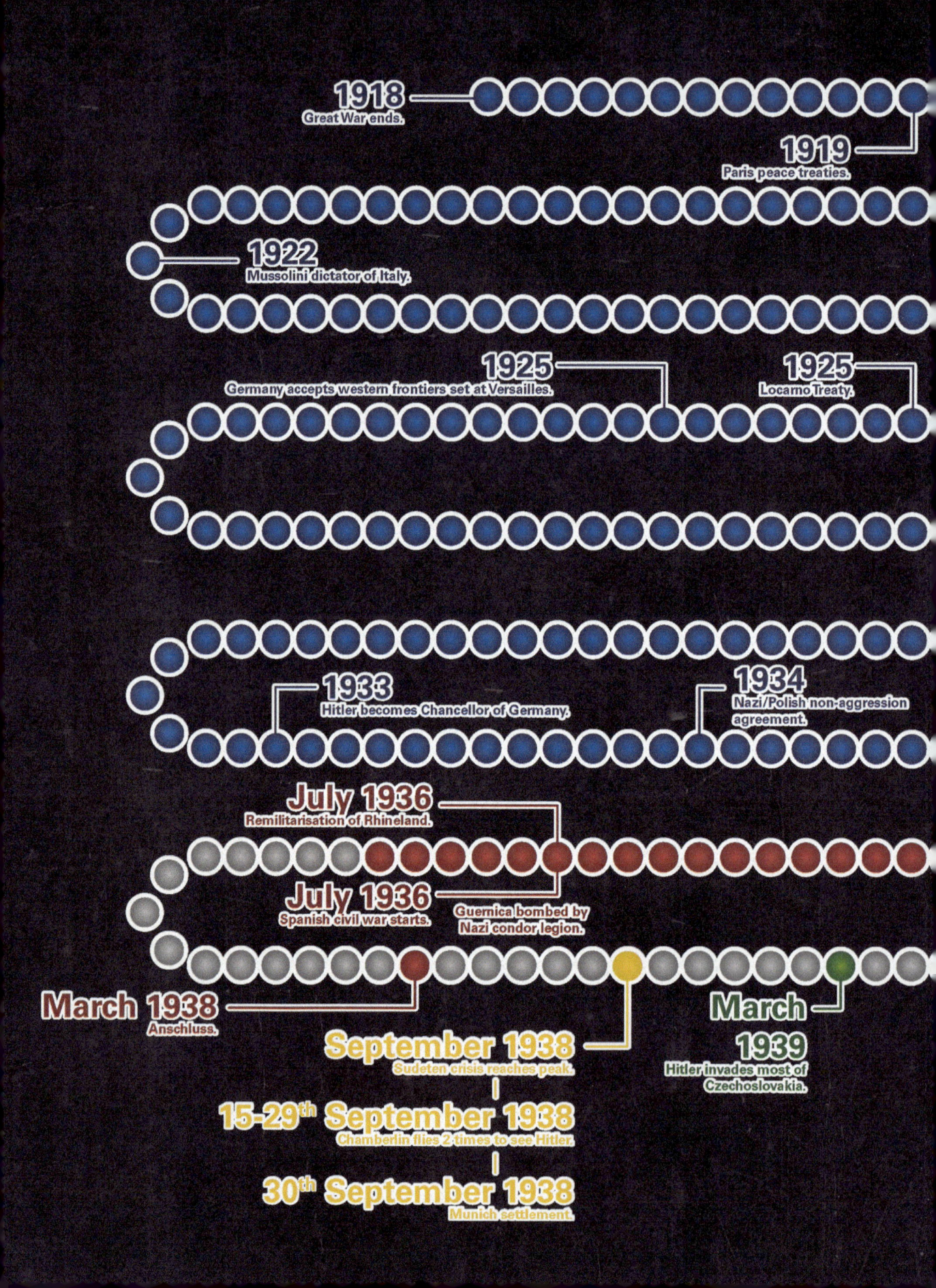

1919
Paris peace treaties.

1922
Mussolini dictator of Italy.

1925
Germany accepts western frontiers set at Versailles.

1925
Locarno Treaty.

1933
Hitler becomes Chancellor of Germany.

1934
Nazi/Polish non-aggression agreement.

July 1936
Remilitarisation of Rhineland.

July 1936
Spanish civil war starts.

Guernica bombed by Nazi condor legion.

March 1938
Anschluss.

September 1938
Sudeten crisis reaches peak.

15-29th September 1938
Chamberlin flies 2 times to see Hitler.

30th September 1938
Munich settlement.

March 1939
Hitler invades most of Czechoslovakia.

Appeasement 1918–1939

Issues 1–2
Issue 4
Issue 5
Issue 6

1935
Hitler announces conscription and rearmament.

1935
Italy invades Abyssinia.

1935
Anglo-German naval treaty.

3rd September 1939
Britain declares war on Germany.

August 1939
Nazi/Soviet agreement.

Question paper 2: Scottish History

Key issue 1: Alexander III and the succession problem 1286–92

For Key Issue 1 you should know about the following:
1. the succession problem
2. the Guardians
3. the Treaty of Birgham
4. the death of the Maid of Norway
5. the Scottish appeal to Edward I — the decision at Norham
6. Bruce versus Balliol
7. the Great Cause and Edward's decision.

What is this section about?

When Alexander fell to his death one stormy night in 1286, Scotland faced a serious problem: there was no obvious successor to the throne. Alexander's own children were dead. His only living heir was a young girl, his granddaughter, living in Norway. Would Scotland really be ruled by a young girl? Would Scotland be ripped apart by powerful nobles all wanting to become king? Or would King Edward of England try to take away Scotland's independence and absorb the nation of Scotland into England?

The reign of Alexander III

Alexander III became king when his father died in 1249. Under Alexander, more of what we now call Scotland accepted his authority. Alexander's law officers, called Royal Sheriffs, spread royal law and order across Scotland and the land became a more peaceful and prosperous place.

Alexander also created a more modern system of law and order that made his own position as king more powerful. Alexander replaced older systems of law and authority with the more modern feudal system. In a feudal state, the king owned all land. The king 'gave' parts of that land to important nobles in exchange for the promises of support and loyalty (fealty). At a special ceremony, the lords receiving the land from the king did homage for the land and made binding promises of support. If the nobles broke their promises of loyalty then they would lose their land. Under the feudal system, the king increased his authority by making it clear to the nobles that it was in their best interests to stay loyal to the king.

Alexander III was King Edward of England's brother-in-law. Old arguments about where the border lay between Scotland and England had been sorted out and both nations saw advantages in the trade that was growing between them. However, by the 1270s the problem of overlordship still rumbled on.

The Wars of Independence, 1249–1328

What was the 'overlord' argument about?

For a long time, Scottish kings had made varying claims over ruling large parts of northern England. On the other side of the argument, English kings persistently claimed that they were more important than Scottish kings and this revolved around the issue of overlordship.

The problem lay in the fact that many Scottish nobles – and even the Scottish king – possessed land in England. They had sworn loyalty for their English land to the English king – so who was the most important king? Could it mean that the English king had authority – or overlordship – over the Scottish king?

The issue came to a head when Edward I of England insisted that Alexander III do homage for the lands that Alexander held in England **and** for the kingdom of Scotland. To do homage meant to make promises of loyalty to the overlord and promise to obey him in everything. Alexander said he would do homage for the land he held in England but refused to do homage for any lands in Scotland. If Alexander had done homage for his Scottish land then he would be accepting that Edward was overlord of Scotland.

During the reign of Alexander III, the issue of overlordship was not solved and it appeared again as a major issue in the years following Alexander's death.

The succession problem

When Alexander III died, he had no living relative ready to become Scotland's next king or queen. It was vital for kings at this time to have an heir old enough and strong enough to take over power, but Alexander had seen his son, daughter and wife all die.

Although Alexander's royal authority had been strong, there were other powerful nobles who were ambitious and saw the empty throne as an opportunity to increase their power. The two strongest families were the Bruce and the Balliol/Comyn families. Both sides built up their armies and it looked like Scotland would face civil war, but then a compromise was reached and it involved his granddaughter, Margaret, who was the daughter of Alexander's now dead daughter and her husband, the King of Norway. Margaret became known as the Maid of Norway.

When Alexander died, his granddaughter was only about 4 years old. Clearly she could not rule Scotland but two years earlier, in 1284, Alexander had made the nobles promise to accept Margaret as queen if the unthinkable happened and he died. Now the unthinkable was reality. Would the nobles keep their promise?

Question paper 2: Scottish History

Who were the Guardians of Scotland?

The Guardians were a group of six men entrusted to rule Scotland until Margaret was old enough to do so herself. The Guardians were also chosen to represent different powerful groups in Scottish society. Two were bishops, two were barons and the remaining two were earls.

The Guardians hoped they could guide and protect Margaret until she was old enough to rule Scotland on her own. Until then, having a young girl as queen was a big risk for Scotland.

Together, the Guardians formed part of what later historians came to call the Community of the Realm. By working as a Community, they were looking to the good of the nation rather than their individual gain. Such concepts were not common in Europe at this time, hence the importance of the Community of the Realm as an important political development in medieval society.

The Community of the Realm is an important concept to understand. It showed that different individuals were prepared to work together for the good of the kingdom (the realm).

Finally, as queen of Scotland , Margaret would inevitably become the focus of ambitious men who would try to gain control over her and also Scotland. The easiest way to do that would be to tie Margaret into a marriage contract for the future. That is exactly what seemed to be happening when Edward of England suggested a marriage between his son and Margaret.

The Treaty of Birgham

King Edward of England saw a way of expanding his influence over Scotland. He suggested a marriage between the young Margaret and his own son who was then only 10 years old. Both sides seemed happy and the Treaty of Birgham signed in 1290 agreed that a marriage would take place between Margaret and young prince Edward.

The threat of civil war in Scotland vanished and the simmering issue of overlordship and boundary disputes would be solved.

However, the Guardians were well aware that they might be giving away Scotland's freedom by agreeing to the marriage so they included several important sections designed to protect Scotland's freedoms. The Guardians intended the Treaty of Birgham to keep Scotland separate and free from control by England.

The main terms:

- the Scottish church would remain free from interference from England
- Scottish nobles who held land from the King of Scots would only do homage to the Scottish king
- no-one accused of a crime in Scotland would have their crime tried under English law
- Scots would only be taxed to pay for Scottish needs and the taxes would not be used by England for its needs.

The Wars of Independence, 1249–1328

The death of Margaret, Maid of Norway

The Guardians were undoubtedly suspicious of Edward's motives, but they seemed satisfied with the conditions laid down at the Treaty of Birgham. Then it all fell apart when Margaret died.

When news of the death of the Maid spread across Scotland, there was a very real danger of civil war. The death of Margaret created a political vacuum and a second disaster for Scotland within 10 years. There was no longer anyone with any automatic right to rule Scotland. The powerful nobles in Scotland prepared to grab power.

It was clear that the Bruce family were raising forces in southwest Scotland and Comyn's allies were doing likewise in the north. The evidence of this fear comes from a letter sent by William Fraser, Bishop of St Andrews to King Edward asking him to come to the Scottish border to help keep the peace.

Bishop Fraser described how powerful families in Scotland were raising armies to fight for the right to be king and Fraser continued by saying how there was a widespread fear of war and slaughter if the succession issue was not settled peacefully. It was clear that only King Edward had the power and strength to make the Scottish nobility stop the rush to civil war.

To avoid civil war, the Guardians asked Edward of England to decide who should be next ruler of Scotland. So began a period of time that came to be known as the Great Cause.

The Great Cause and Edward's decision

The Great Cause is the name given to the time when Edward sat in judgement over the question of who should be next king of Scotland.

Although there were 13 Competitors (as the claimants were called) only three really mattered – John Hastings, Robert Bruce (the grandfather of Robert the Bruce) and John Balliol (a close ally of the Comyn's).

Edward now saw an opportunity to assert his power over Scotland and he manipulated the situation carefully. First, Edward arrived with a large army and set up his base at Norham castle on the banks of the river Tweed, near Berwick.

The Guardians of Scotland rode to meet Edward but right away Edward was playing political games. The Guardians expected Edward to cross the Tweed and meet them on Scottish soil but instead he insisted the Scots cross the Tweed and come to him.

Then Edward insisted the Scots recognise him as their overlord. Edward argued: how else could he give the right to rule Scotland to someone else if he did not already own it first?

The Scots tried to delay making an answer but Edward was not prepared to wait. He had already asked all English monasteries (where official records were kept) to search for any documents supporting his claim to overlordship. Edward had also begun the build-up of a large army to enforce his will over Scotland if necessary. It was clear that Edward's ambitions towards Scotland had changed, at least in terms of the speed with which he wanted to assert his influence.

The Scots gave in. They had little choice.

Question paper 2: Scottish History

The Award of Norham is the name given to the acceptance of Edward's overlordship by the claimants to the throne of Scotland.

Edward had successfully outmanoeuvred not only the Guardians but also all the claimants to the throne. If they wished to be considered for the title of King, each claimant would have to accept Edward as his overlord. If they did not, then their claim would be rejected.

The claimants had no choice but to accept Edward as judge and agreed that he should have possession of the lands of Scotland, on the condition that when the case was settled, Edward would restore the realm of Scotland to the successful candidate. The date was 3rd June 1291.

Edward was now the legal owner of Scotland.

Once the agreement about temporary overlordship was reached, 104 (40 chosen by Balliol, 40 by Bruce and 24 by Edward) 'auditors' heard and discussed the evidence. They then reported directly to Edward so he could reach his decision.

Bruce versus Balliol

Although all the claimants to the throne were in some way related to the royal line of Scotland, none had a clear and close connection.

The first Competitor, John Hastings, argued that Scotland should be divided into parts and divided among the other claimants. Neither the other claimants nor Edward would agree to that so Hastings' claim was quickly rejected. That left Robert Bruce and John Balliol.

Robert the Bruce was nearly 80. He claimed he was nearest relative to the Scottish royal family. On the other hand, John Balliol was also a close relative of the royal family. The problem for Bruce was that he was the son of the second-born child. Under the law of primogeniture (the law that states inheritance of titles or property passes through the first-born child) Balliol was clearly the correct legal choice and on 17th November 1292 Edward announced that Balliol would be the next King of Scotland.

got it? ▢ ▢ ▢   **The Wars of Independence, 1249–1328**

Check Your Understanding

ESSENTIAL KNOWLEDGE

1. Why did the death of Alexander III cause such problems for Scotland?
2. Why did Edward of England get involved in the search for a new Scottish king?
3. Why were Scots unhappy at Edward's demand to be overlord of Scotland?

THEME QUESTION

1. Why did the appointment of six Guardians seem a sensible solution to Scottish problems after 1286?
2. In what ways did Edward of England pursue his own agenda to control Scotland throughout the time from the death of Margaret until his choice of John Balliol?

TEST YOURSELF

Do you know the meaning of these key words?

Succession
Birgham
Guardians
Overlord
Homage
Fealty

Question paper 2: Scottish History

Key issue 2: John Balliol and Edward I, 1292–1296

For Key Issue 2 you should know about the following:
1. Balliol's rule
2. Edward's overlordship
3. the Scottish response
4. the Anglo–French war and the Franco–Scottish Treaty
5. the subjugation of Scotland.

What is this section about?

Between 1292 and 1296, Scotland was ruled by King John Balliol but as soon as he became king, John faced problems. Many in Scotland did not respect his authority and throughout his reign King Edward of England tried to assert his authority over King John. Eventually war broke out between Scotland and England.

Balliol's rule

When Balliol became king he took over a country that had been without royal authority for seven years and where the rule of law and royal administration had become weak. Not only that, many Scots nobles disagreed with Edward's choice of king and would do all they could to ignore or undermine Balliol's authority in their regions.

Away from the traditional power base of the Lothians and southern Scotland, the power of Scottish kings in the Western Isles and Highlands had always been relatively weak. Now the lords of the far-away regions of Scotland felt they could do as they wanted. Balliol lacked power, time and assertiveness to rebuild royal authority in Scotland.

Balliol was in a difficult position. With so many powerful nobles against him, how could he trust them to administer Scotland on his behalf? The answer lay in using members of his own Balliol / Comyn family to fill important posts, but that of course made relationships with other noble families more difficult.

Nevertheless, Balliol did set up several royal parliaments and appointed his own royal officials to enforce royal authority, not only in friendly areas such as Lothian and Moray but also in more troublesome areas such as Galloway and the Western Isles. Balliol also managed to keep tension between the Bruce and Comyn families quiet, although the Bruces may just have been waiting for their opportunities.

Balliol needed time to establish himself as king and to let Scotland see how his reign could bring stability, peace and prosperity back again; but it was time that Edward was not prepared to allow Balliol to have.

The Wars of Independence, 1249–1328

Edward's overlordship

Almost as soon as Edward announced his decision on 17th November 1292 that John Balliol should be king of Scotland, Edward put pressure on Balliol and undermined his authority in Scotland.

Balliol was in a difficult position. Edward insisted Balliol pay homage to Edward and accept Edward as overlord. That meant Balliol promised to be Edward's 'man', which in turn meant Balliol had promised to be loyal and promised to support Edward in all he was asked to do.

Those who try to repair the reputation of Balliol argue that previous Scottish kings had sworn fealty, or loyalty, to the English king, but that is to forget the way that Alexander III had asserted his authority over the land of Scotland and drew a line under the extent of Edward's power in Scotland. The argument that Balliol's promise meant nothing also ignores Edward's clear tactical moves during the Great Cause to gain overlordship and the fact that a feudal oath of fealty was binding.

Edward also consistently undermined the authority of King John.

When the Guardians negotiated the terms of the Treaty of Birgham, they insisted on certain conditions to maintain Scottish independence. One of these was that any English court could not overturn legal decisions made in Scotland. Of course the treaty was abandoned with the death of Margaret and Edward lost no time in taking every opportunity to weaken King John's status.

In 1292, Edward held a parliament in Newcastle. There, a merchant from Berwick made a complaint about a decision taken by the Guardians against him. King John upheld the decision of the Guardians. That should have been the end of the complaint as the merchant in Berwick was Scottish, Berwick was Scottish and Edward had no authority there. However, Edward did intervene, supported the merchant and ordered King John to change his decision. It was clear that Edward had no respect for King John or Scottish independence. The issue of Edward's overlordship and feudal superiority was once again at the heart of English/Scottish relations.

Although King John protested about Edward's actions, he soon backed down. King John not only accepted Edward's decision but also announced that the Treaty of Birgham was officially ended and Edward was freed from all and any promises he made, including the conditions that protected Scottish freedoms and independence.

Edward took full advantage of the changed relationship between himself and King John. A case similar to that of the merchant of Berwick involved an important noble called Macduff who complained that he had been disinherited from lands he thought should belong to him. The argument seemed to have been settled once Balliol became king, but Macduff renewed his complaint. Once again Edward supported a complaint made against a Scottish decision. King John Balliol was ordered by Edward to appear in person before the English Parliament to explain his decision. Clearly, Edward was making a point of showing that his authority was greater than Balliol's despite Scotland being an entirely separate country and beyond Edward's jurisdiction. Despite protests from the Scots, Edward agreed to hear more appeals on cases that had already been decided upon and settled by the Scottish courts. In effect Edward was stating that he refused to recognise Scotland's right to make and enforce its own laws. Edward was once again asserting his right to be overlord of Scotland, and to treat Scotland as a land over which he had final authority.

Question paper 2: Scottish History

And so it went on with more and more cases being taken to Edward by individuals unhappy with the decision of the Scottish courts.

Edward continued to undermine Scottish independence by forcing Balliol to accept Edward's men in important positions in the government of Scotland. Edward even redesigned the Royal Seal of Scotland.

Why did war break out between Scotland and England?

The immediate cause of war was Scotland's alliance with France but the roots of the war lay in Edward's treatment of Scotland. Later historians argue that the Guardians could take no more of Edward's bullying tactics, while others argue that Balliol was finally driven into a position where he had to stand up for himself and Scotland.

The immediate cause of war came in 1294 when Edward demanded that Scotland pay taxes to finance his war in France **and** supply troops to help him fight it.

The Scots refused to help Edward or pay for his war.

Scotland had no quarrel with France and in fact France was an important trading partner with Scotland. Merchants from Flanders in northern France had a large and very important trading base in Berwick.

In 1296, Scotland agreed a treaty with France. Clearly Edward could not fight a war in France while he faced a threat of invasion from Scotland on his northern frontier.

Edward now had no option but to deal with the enemy threatening his northern frontier.

Why did the war go so badly for Scotland?

Edward assembled a large army and moved against Berwick. The speed of his advance with such a large army suggests he had been planning such action for a long time and perhaps war was the final part of his plan to establish complete overlordship over Scotland.

The Scots also reacted quickly and advanced south to reinforce Berwick. Perhaps as many as 10,000 men were gathered to meet the English invasion. The Scots were confident but their confidence was short-lived. The Scottish troops were untested, mostly untrained and poorly equipped. The common army of Scotland was mostly made up of levies – men taken from the farms and fields of Scotland and ordered to fight as part payment for the right to farm their land. They were often equipped with little more than sharpened farm tools.

Nevertheless, the Scots took the war to England and raided into north-west England and headed towards Carlisle. English reports from the time described the Scots as people who killed and burned without mercy.

By March 1296, Edward was ready to attack Berwick. Berwick was a well-defended town and resisted Edward's first attacks. To make matters worse, the local people insulted

The Wars of Independence, 1249–1328

and taunted Edward. He was furious. Edward reacted predictably. He ordered huge war machines to batter down Berwick's defences, then ordered that none of Berwick's defenders should be spared.

Berwick was soon captured. Reports suggest that soldiers defending Berwick were allowed to leave on condition they did not fight against Edward again but there was no protection for the civilian inhabitants of Berwick. Edward ordered the dead and wounded of Berwick to be hung on hooks and spikes around the remaining town walls.

Why did the Scots lose the battle of Dunbar?

After taking Berwick, Edward's forces advanced up the east coast to the next major Scottish strong point – Dunbar Castle.

The castle was held by the wife of the Earl of Dunbar, a member of the Comyn family and a relative of John Balliol.

Meanwhile, a Scottish army had advanced towards Dunbar and had stopped on a hill. From their position the Scots could watch the English organise their troops ready to attack uphill. The Scots held the advantage – then they threw it away!

For some reason the Scots seemed to think the English were retreating rather than preparing for attack. The Scots rushed downhill, lost their advantage and were destroyed by the disciplined English troops.

The subjugation of Scotland

Subjugation means to take over something totally and destroy its separate identity.

After the defeat at Dunbar, the war was all but over. So many Scottish nobles were captured at Dunbar that there was no organised resistance to Edward as he moved north.

Edward's tactics at Berwick also helped win the war. As news spread of the Berwick massacre, other towns were terrified as Edward's advance continued.

Roxburgh castle surrendered, Jedburgh and Edinburgh were battered to surrender by Edward's siege engines and Stirling Castle was simply abandoned as Edward moved closer. By July, Edward was in Elgin, having marched up the entire east coast of Scotland meeting almost no resistance.

On 2nd July 1296, King John Balliol surrendered to Edward. Balliol's apology to Edward was pathetic. He blamed his resistance to Edward on bad advice and his own foolishness. Balliol then claimed that the Scots had surrendered of their own free will and were under no pressure to do so. Balliol ended his apology to Edward by accepting him as overlord of Scotland.

Question paper 2: Scottish History

What happened to King John Balliol?

Remember that Edward had destroyed the Scottish army and now occupied most of eastern Scotland. Balliol had been defeated and captured and Edward increased the humiliation.

Balliol had the royal coat of arms ripped from his clothing and was then taken to England as a prisoner. Edward eventually released Balliol into the control of the Pope and Balliol lived out the rest of his life on his lands in France. Balliol never returned to Scotland.

Balliol became known as Toom Tabard – or Empty Coat, a reference to his loss of title and the removal of the coat of arms.

That is what Edward tried to do after the defeat of Scotland. Edward's aim was to take away Scotland's identity as a separate and independent nation.

The Stone of Destiny on which Scottish kings had been crowned was taken away to London.

All Scottish legal records went south (and were lost at sea) while all taxes raised in Scotland were taken to London to be spent as Edward wished.

The Scottish crown jewels soon followed southwards and Scotland was now referred to as a 'land', not a nation and not a kingdom.

As far as Edward was concerned his 'Scottish problem' was over.

Finally, in August 1296, Edward made sure there was there no more trouble from Scotland. He insisted that all Scottish nobles must swear an oath of loyalty to him personally. The document that they all signed became known as the Ragman Rolls. Almost all of Scotland's important families now swore an oath of loyalty to Edward, accepting him as their overlord.

Was John Balliol really Toom Tabard – an empty and worthless King?

Even today most Scots dismiss John Balliol as a weak king of Scotland, defeated and humiliated by Edward of England. How true is that simple story?

Several things have damned Balliol's reputation. The first is his lack of time to establish his authority in Scotland. The second is the growing ambition of the politically and militarily powerful Edward of England. Could any king have stood against Edward at that stage?

Finally, to understand the image of Balliol as a weak king, one should think about who created that image of Balliol.

We have very little first-hand evidence from this time. Most of what we know about Balliol comes from chronicles written many years after the events – when Bruce and his successors were in power. As you will read, Bruce seized power through murder and violence and he made great efforts to legitimise his reign by clever and careful propaganda. Part of that legitimising was to make Balliol look as useless and weak as possible. After all, Balliol ws a member of Bruce's great rival, the Comyn family. So, after seven centuries most Scots now believe the Bruce version of history!

Got it? ☐ ☐ ☐   **The Wars of Independence, 1249–1328**

Check Your Understanding

ESSENTIAL KNOWLEDGE

1. Why did Balliol face problems from within Scotland when he became king?
2. How did Edward undermine Balliol's authority and why did he do so?
3. Was Edward entitled to claim overlordship over Balliol?

THEME QUESTION

1. Why do you think Balliol had such problems with asserting his authority throughout his reign?
2. How would Edward's claim of overlordship over Balliol present problems for Balliol and Scotland's independence?
3. Consider all the things that were done to subjugate Scotland. Explain which you think were the most significant in the attempt to destroy Scottish nationality and independence.

TEST YOURSELF

Do you know the meaning of these key words?

Feudal

Royal Seal

Toom Tabard

Subjugation

Question paper 2: Scottish History

Key issue 3: William Wallace and Scottish resistance

For Key Issue 3 you should know about the following:
1. Scottish resistance
2. the roles of William Wallace and Andrew Murray
3. the victory at Stirling and its effects on Scots and on Scotland
4. the defeat at Falkirk and continuing Scottish resistance.

What is this section about?

In 1296, Scotland was defeated by England, King John Balliol was captured and stripped of his authority. Edward of England began to rule Scotland as a conquered land and tried to establish his control over all of Scotland.

Edward's harsh treatment of Scotland caused resistance to grow. The most famous leaders of that resistance were Andrew Murray and William Wallace.

Why did resistance to Edward's rule grow?

If Edward thought the capture of Balliol and the Ragman Roll would end Scottish resistance then he was wrong. Edward's attempts to administer Scotland as a part of England led to growing resentment and resistance.

Edward's mistake was to treat Scotland as a province of England. Edward's officials in Scotland made no attempt to learn the language or adapt to local customs. They in turn were seen by the local people as part of an army of occupation, to be resisted whenever possible. Even the collection of taxes proved impossible in many areas without the use of force and that only made hatred of the English occupation all the greater.

When Edward appointed John de Warenne as 'warden of the kingdom and land of Scotland' in August 1296 and gave him responsibility for law and order in the land, Edward's problems were just beginning.

Many of the administrators resented being in Scotland and made no secret of their dislike of the place or the people. Even John de Warenne returned to England after a few months, claiming that the Scottish climate was bad for his health.

Another of Edward's officials in Scotland was Hugh de Cressingham – the king's Lord High Treasurer and the man responsible for collecting English taxes in Scotland. Cressingham was always looking for the cheapest option in any military action and that was to lead to disaster for the English.

The Wars of Independence, 1249–1328

Given such resentment of English occupation and the lack of strong central government in Scotland for over 10 years, it is not surprising to find that resistance and rebellion against the English broke out all over Scotland.

By 1297 there were not one but several rebellions in full swing. Robert Wishart, Bishop of Glasgow, James Stewart, Sir William Douglas, Robert Bruce, William Wallace and Andrew Murray all led uprisings. The Bishop and his friends were able to accomplish little, but Wallace and Murray were more successful.

Who was Andrew Murray?

Murray was the son of an important nobleman who owned lands around Avoch, north-west of Inverness. He was a trained soldier and fought in the Scottish army under Balliol. Murray was captured at the battle of Dunbar but he escaped, travelled back north and found his family lands under English control.

Murray had no trouble assembling a small army and by the end of 1297, Murray had thrown the English out of northern Scotland, even as far south as Dundee where he met up with Wallace. They hastily joined forces and marched to Perth. They knew a powerful English army was heading north to crush them, but that force had to use Stirling Bridge to reach into northern Scotland. Murray and Wallace made their plans.

What do we know about Wallace's early life?

The first we really know about William Wallace is that his name appears on an English list of outlaws wanted for crimes. In Wallace's case, he was accused of murdering William de Hazelrig, the English sheriff at Lanark.

The most important fact about Wallace is that William Wallace led sustained resistance to the English after the Hazelrig murder and was, along with Murray, victorious over a much larger English army at the battle of Stirling Bridge.

Victory at Stirling

Even today the main transport routes between south and north Scotland hinge around the Stirling area.

In medieval times the easiest route from England to Scotland was up the east coast. Armies marched from Berwick northwards, skirting the Lammermuir Hills, past Dunbar and then across the relatively flat Lothians to Edinburgh. Then there was a problem – how to get further north. The Firth of Forth was an impassable obstacle to armies and all had to march upstream until they reached the first bridge across the Forth. That bridge was at Stirling, near to Stirling castle.

Question paper 2: Scottish History

Control of that bridge was vital, both to attackers and defenders. By 11th September 1298, the English army was camped on the southern side of the Forth, near the castle. Hidden just across the river in the woods covering Abbey Craig was the Scottish army led by Wallace and Murray. From their position high up in the wooded hillside, the Scots had a clear view of the English camp and their preparations to cross the river.

How did the two sides prepare for battle at Stirling Bridge?

The English army that arrived at Stirling numbered about 7,000 men, including about 1,000 on horseback.

The force was led by the Earl of Surrey and Hugh Cressingham. While the latter was an experienced manager of Edward's administration of Scotland, he had very little military experience. Surrey was a military commander but was in bad health just before the battle.

Facing the English army were the followers of Wallace and Murray. In total, the Scots numbered about 2,500 and most were armed with long poles called pikes. The pikes were about 5 metres long with sharp blades attached to the top. These pikemen were trained to fight in tight formations called schiltrons. With hundreds of men huddled together in the formation, each one holding out their pikes, schiltrons were like giant hedgehogs, bristling with sharp blades and almost impossible to break with cavalry charges.

The Battle of Stirling Bridge

Crossing the bridge at Stirling was a difficult military move because it was so narrow. The English army would be in a slow-moving bottleneck while it crossed.

The battle began with the Scottish schiltrons advancing downhill out of the woods. The Scottish schiltrons that waited on Abbey Craig had been trained to move as a unit and the mobility of the schiltrons was to surprise the English forces so that less than half of the English force had crossed the river and few were ready for battle when the Scots attacked. By attacking quickly, the Scots had trapped the English forces and cut them off from the bridge, their only means of escape.

Thousands of English soldiers died either on the points of the pikes or drowned while trying to swim to safety.

Although the English who had not yet crossed the bridge still outnumbered the Scots, their confidence had gone. The English army retreated all the way back to Berwick, taking their commander, the Earl of Surrey, with them. Stirling Castle surrendered after a few weeks.

The Wars of Independence, 1249–1328

What was the effect of the battle on Scots and Scotland?

In the short-term, victory at Stirling gave a huge morale boost to the Scots, and Wallace and Murray were made joint Guardians of Scotland. However, the reality of the situation is that Wallace and Murray had got lucky with a perfect choice of battle ground and a careless English army. Nor did the victory at Stirling force the English from Scotland. In the long term, the battle had very little importance to the wars of independence. When Edward came back north for revenge, the English would not underestimate the Scots again.

Why was Wallace made Guardian of Scotland?

Strictly speaking, Wallace was made joint leader of the army of Scotland and Guardian along with Andrew Murray, but Murray had been seriously wounded in the battle and died soon afterwards.

Some writers have expressed surprise that the nobles of Scotland allowed Wallace to become a Guardian, but was it such a surprise?

Wallace was not a threat to the Scottish nobility. At no point did Wallace seek power for himself. He always worked to restore Scotland's strength on behalf of its absent king, John Balliol. There was therefore little opposition to the move to make Wallace 'Sir William' and joint Guardian of Scotland.

Defeat at Falkirk

By the summer of 1298, Edward was back in Scotland looking for revenge. Edward heard that Wallace was near Falkirk and moved towards the Scots.

The English army that advanced towards Falkirk was much stronger and more organised than the army defeated at Stirling Bridge, and it was led by Edward himself, determined to have his revenge.

Facing Edward stood a Scottish army of around 500 cavalry and about 6,000 pikemen grouped into three large schiltrons. Between the schiltrons stood Scottish archers. In front of the schiltrons there was a large marshy bog and behind the Scots there was a wooded hillside.

The position of the Scots was weak and their battle plan made the Scots' position worse. Immediately, the English moved around the bog attacking the Scots at their left and right wings.

The Scottish schiltrons had little room to move and simply stood their ground. They were sitting targets for the English archers who poured clouds of arrows into the massed Scots schiltrons. At Stirling Bridge and later at Bannockburn the schiltrons were mobile, trained men who moved as a huge bristling mass. Clearly it was possible to train for and plan such mobility, so why it was not done at Falkirk is a mystery.

Question paper 2: Scottish History

> Wallace escaped from the battlefield but his reputation as a successful war leader was dead; Wallace resigned the Guardianship and Scotland was almost back to where it was before Wallace's rising. Edward was victorious and Scotland was divided again between the Bruce and Comyn families when the two family heads became joint Guardians of Scotland.

Did Scottish resistance continue?

Edward had learned from his earlier mistakes. By trying to destroy Scotland's identity as a nation and put his own English managers in charge of 'the land' of Scotland after Balliol's defeat, Edward had simply provoked anger and resistance. Now Edward decided to get the Scottish nobles on his side. In the 'Ordinance for the Order of Scotland' issued in September 1305, Edward declared that Scots noblemen could once again become sheriffs, this time enforcing English laws in exchange for which the Scots lords had to stop their rebellion, accept Edward as king and swear allegiance.

Even John Comyn, one of the main leaders of the resistance to Edward, accepted Edward's offer of peace. It was as if the Scottish resistance had never happened, the Comyn family now became loyal supporters of Edward and all demands for a return of King John Balliol were forgotten.

What happened to Wallace?

Edward had made it known that the only person he would not forgive was Wallace, so any person helping Wallace would also face the anger of Edward.

On 3rd August 1304 Wallace was captured, his hiding place betrayed by Sir John Menteith. Wallace was taken to London and put on trial for treason.

Wallace stood trial with no right of defence and the verdict was never in doubt. Edward had decided Wallace had to be made an example of so as to discourage any future rebellion.

Wallace was sentenced to be hanged, drawn, quartered then disembowelled and beheaded. His head was sent to the Tower of London while the rest of his body was quartered and each quarter was sent to Newcastle, Berwick, Stirling and Perth as a warning to those who might think of rebelling against Edward I again.

From one point of view Wallace was not important.

After one victory that inspired Scottish resistance, his next battle was an outright defeat that demoralised the Scots and led to English domination once again. Even Mentieth, the man who betrayed Wallace, suffered no punishment from the Scots. A few years later Bruce rewarded him with lands and titles.

There was not even public protest at Wallace's death or the display of his body parts.

GOT IT? ☐ ☐ ☐   The Wars of Independence, 1249–1328

Check Your Understanding

ESSENTIAL KNOWLEDGE

1. Why did resistance to King Edward of England grow in Scotland after 1296?
2. Why was victory at Stirling Bridge so important?
3. Was Andrew Murray important?
4. Why was the battle of Falkirk important?

THEME QUESTION

1. Why did Edward continue to want to capture Wallace despite making peace with all other Scottish nobles in his 'Ordinance for the Order of Scotland'?

TEST YOURSELF

Do you know the meaning of these key words?

Resistance

Schiltron

Ordinance

Allegiance

Question paper 2: Scottish History

Key issue 4: The rise and triumph of Robert Bruce

For Key Issue 4 you should know about the following:

1. the ambitions of Robert Bruce:
    a. — his conflict with and victory over Scottish opponents
    b. — his victory at Bannockburn
2. continuing hostilities
3. the Declaration of Arbroath
4. the Treaties of Edinburgh/Northampton, 1328.

What is this section about?

In 1305, Robert the Bruce was involved in the murder of his main rival for the crown of Scotland, John Comyn. Almost immediately Bruce was an outlaw, hiding from his enemies as he tried to survive. Yet in 1314 Bruce led the Scots to the famous victory at the battle of Bannockburn. How did he rise to a position of such power that he could lead a Scottish army as its king and triumph over the power of Edward II's army? And how did that success lead finally to the winning of Scottish independence and freedom guaranteed by the treaties of Edinburgh and Northampton in 1328/9?

The ambitions of Robert Bruce

The Bruce family was ambitious. At the time of the Great Cause, Robert the Bruce's grandfather had been one of the claimants for the throne after the death of Margaret. In the years that followed, Bruce had been made Guardian after the resignation of Wallace but had changed sides to support Edward on separate occasions when he felt it suited his best interests.

Critics have argued Robert the Bruce was unreliable and treacherous, breaking promises when it suited him. That is true. During the Great Cause, Bruce had signed the Ragman Rolls promising loyalty to Edward only to lead resistance to Edward a few years later.

In 1298, Bruce surrendered again but after Wallace's defeat at Falkirk, Bruce became a focus of resistance to the English. But Bruce once again made peace with King Edward in exchange for keeping his lands and titles for the Bruce family. As one of the first Scottish nobles to make peace even before the Ordinance of Scotland, Bruce expected big rewards from Edward. Although Bruce became joint Guardian of Scotland alongside John Comyn, by 1304/05 Bruce was resentful and jealous of John Comyn.

There is no evidence to prove that Bruce had a precise plan to grab the crown for himself but there is evidence that Bruce was plotting and planning to increase his influence.

In a secret meeting at Cambuskenneth Abbey near Falkirk on 11th June 1304, an agreement was reached between Bruce and the Scottish bishops including Lamberton and Wishart.

The Wars of Independence, 1249–1328

Each side promised to support the other. It is unclear exactly what was meant by 'support' but if either side broke their promise a penalty of £10,000 had to be paid.

Quite simply, Robert the Bruce and John Comyn were both ambitious and powerful. The Comyns were closely related to John Balliol and Bruce's grandfather had been one of the Competitors claiming the throne when Margaret, Maid of Norway died. In February 1306, Bruce and Comyn met at the Church of the Grey Friars in Dumfries. No one is sure why they met, but when Bruce left the meeting, Comyn lay dying.

Why did the murder of John Comyn almost destroy Bruce and his family?

Bruce had murdered a man in a church. That was the sin of sacrilege and for that crime Bruce would surely be excommunicated. If that happened then all oaths of loyalty to Bruce would be cancelled. He would lose his power. But Bruce had friends in high places of the Scottish church, especially Bishop Wishart who saw in Bruce a man who would help maintain the Church's independence. Bishop Wishart therefore delayed and avoided excommunicating Bruce.

Excommunication would also deny Bruce the chance to be crowned King of Scots and here again Wishart helped Bruce by pardoning him. At Scone on 25th March 1306 Bruce was crowned King by the Countess of Buchan and some supporters. But Bruce's actions had offended many Scots nobles and others were scared of the consequences if they supported Bruce. Was there any point attending a crowning that would infuriate the Church, Edward of England, the Comyns and all their allies?

It seemed that Bruce had no chance of long-term success. Across Scotland the relatives and friends of the Comyn family made it their business to hunt down Robert the Bruce. It seemed clear that Bruce was finished but just to make sure, friends and family of Bruce were targeted.

His wife and daughters were captured at Kildrummy Castle and remained in captivity for almost 10 years. The Countess of Buchan who had crowned Bruce King of Scotland was left in a cage hanging from the walls of Roxburgh castle. Neil, brother of Robert Bruce, was executed along with other supporters of Bruce. They were hanged, drawn and quartered.

How did Bruce manage to recover his power and authority in Scotland?

The short answer is that Bruce had luck. Although King Edward was ill and tired, he wanted one last chance to kill or capture Bruce. However, Edward died at the head of his invading army in July 1307. Edward's son (now Edward II) led the army back into England. Bruce now had a breathing space and time to deal with his enemies in Scotland.

Question paper 2: Scottish History

How did Bruce defeat his enemies in Scotland?

Bruce had to remove the threat from the Comyn family if he was to remain king. Bruce also knew that as long as Scotland remained divided between his supporters and those of Comyn it would be impossible to organise united resistance against the English.

The core of Comyn power lay in the north-east of Scotland and in the winter of 1307/8 Bruce was there attacking both English and Comyn bases.

By spring Bruce was even stronger and in March 1308 the armies of Bruce and Buchan came face to face again, this time at Inverurie.

The Battle of Inverurie was a decisive victory for Bruce. After winning the battle Bruce ordered all the lands of the Earl of Buchan to be destroyed. The 'Herschip of Buchan', as the destruction of Comyn lands was called, destroyed the Comyn power base. People loyal to Comyn were killed, animals and crops destroyed and property was burned to the ground.

Bruce's campaign against the Comyns in the north-east and then 'the Herschip of Buchan' meant that Bruce had almost won his civil war.

How did Bruce increase his power from 1309 onwards?

By 1309, Bruce had defeated his enemies in Scotland and he used his parliament at St Andrews to start a propaganda campaign aimed at justifying himself as king.

In the Declaration of the Clergy, Scotland's bishops accepted Bruce as the legitimate Scottish king. Certainly by 1309 Bruce seemed safe within Scotland as its king. Even the French king sent word that he recognised Bruce as Scottish king, rightfully replacing the absent John Balliol. However, although the civil war in Scotland seemed to be settled, the war with England was not.

Bruce knew that his army was unlikely to win a pitched battle with Edward II, so Bruce developed his 'secret war' – what we would call guerrilla warfare. He launched sudden surprise attacks then vanished into the hills and forests again.

English armies marching into Scotland were forced to retreat as a result of Bruce burning and destroying any food, shelter or water that could help the enemy. Meanwhile, Scottish troops raided into northern England. Not only did the Scots return with all the loot and livestock they could bring back, the persistent Scottish attacks into England increased pressure on Edward. English nobles in the north of England asked why their king could not protect them.

By 1314, Edward was facing the possibility of being forced out of Scotland. Most of Scotland's major castles including Dundee, Perth, Dumfries, Linlithgow, Roxburgh and Edinburgh had all been retaken by the end of 1313.

Only Stirling and Berwick castles remained in English hands. Edward II could not let Stirling castle surrender without making an attempt to break the siege, so in the summer of 1314 he marched north with a huge army. The scene was set for the battle of Bannockburn.

The Wars of Independence, 1249–1328

How did each side prepare for battle?

By the middle of June 1314, Edward II's army was approaching Stirling Castle. In the army there were about 15,000 foot soldiers, about 1,000 archers and around 2,000 cavalry.

Facing the advancing English force was a Scottish army of about 5,000 men.

The Scots waiting in the woods near Bannockburn were organised, well trained and confident.

Bruce's men were grouped in three huge schiltrons with about 1,500 men in each.

Bruce also used the terrain around the Bannock burn to his advantage, which helped make up for the difference in size between the two armies.

In contrast, the English army was disorganised. Edward appointed many of his friends to important positions in the army regardless of their military experience and removed experienced army commanders if he disagreed with them.

Predictably, the English army planned to use the road that led straight to Stirling Castle along a high dry ridge for their advance.

Bruce was determined to deny the English use of that road. After the main road to Stirling crossed the Bannock burn there were hills to the left and a narrow area of flat, rough ground to the right that stretched off into an area of rough, boggy marshland that was bounded by the Bannock burn and the Firth of Forth. Bruce ordered potholes (called potts) to be dug on and around the road to make the road almost unusable to the advancing forces. He also ordered caltrops, which were iron spikes, to be scattered in their thousands across the rough ground. Horses could not travel easily over such booby-trapped ground and Bruce intended to trap the English army on land where they would lose all their advantages.

The first contact between the Scots and English forces happened almost by accident.

A force of about 300 English cavalry rode up the road, avoiding the potts as best they could. Their intention was to scout the land ahead and if possible make contact with the garrison in Stirling castle. Suddenly, the English cavalry found Bruce out in the open inspecting his troops and unaware that English troops were anywhere nearby. For brief seconds neither side knew what to do. Suddenly, a lone English knight called Henry de Bohun saw his change for fame and glory and charged at Bruce.

De Bohun was a fully armed experienced knight on a warhorse. Bruce was lightly armed on a much smaller horse and not expecting to fight. As the English knight charged closer, Bruce sat still on his horse until the last minute, then sidestepped de Bohun's charge. At the same moment Bruce crashed his battle-axe into the head of de Bohun.

The Englishman crashed to the ground dead. The rest of the English cavalry charged to avenge de Bohun but by then it was too late. A Scottish schiltron had moved from the woods to protect Bruce. The cavalry crashed against the wall of pikes but failed to break through. They then retreated.

While the combat between Bruce and de Bohun was taking place, the main English force tried to move across very rough ground towards Stirling castle. However, once again a Scottish schiltron blocked the English move and the English were undecided what to do next. Instead of moving quickly against the Scots, arguments broke out between two English commanders and the delay gave the Scots time to prepare their schiltron

Question paper 2: Scottish History

formation fully. When the English knights charged at the Scots they were met with a forest of pikes. The English knights either died on the Scottish pikes or rode around the schiltron ineffectively.

That night, as the English regrouped on open boggy ground, English morale was at rock bottom, but even so the Scots were still not confident of victory.

The Scots were preparing to retreat away from Bannockburn and resume hit and run tactics when news reached them of the disorganised and miserable state of the English forces. Bruce decided to fight. It was all or nothing.

What happened on the second day of the battle of Bannockburn?

Overnight, English preparations were chaotic. The Scots knew the English were trapped and crowded together with the steep-sided Bannock burn behind them and the advancing Scots in front of them. The English commanders had no room to use their archers to wreck the schiltrons as had happened at Falkirk.

The final stage in the battle came when the English saw what appeared to be another Scottish army charging down from nearby Coxet Hill. Later historians call this 'new army' the small people or 'wee folk'. Where this force came from, no one is quite sure. Some say it was made up of cooks, women and the families of the fighting men who charged downhill to give the Scots support just when the English looked to be on a point of collapse. Other historians argue they were Highland forces who had arrived late for the battle. Either way, the sight of apparently fresh forces arriving was the final straw for the English and they began a headlong retreat back across the Bannock burn, slipping, sliding and drowning.

Edward II escaped but thousands of English soldiers did not. Reports from the time refer to thousands of English soldiers dying as they tried to cross the Bannock burn and run to safety.

Was did the English lose the battle of Bannockburn?

Historians still argue about whether the Scots won a great victory or if the English caused their own defeat.

English errors included overconfidence, a confused command structure made worse by Edward II dabbling in military planning he did not fully understand and an utter failure to learn from mistakes on the first day of the battle.

Why did the English not just send wave after wave of arrows into the Scottish schiltrons as they did at Falkirk?

Finally, why did the English army choose to move on to boggy land on which their room for manoeuvre was severely restricted by the Bannock burn and the Firth of Forth?

The Wars of Independence, 1249–1328

Was the Scottish victory the result of careful planning?

Those who claim that Scottish planning won the battle do have some strong arguments to make.

Remember that the whole point of the English advance was to relieve Stirling Castle. They had to get there and the Scots knew that. Scottish control over the high road to Stirling was vital for victory. By digging the potts around the high road and scattering caltrops in the rough grass, the advancing English were forced to look for alternative routes.

The Scottish troops were well trained. Remember these groups of pikemen were huge – over a thousand men in each and there were at least three if not four such groups on the battlefield. By keeping the schiltrons pushing forward, the Scots gave the English no room to move or to regroup.

Finally, Bruce is even credited with using the 'wee folk' to charge at a crucial moment of the battle to demoralise the English.

How important was the battle of Bannockburn?

Victory at Bannockburn gave the Scots huge confidence. Without doubt the victory made Bruce's position as King of Scotland secure.

He was a successful warlord and with military success comes more support.

The Scots also captured many English knights and they were used not only to earn ransoms but also to exchange for Scottish prisoners. In this way Bruce won back his wife, daughter and sister after almost 10 years in captivity.

Finally, the aftermath of victory gave Bruce the time to stabilise and secure his authority over his kingdom.

However, the battle did not end the Scottish Wars of Independence.

It did not force England to give Scotland its freedom and the battle did not significantly weaken English power.

Immediately after the battle of Bannockburn, Bruce secured his position as King of Scots.

For a long time Scottish nobles had been torn between their loyalty to the King of Scotland and their promises of loyalty to the English king to whom they did homage for the lands they held in England. The Scottish lords were given a straightforward choice. They could keep their lands in England but lose all their lands and title in Scotland. At a parliament held at Cambuskenneth Abbey in November 1314 the new arrangements became law. To Bruce and his supporters the action to stop the problem of divided loyalties made good political sense. Bruce had to be sure of his nobles' loyalty. Bruce rewarded those who now sided with him with land taken from the disinherited nobles and from and Bruce's enemies who had died at Bannockburn.

The nobles who decided to keep their lands in England became known as 'the Disinherited'.

Question paper 2: Scottish History

Continuing hostilities

By 1315, Bruce was secure in Scotland but the war with England continued. Bruce decided to take the war to Edward II in two ways. The first was to threaten English control in Ireland.

The Irish campaign made sense to Bruce. The English used men from Ireland to fight against the Scots. Ireland was also a base used by the English to launch attacks into Scotland. Edward Bruce, brother of Robert, led the Scots campaign into Ireland.

At first the campaign seemed to be a success. The Irish lords seemed happy to see the Scots and in the summer of 1316 Edward Bruce was accepted as High King of Ireland. But promises made are not the same as promises kept and very soon the alliance of Irish Lords fell apart along with their promise to accept Edward Bruce as High King of Ireland.

The Scots only had limited success. They failed to capture Dublin and only managed to keep control over the northern part of Ireland called Ulster. Finally, the ambitions of the Bruce family in Ireland ended when Edward Bruce was killed.

Nevertheless, the Irish campaign had distracted English attention from Scotland alone and that was useful to Bruce.

English forces that could have been used against Scotland or to protect northern England were diverted to deal with the trouble in Ireland.

Edward II and his advisers could not plan campaigns against Scotland while they were more concerned about the possibility of a Celtic fringe alliance – in other words Scotland, Wales and Ireland uniting together to fight against the English.

Why did Bruce continue raids into northern England?

Meanwhile, Bruce continued to cause King Edward of England problems by raiding into northern England. It was increasingly obvious to the lords of northern England that Edward could do little to protect them and several made private arrangements with Bruce, mostly involving the payment of 'protection money'.

By 1319, Edward II had been defeated in battle, his lands in the north of England were raided with ease by the Scots, his own nobles in the north were very unhappy with his kingship and Bruce had even threatened to open a Celtic alliance against him by invading Ireland. Edward II had even been forced to make a truce with Bruce but Edward would still not accept that Scotland was an independent nation, free from English expansionist ambitions.

The Wars of Independence, 1249–1328

What part did the Pope play in winning Scotland's independence?

A main issue that was central to the independence of Scotland was Bruce's right to be king. Remember that Bruce had committed a great sin by murdering John Comyn in a church. For that crime Bruce should have been excommunicated. In 1319, the Pope ordered Scotland's bishops to explain why they had never enforced the excommunication.

This was an opportunity Bruce turned to his benefit. Edward had tried to use international diplomacy to create pressure on Bruce. Now Bruce turned the tables on Edward and ordered three documents to be prepared for the Pope, each in their different ways justifying Bruce as King of Scotland. Two of the three have been lost to historians but the third, The Declaration of Arbroath, still survives.

Why is the Declaration of Arbroath so important?

Today, the words of the declaration are used for many purposes. Are they the first stirrings of a basic democracy in Europe, where kings could be removed if they displeased the people of the country? The Declaration stated, 'If he (Bruce) should agree to make our kingdom subject to the King of England, we should drive him out as our enemy'.

Are the words, 'for as long as a hundred remain alive we shall never on any conditions be brought under English rule' clear statements of national identity and pride in a nation?

Even the words, 'It is in truth not for glory, nor riches, nor honours that we are fighting, but for freedom' have been seen as a statement made by the Community of the Realm, making clear that their actions were carried out in the interests of the country as a whole rather than personal gain.

Or were the words just propaganda? Is the Declaration of Arbroath just a carefully worded document written on the orders of Bruce to justify Bruce's kingship and also to persuade the Pope to drop his opposition to Bruce as King of Scots? It is true that most of the Scots nobles who attached their seals to the document would never have read the document. However, the Declaration survives today as a truly important document that can legitimately be interpreted in all the ways outlined above.

Question paper 2: Scottish History

Did the Declaration of Arbroath achieve Scottish freedom and independence?

In the short term it did not. Although the truce between England and Scotland limped along, there was no formal making of peace between the two countries. Later negotiations with a new Pope in 1323 helped to ease relations between the Papacy and Scotland but events in England were about to change the situation completely.

After three years the truce between England and Scotland broke down. In England, discontent with Edward II's reign reached such a peak that Edward was overthrown by his own wife Isabella and her lover, Mortimer. As far as Scotland was concerned this was an opportunity not to be missed and they continued with their hit-and-run raids. Bruce even began granting land in Northern England to his followers. While these land grants were only made in name, because Bruce did not control the land, the symbolism of the action was obvious. English authority was so weak that perhaps Bruce would absorb the northern English counties into Scotland.

Meanwhile, Bruce launched a new attack into Ireland, raiding into Ulster and raising English fears once again of a new Celtic alliance against England.

The pressure on Mortimer and Isabella's government was just too much. They agreed to negotiate with Bruce.

What was the Treaty of Edinburgh and Northampton?

The Treaty of Edinburgh was signed on 17th March 1328.

Bruce gave up Scotland's claims to Northumbria and he agreed to pay compensation for damage caused totalling £20,000. In exchange, England accepted that Scotland was a free and independent country with Robert the Bruce as its officially recognised king. The matching Treaty of Northampton confirmed the Treaty of Edinburgh.

Three months later Bruce died, but he had lived long enough to see Scotland recognised as a free and independent nation with himself as the accepted King of Scots. Bruce knew his arrangements about who should be king after him (the succession) were secure and the Bruce dynasty would continue.

The treaties of Edinburgh and Northampton did not end conflict between Scotland and England. Soon after the treaties were signed a pattern similar to before was re-established with English invasion being met by Scottish counter-attack. However, the conflict between England and Scotland had become conflict between two separate countries, no longer a struggle in which one country was trying to win its freedom and independence from another.

Got it? ☐ ☐ ☐   **The Wars of Independence, 1249–1328**

Check Your Understanding

ESSENTIAL KNOWLEDGE

1. Why was it important for Robert the Bruce to be crowned King of Scotland as fast as possible after the murder of John Comyn?
2. Why was it important for Bruce to capture Scottish castles held by the English?
3. What was the Herschip of Buchan?
4. What was the issue concerning the disinherited?

THEME QUESTION

1. Why were the Comyns and Bruces such rivals even before the murder of John Comyn?
2. Why did Bruce need to win the civil war in Scotland before taking on English power in Scotland?
3. What was the 'secret war' fought by Bruce after he returned from hiding?
4. Why did Bruce change from guerrilla tactics to fight the battle of Bannockburn?

TEST YOURSELF

Do you know the meaning of these key words?

Sacrilege
Competitors
Civil war
Deploy
Disinherit
Clergy
Celtic fringe alliance
Papacy

137

Scottish Wars of Independence

Issue 1
Issue 2
Issue 3
Issue 4

1249
Alexander III crowned King Of Scots.

1272
Edward I crowned King of England.

March 1286
Alexander III dies in accident. All his children already dead.

April 1286
Six Guardians of Scotland selected at Scone.

September 1290
Margaret, Maid of Norway dies on her way to Orkney. Who will now lead Scotland?

1294
Edward I orders King John to fight in France. The Scots refuse and instead make an alliance with France in 1295. Edward furious.

1300–1301
Edward I and son campaign in south Scotland.

August 1305
William Wallace captured and executed.

February 1306
Robert Bruce murders John Comyn at Dumfries Abbey.

March 1306
Robert I inaugurated at Scone.

1307
May: Battle of Loudon Hill.
July: Death of Edward I, succeeded by Edward II.

1314
Scottish victory at the Battle of Bannockburn. Bruce disinherits Scots nobility who will not swear oath of loyalty to Bruce alone.

1320
April: Declaration of Arbroath.

1322
Edward II's last invasion of Scotland fails.

1327
Jan: Edward II deposed and murdered by English opposition.
Feb: Coronation of Edward III.

1328
March: Treaty of Edinburgh-Northampton. Scottish Independence recognised.

1329
June: Death of Robert I.

1281
Princess Margaret, daughter of Alexander III marries Eric, King of Norway. They have a baby, called Margaret. She is granddaughter of King Alexander.

1283
Princess Margaret, now Queen of Norway, dies. She is last remaining child of Alexander III. Now baby Margaret is next in line for a Scottish throne.

1291
Aug: The Great Cause begins. Edward 1 invited to manage the process of selecting a new Scottish King.

1292
Nov: John Balliol chosen as new Scottish King. Almost immediately Edward claims his overlordship over King John Balliol.

1296
March: Edward1 attacks and captures Berwick upon Tweed.
April: Battle of Dunbar. Scots loose battle and almost immediately Scots resistance crumbled.
July: King John surrenders to Edward I. He is humiliated by Edward and then imprisoned.

1297
William Wallace and Andrew Murray rebel Sept: Scottish victory at the Battle of Stirling Bridge
Nov: Death of Andrew Murray.

1298
Scottish defeat at the Battle of Falkirk.

1301
After Papal urging, John Balliol released into custody of King Philip of France.

1303
King Philip forced into treaty with Edward I. Scotland now isolated.

1303–1304
Edward I invades Scotland again. John Comyn and nobles surrender to English king. After an agreement at Strathord almost all Scots nobles get their lands back.

1308
Aug: King Robert's campaigns in Scotland; wins the Battle of the Pass of Brander. Bruce continues guerrilla war again English forces and their Scots allies up until 1314.

1309
King Robert's first parliament in St Andrews.

1310–1311
Edward II invades Scotland but by 1314 all Scottish castles recaptured by a Bruce – apart from Stirling Castle.

1315–1318
Scots launch campaign in Ireland led by Edward Bruce.

1315
onwards – Scots raid into a Northern England creating problems between Edward 11 and his northern nobles.

1318
Death of Edward Bruce Robert I excommunicated by Pope John XXII.

Question paper 2: Scottish History

Key issue 1: The migration of Scots

What is this section all about?

Roughly two million people emigrated from Scotland overseas between 1830 and 1914. First of all you need to know a bit about how ordinary Scots were affected by the social effects of the changes in the Scottish economy, in particular working and living conditions.

Scots left Scotland for a variety of reasons: some were attracted by opportunities such as higher wages and cheap land abroad, while others were forced to move by events such as the Highland Clearances.

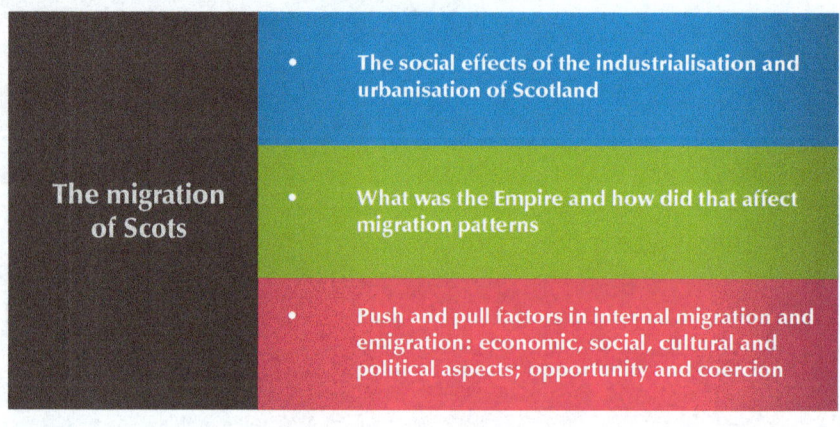

The migration of Scots
- The social effects of the industrialisation and urbanisation of Scotland
- What was the Empire and how did that affect migration patterns
- Push and pull factors in internal migration and emigration: economic, social, cultural and political aspects; opportunity and coercion

What were the Highland Clearances?

In brief, the Highland Clearances meant the eviction of Highland crofters from their homes and small farms (crofts), sometimes by force. Public opinion at the time sympathised with those being evicted and criticised 'wicked landowners' for putting money before people. It was true that landowners often used emigration as a way of removing the surplus population and to try to make their estates profitable. In reality the Highland communities also suffered from overpopulation with too few resources in terms of land and food to allow the communities to prosper.

Something had to change. The Clearances left a bitter folk memory about evictions and the unfairness of the landowners while in reality it was the landowners' land, the Highland population was getting too big and many landowners helped the population move by building new villages or paying fares to emigrate.

Migration and Empire, 1830–1939

Moving to the towns

Moving from one part of Scotland to another is called internal migration because it is movement within Scotland. The most common pattern of internal migration was from countryside to town. Migration to the growing towns and cities offered opportunities socially as well as economically. Farming life was hard work with long hours and few holidays. Pay was poor and life in the countryside offered limited opportunities for socialising. With the arrival of railways across the country, moving to the towns became easier and many rural workers chose to leave for the bright lights of the town. The young in particular did not find country employment particularly attractive. It was isolated and lacked access to leisure opportunities such as the pub, cinema, dance hall and football ground. By the early 20th century, rural depopulation was still a feature of the changing pattern of Scotland's population. England was also an important destination for internal migrants as it offered higher wages and better opportunities in trades and professions.

What are push and pull reasons for migration?

Push reasons are things that make you want to leave because conditions are difficult or unpleasant. Unemployment, bad housing and lack of opportunity would be push factors. Pull factors are things that attract you to move such as free land, easier transportation or the expectation of greater and better opportunities.

The importance of transport

Migration and emigration were also encouraged by cheaper, more efficient transport. Developments in the technology of steam ships meant that a journey time of six weeks for a crossing between Scotland and North America had been reduced to one week by 1914. The development of railways also meant travel to ports like Glasgow became easier, and allowed for swift movement once within a new country like Canada or America. In fact Canada was such a popular destination mainly because travelling time was short and once there it was a fairly easy way into the USA.

April 1923: Emigrants from the Hebrides boarding the 'Matagama' at Glasgow docks on their way to Canada.

Question paper 2: Scottish History

What was the attraction of moving abroad?

Canada, Australia and New Zealand were important and popular places of emigration because of the availability of land and the opportunity to earn more money. Higher wages could be earned overseas and often financial help was given to encourage emigration by individual landowners, government organisations such as the Colonial Office and charities like the Highland and Island Emigration Society. Scots were also encouraged by other Scots who had already moved. A letter home from a relative or friend who had already emigrated was an important factor in persuading Scots to move. The fact that there was a support network of fellow Scots in existence abroad was a huge reason why many emigrated.

Scots were also welcomed due to their skills and the fact that many brought money with them, these factors combining to help develop the economies of the Empire. Countries like Canada put considerable effort into attracting Scots through agents and advertising. Once in their new homelands, Scots developed a system of support for each other when abroad that led to an increased sense of their Scottish identity. By the time of the 1922 Empire Settlement Act, the British government paid up to three million pounds a year to encourage emigration. It was hoped that this would relieve rising unemployment in Scotland in the 1920s.

In the 1920s and 1930s Scotland had the highest rate of emigration of any European country. Many Scots saw emigration as an escape from a Scotland locked in unemployment and decline. Migrants were not only from the Highlands but also from the depressed industrial areas of central Scotland.

Many Scottish people made the journey to Canada, which offered new beginnings and job opportunities.

Check Your Understanding

ESSENTIAL KNOWLEDGE

1. Why did so many Scots emigrate to Canada, New Zealand and Australia?
2. Why was Canada so popular?
3. What is the difference between a push reason and a pull reason?

THEME QUESTION

1. Recently, the reasons for migration have been summarised as coercion and opportunity. What examples can you give for each?
2. What is the difference between emigration and internal migration?

TEST YOURSELF

Do you know the meaning of these key words?

Overpopulation

Emigration

Internal migration

Depopulation

Crofters

Coercion

Opportunity

Migration and Empire, 1830–1939

Key issue 2: The experience of immigrants in Scotland

What is this section all about?

Between 1830 and 1939 there were four main groups of people who came to Scotland from overseas. These were the Irish, Jews, Lithuanians and Italians. All those groups had an effect on Scotland and the Scots. Some immigrants were welcomed and some were not. This section is about how the new immigrants were welcomed, how they retained their original identity and how they assimilated into Scottish life.

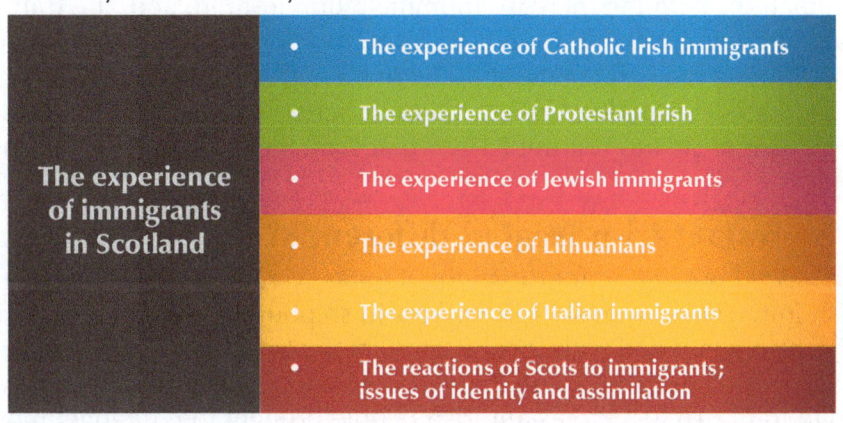

The experience of immigrants in Scotland:
- The experience of Catholic Irish immigrants
- The experience of Protestant Irish
- The experience of Jewish immigrants
- The experience of Lithuanians
- The experience of Italian immigrants
- The reactions of Scots to immigrants; issues of identity and assimilation

The Catholic Irish experience

Most Irish people came to Scotland to escape poverty, unemployment and hunger and most of those immigrants were Catholic. In contrast, most Scots were Protestant and rivalry between those two groups was still raw in 19th century Scotland. Irish immigrants in Scotland often settled in the west of Scotland, around Glasgow. There were thousands of jobs in the new growing industries such as cotton factories, coalmines, ironworks and building the railway network. As the industrial economy of Scotland developed, so did the demand for workers. Immigrants from Ireland arrived in large numbers to meet the demand for unskilled and semi-skilled labour in Scotland's growing industries. The Irish arrivals found living and working conditions in the industrial cities and factories of Scotland were hard but better than the life left behind in Ireland. Pay in Scotland was also better than back in Ireland.

Why were the Catholic Irish not always welcome?

The Catholic Irish immigrants were met with persecution and discrimination from Scots. Many immigrants were poor and tended to live in the cheapest, and therefore poor quality, housing. Scots saw the poverty of the Irish as evidence of their bad habits and blamed them for spreading disease and hardship. It was easier to blame people who could be picked on and persecuted than look for the real causes that lay in the effects of industrialisation and urbanisation.

The number of poor Catholic Irish flooding into Scotland looking for jobs led to a growing resentment among Scots. Irish workers were accused of being strike-breakers and being

143

Question paper 2: Scottish History

willing to work for less money than Scottish workers. Stories spread that the Irish came to Scotland to get poor relief help, available after three years living in Scotland.

The 1920s saw widespread violence between Catholic and Protestant communities. The Church of Scotland published its pamphlet, 'The Menace of the Irish Race to our Scottish Identity', in 1923 which showed that anti-Irish Catholic feelings remained in Scotland. The Scottish Protestant League was a political party in Scotland during the 1920s and 1930s that wanted to stop Irish immigration to Britain, send Irish immigrants already settled here back to Ireland and stop Irish immigrants receiving any welfare benefits.

Did the Catholic Irish assimilate easily into Scottish life?

For many years the answer was no. The Catholic Church was a place of safety, security and identity for many Irish immigrants, especially when they faced hostility from the local Protestant population. With the increase in immigration from Ireland, the Catholic Church expanded its services in Scotland. Even a separate sporting identity was created with the emergence of differing football teams, still clearly in evidence today with Rangers/Celtic, Hibs/Hearts and Dundee/Dundee United. Catholic schools developed in this period, funded by voluntary donations. It was not until 1918 that Catholic schools received funding from the government.

Were the Protestant Irish treated differently?

The answer is yes. About one in four Irish immigrants were Protestants. Many of the Protestant Irish immigrants were skilled workers in shipbuilding and the iron industry. The Protestant Irish also combined with local Protestant Scots in their dislike of the Catholic population. Sectarian trouble between the two communities existed in Glasgow, Ayrshire and Lanarkshire in the 1830s. Protestant Irish people brought the 'Orange' movement to Scotland. By the 1920s and 1930s, football-related sectarian violence had increased.

Jews

Large numbers of Jews arrived in Scotland between 1880 and 1914. Most were poor and came from Russia and Poland. Many Jews migrated to escape pogroms. A pogrom is an organised massacre of a particular ethnic group back in their home countries. Many Jews also migrated because they were not able to become skilled craftsmen or professional people in their home countries because of prejudice and religious persecution.

Jews formed a distinct community owing to their religion and language (many spoke Yiddish, the Jewish language). Most lived in the Gorbals, which had the advantage of cheap lodgings. Jews worked in jobs that were not a direct threat to the native Scots. The Jewish population kept their identity separate from local Scots. They built synagogues to worship. Jewish immigrants tended to work in particular jobs such as peddling and hawking (selling door-to-door), cigarette making and also as tailors specialising in cheap suits for the local population.

A Jewish drapery shop in the Gorbals, Glasgow.

In fact, the immigrant Jews lived a fairly self-contained and independent existence. Local groups of wealthier Jews often helped poorer members of their community. It would be fair to say that Jews tended to be tolerated, but not totally accepted, in Scottish society.

Got it? ☐ ☐ ☐　　　　　　　　　　　**Migration and Empire, 1830–1939**

Lithuanians

About 7,000 Lithuanians settled in Scotland between the 1860s and 1914.

Lithuanians moved because taxes were very high in their home country and income from farming had fallen. Another reason why many Lithuanians moved was because the population was increasing and good farming land became scarce.

Many Lithuanians settled in Lanarkshire and Ayrshire and took jobs in the coal, iron and steel industries. At first Lithuanians were unpopular as Scottish miners saw the immigrants as a threat to their jobs. Lithuanians were used as strike-breakers, working while Scottish miners were on strike for better wages. Lithuanians were also Catholic so there was some anti-Catholic prejudice. It's more difficult to check how Lithuanians mixed with the Scottish community in the past because many Lithuanians simply changed their surnames to local-sounding names.

Italians

By 1914 there were 4,500 Italians in Scotland but unlike other immigrant groups, Italians settled all over Scotland. They settled in Scotland in large numbers after 1880 and prospered because they provided two things that became hugely popular to Scots, ice-cream and fish 'n' chips.

At first the Italians worked from barrows, which they pushed along streets. Soon, however, hardworking Italian families opened up shops and cafes. Some Scots complained that Italian cafes opened on a Sunday. This offended some strict Protestant Scots. They also complained that Italian cafes opened late in the evening and that the shops attracted groups of youngsters.

Other Scots liked the Italian cafes because they did not sell alcohol and provided a place for youngsters to meet up with their friends. The long hours of work in the cafes and fish and chip shops meant that they did not always integrate with the local Scottish population. Italians settling in Scotland often had the intention of working for a while to raise money, then returning home to Italy.

Check Your Understanding

ESSENTIAL KNOWLEDGE

1. Why was there such resentment of Catholic Irish people?
2. Why was integration and assimilation difficult for many immigrant groups?
3. Did immigrants leave their mark on present-day Scotland?
4. Why did Irish migration to Scotland cause so much more discontent than other immigrant groups?

TEST YOURSELF

Do you know the meaning of these key words?

Lithuanians
Assimilated
Integrated
Industrialisation
Urbanisation
Synagogues
Catholic Irish
Protestant Irish
Sectarian

Question paper 2: Scottish History

Key issue 3: The impact of Scots emigrants on the Empire

What is this section all about?

Scots played an important part in developing the new lands where they settled. Scots influenced the development of the Empire as politicians, engineers, manufacturers and farmers. Scots also influenced the development of the education systems of countries in the Empire. Scots emigrants took with them their customs and culture but a darker side of the Scots' arrival in new lands is what happened to native societies.

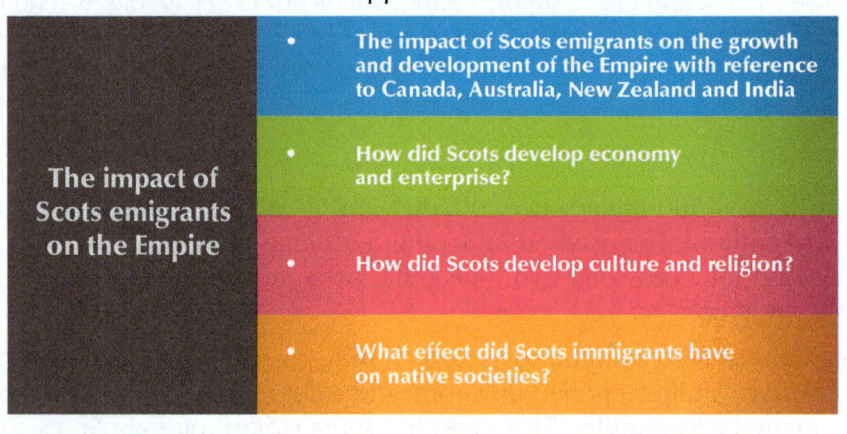

The impact of Scots emigrants on the Empire
- The impact of Scots emigrants on the growth and development of the Empire with reference to Canada, Australia, New Zealand and India
- How did Scots develop economy and enterprise?
- How did Scots develop culture and religion?
- What effect did Scots immigrants have on native societies?

Canada

Economic, political and cultural development

In Canada, Scots were very important in the development of trade in furs and timber as well as agriculture. They were also heavily involved in the iron, steel, oil and gas industries. By the 1920s it has been calculated that one-quarter of Canada's business leaders were born in Scotland. Scots were important in the development of the Canadian education system. Scottish influence can also be seen in the development of the curriculum in Canadian universities. In politics, Sir John MacDonald, Glasgow born, was the first Prime Minister, while Scotsman George Brown founded the influential newspaper the *Toronto Globe*.

Scots quickly gained a reputation for being hard-working, risk-taking and seeking to improve their life. They brought with them new ideas on how to farm Canada. One example of an industrial development that shows the importance of Scots in the Canadian economy is their involvement in the building of a railway across Canada – the Transatlantic Canadian Pacific Railway. The railway was completed in 1885 and played a vital part in opening up Canada to new immigrants who could now settle in areas around the railway.

Migration and Empire, 1830–1939

Native societies

Native American tribes, who used to be called 'Indians', are now referred to as First Peoples. Scottish immigrants had a big effect on the First Peoples. At first immigrants depended on the First Peoples for their survival: when Scottish fur traders first began to develop their business, they traded with the Native American tribes that existed in Canada. Soon personal relationships developed and the children of the union of Scots and local native people became known as Métis people. They were extremely useful people in the development of the fur trade, acting as trusted links between Scottish traders and the local people.

However, the traditional life of the First Peoples was changed forever by contact with immigrants like the Scots. Some immigrants saw them as 'savages' who were not 'civilised'. As the numbers of immigrants increased, thousands of First Peoples were moved from their lands. The immigrant Scots who had been pushed off land in the Highlands now did the same thing to First Peoples in Canada.

Australia

The economy and politics

Scots were central to the development of the Australian sheep farming economy where they created huge sheep runs in New South Wales and Victoria with big centres for the wool trade established in Melbourne and Adelaide. Scots also played important parts in the sugar industry, mining, manufacturing, shipping, engineering and finance. They also owned shipping company lines that were used to carry even more immigrants to Australia.

Scots were also involved in Australian politics. Perhaps the most famous Scottish Australian politician was Andrew Fisher who arrived in Queensland in 1885 and became Prime Minister three times.

Culture and religion

Scottish education reformers took their thoughts and skills to Australia where schools were needed to educate a new generation of Australians. As a result, schools organised by Scots were important as they produced many of the Australian leaders of the future, whether it be in politics, business and the economy or the military.

Native societies

In some cases new Scottish settlers took Aboriginal women as their wives but more often the relationship between Scots looking to expand farms and businesses led to conflict with Aboriginal people. The 'Hornet Bank' massacre of 1853 shows the conflict that happened as land newly used for farming began to eat into traditional Aboriginal land. As a result of a massacre involving the Frasers, a Scottish emigrant family, as many as 300 Aborigines were shot in retaliation. Soon afterwards, the entire Yeeman tribe and language were exterminated. The irony of migrant Scots forcing people off the land they had lived on for generations to make way for sheep seems not to have been noticed by most migrants.

New Zealand

Economy and culture

Scots were very important in the development of New Zealand. As with other parts of the Empire, Scots were considered to be good immigrants because they were Protestant, hard-working and well educated. Scots founded New Zealand's papermaking industry and were important engineers and shipbuilders. They were skilled farmers and influenced the development of New Zealand by developing the wool and sheep rearing industry.

In the 1860s, discovery of gold started a gold rush in Otago. The Free Church of Scotland, through a company called the Otago Association, founded the town of Dunedin. The name comes from the Scottish Gaelic name for Edinburgh. The Otago Association actively recruited settlers from Scotland and as a result, some parts of New Zealand became more Scottish than others. All over New Zealand, Caledonian societies were formed that helped maintain Scottish culture and traditions such as annual Caledonian Games. Dunedin's main rugby team is called The Highlanders.

Politics

Peter Fraser from a village near Tain in Easter Ross was one of the most famous New Zealand Scots. He became politically active around the time of the First World War. Fraser was involved in the creation of the New Zealand Labour Party, became an MP in 1918 and eventually Prime Minister of New Zealand in 1940.

Native societies

Immigration had a big impact on the Maori people of New Zealand. By 1830 the population of Maori living in New Zealand was over 100,000. Many Maori chiefs welcomed trade with the European settlers, but were worried by the Europeans taking their land. The Treaty of Waitangi in 1840 between British and Maori chiefs seemed to establish British authority and gave immigrants legal rights as citizens.

The combination of war, land loss, disease and intermarriage caused a fall in the Maori population so that by 1896 it had dropped to 40,000.

Got it? ☐ ☐ ☐   **Migration and Empire, 1830–1939**

India

After 1850, Scots were important in changing Indian society, especially Charles James Napier and Lord Dalhousie, Governor-General of India 1848–1856. Napier created a police force to keep the peace as well as seeking to develop the country economically. Critics of Dalhousie say his encouragement of the railway, telegraph and postal services was all to do with controlling India for the benefit of Britain.

The British also justified their mission to 'civilise' India by using the examples of Thuggee (a religious sect that existed to strangle travellers) and Sati (widows burned alive on the funeral pyres of their dead husbands). Both of these activities were banned by the British.

Many Scots worked in India as missionaries and they believed their mission was to convert Indians to Christianity and to educate them. Critics argued this was an attempt to destroy Indian cultures and create a class of Indians to serve the Empire.

Reaction to change

In 1857 the Indian Mutiny broke out. From the point of view of some Indians the Mutiny was really a rebellion against British rule but for people in Britain the image of the Scot in India was of a heroic soldier saving the Empire and avenging the slaughter of British women and children during the Mutiny.

India remained very important for trade and as a place where Scots saw service and made their fortunes. The Scottish middle classes had many family, investment and business links with India, and India in turn gave many families in Scotland a steady income from their investments.

Check Your Understanding

ESSENTIAL KNOWLEDGE

1. To what extent can Scots emigrants be accused of doing to others what was done to themselves?

THEME QUESTION

1. In what ways did Scots influence the Empire most?
2. Did Scots have a negative or positive impact on Empire?

TEST YOURSELF

Do you know the meaning of these key words?

Métis
First peoples
Aboriginal people
Maori
Mutiny

Question paper 2: Scottish History

Key issue 4: The effects of migration and Empire on Scotland, to 1939

What is this section all about?

The British Empire helped to make the Scottish economy very strong. The Empire was a very important market for Scottish-made products, while the Empire provided raw materials for Scottish industries such as sugar and tobacco. In turn, Scotland then sold its products to the Empire, usually transported on ships built in Scotland or packed in jute sacks made in Scotland. The Empire was also a place where Scots found jobs and Highland Regiments gained fame fighting to protect the British Empire.

The effects of migration and Empire on Scotland, to 1939:
- The contribution of immigrants to Scottish society, economy and culture
- The impact of Empire on Scotland
- The significance of migration and Empire in the development of Scottish identity

How big an effect did immigrants have on Scotland?

What was the contribution of the Irish to Scottish society?

Irish labourers were prepared to tackle the hardest of jobs. They helped to build Scotland's roads, canals and railways. Irish Catholics developed schools and churches across central Scotland and even today the effect of Catholic Irish culture can be seen in the development of Scottish football. Other contributions of the Irish to the culture of Scotland can be seen through the Protestant Orange Lodge order that is most obviously seen each summer in the 'marching season' with their annual parades in many Scottish town centres. A negative impact of this is that sectarian tensions continue due in part to historic reminders of the divide that existed between Scots and Irish.

An Orange Order parade makes its way through Dumbarton.

Migration and Empire, 1830–1939

Immigrants and Scottish politics

Until the early 20th century, most Irish Catholics voted for the Liberal Party but after the Easter Rising of 1916 in Dublin, many Irish Catholics in Scotland moved their support to the Labour Party. This was a major reason for the rise of the Labour Party in Scotland. In the 1922 election, the Independent Labour Party won 10 out of 15 Glasgow constituencies, achieved partly by increased support from Catholic Irish voters. Many Protestant Irish immigrants voted for the Conservative/Unionist Party because they wanted Ireland to remain part of the UK.

Lithuanian and Jewish immigrants became politically active in two ways. One was to join a trade union and campaign for better working conditions. The second route into political action was to vote for and work within the Independent Labour Party, campaigning for better living conditions and political reform.

Italian immigrants were less influential in politics, partly because it was the intention of many Italian immigrants to return home when they had made their fortunes.

What was the contribution of Italians, Jews and Lithuanians to Scottish society?

The Italian contribution to Scottish society has been both visible and welcome with most Italians linked to fish 'n' chip shops and ice cream cafes. Jewish immigrants were very important in the tailoring trade (especially making cheap men's suits) and the tobacco industry: cigarette making was a common job for Jewish immigrants to Scotland and there was no local workforce that could produce cigarettes. Many Lithuanian immigrants worked in the coal-mining industry but when the First World War broke out many returned to Eastern Europe.

Empire and economy

In the years before 1914, the wealth of Glasgow increased hugely. By 1921 Glasgow was referring to itself as the 'second city of the Empire'. Many Scots found jobs and built up businesses in the Empire and many then invested their profits in their home country. For example, money made in the jute industry was used by wealthy merchants to buy and improve Scottish rural estates, or to build large mansions in the suburbs of large towns and cities.

Trade with the Empire certainly benefitted the Scottish economy before 1914, but once areas of the Empire developed their own agriculture and industry, they became serious competitors for Scottish producers. By 1914, Bengal jute mills, developed by Scottish business people, were making huge profits based on the very low wages paid to their Indian workers. Demand for British-produced jute fell after 1920 and employment fell from 35,000 to 26,000 workers between 1929 and 1939. Competition from India also ended the cotton industry in Glasgow and the west of Scotland by the end of the 1920s.

Workers drumming Jute in Bengal.

Question paper 2: Scottish History

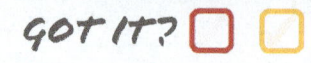

Got it? ☐ ☐ ☐

Locomotive production was also an important industry for Scotland with railway engines produced in the Springburn Works in Glasgow exported across the Empire. The other large industry that benefited from Empire was shipbuilding – making the ships that linked the British Empire together.

Many Scots travelled abroad and came home again with the money they had made, and for many people that money made an important contribution to the local economy. Scots also invested money abroad, especially Australia, New Zealand and India. In return, Scottish estates benefitted from a flow of money from Empire investments that allowed these older estates to spend money on improvements and repairs.

How did the Empire create the image of the brave, kilted soldier?

The simple answer is that Scottish soldiers, often from the Highlands, were used in the Empire's trouble spots to fight any threat to the Empire. In the late 18th century the British government was trying to pacify the Highlands after centuries when the dreaded Highland horde of warriors was feared by the more peaceful southern Scots and the English. After the Jacobites were defeated at Culloden in 1746, the British government tried to pacify the Highlands by banning weapons, bagpipes and the tartan kilt. In other words, the government tried to end the Highland clan identity. However, the government also offered jobs to any Highlander who wanted to join and in the British army the soldiers could continue their identity with weapons, bagpipes and kilts and use them against the enemies of the Empire.

By the late 19th century the Highland soldier was the usual image of British military power in the Empire, so it was the Empire that gave the Highland kilted soldier its status and authority.

The later 19th century saw a 'Highland craze' in the UK. In Scotland the Highland craze meant that even Lowland regiments were wearing tartan and had pipe bands by the end of the 19th century. The Highland identity had become Scottish identity.

Check Your Understanding

ESSENTIAL KNOWLEDGE

1. Why was the Empire so important to the Scottish economy?
2. Why did Irish immigration seem to have a much greater effect on Scotland than all other groups?

THEME QUESTION

1. Which was greater – the impact of Scotland on the Empire or that of the Empire on Scotland?
2. Was emigration from Scotland a force for good in the world?
3. Economic, social or political – which were the greatest causes of migration?

TEST YOURSELF

Do you know the meaning of these key words?

The British Empire/The Empire

Constituencies

Jute

Identity

Investments

Migration and Empire 1830–1930s

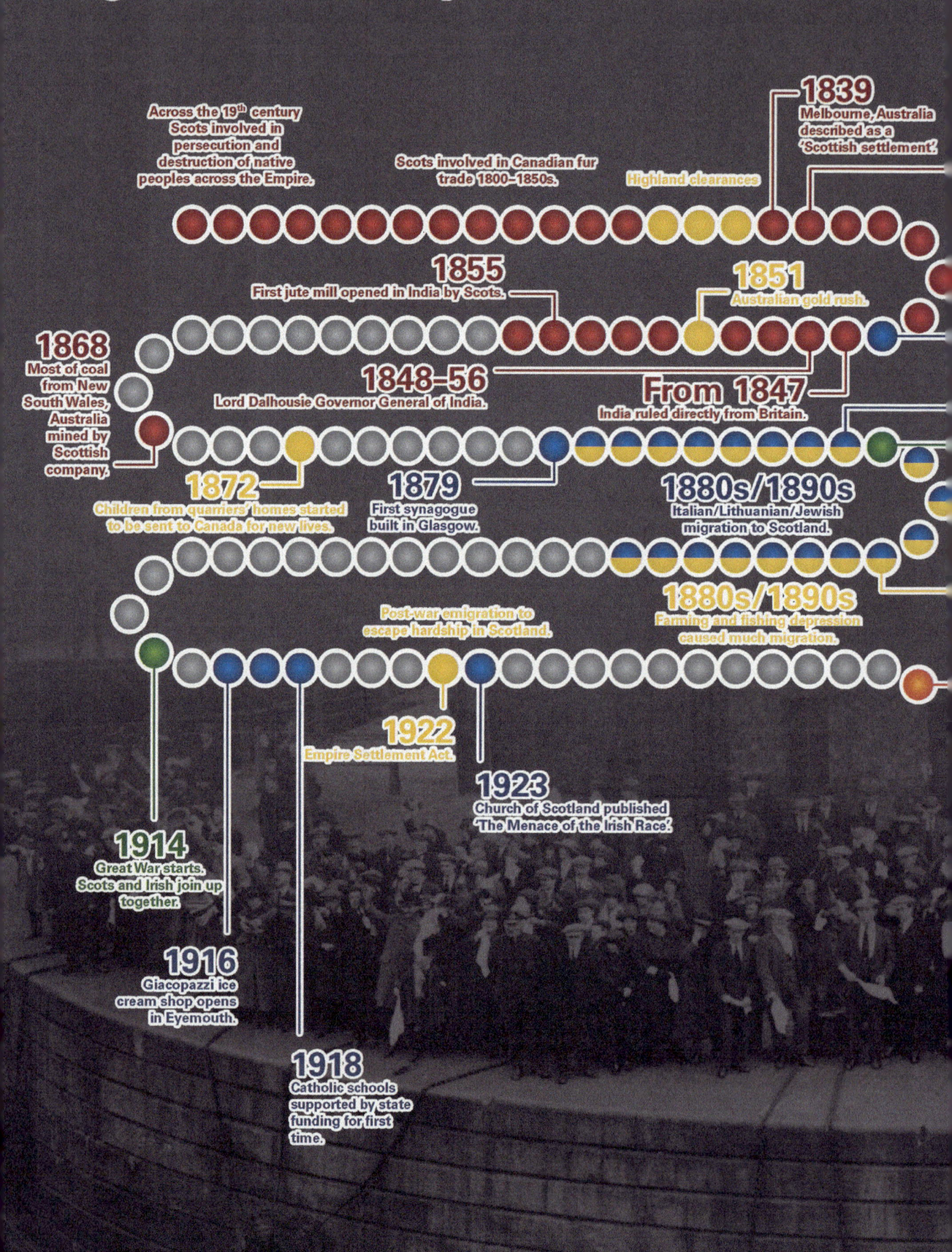

Across the 19th century Scots involved in persecution and destruction of native peoples across the Empire.

Scots involved in Canadian fur trade 1800–1850s.

Highland clearances

1839 Melbourne, Australia described as a 'Scottish settlement'.

1855 First jute mill opened in India by Scots.

1851 Australian gold rush.

1868 Most of coal from New South Wales, Australia mined by Scottish company.

1848–56 Lord Dalhousie Governor General of India.

From 1847 India ruled directly from Britain.

1872 Children from quarriers' homes started to be sent to Canada for new lives.

1879 First synagogue built in Glasgow.

1880s/1890s Italian/Lithuanian/Jewish migration to Scotland.

1880s/1890s Farming and fishing depression caused much migration.

Post-war emigration to escape hardship in Scotland.

1922 Empire Settlement Act.

1923 Church of Scotland published 'The Menace of the Irish Race'.

1914 Great War starts. Scots and Irish join up together.

1916 Giacopazzi ice cream shop opens in Eyemouth.

1918 Catholic schools supported by state funding for first time.

Issue 1
Issue 2
Issue 3
Issue 4
Issues 2 & 4

1840s
Otago, New Zealand developed by Free Church of Scotland.

1846
Irish potato famine leading to large-scale Irish migration.

1887
Celtic football club founded.

1888
Kelvingrove museum built from profits of Empire trade.

1892
Canadian government has two full-time agents in Scotland to promote emigration.

1935
Nardini's Ice Cream Palour opened in Largs.

Question paper 2: Scottish History

Key issue 1: Scots on the Western Front

What is this section all about?

When war broke out, tens of thousands of young Scots volunteered to join the armed forces. When fully trained these young Scottish soldiers served mainly on the Western Front – that means you must know about trench warfare and especially Scottish involvement in the battles of Loos and the Somme. You should also be able to give examples of individual Scots and describe and even assess the part they played in the war. Finally, you should be able to make some informed comments on how important Scots were to the British war effort in the Great War.

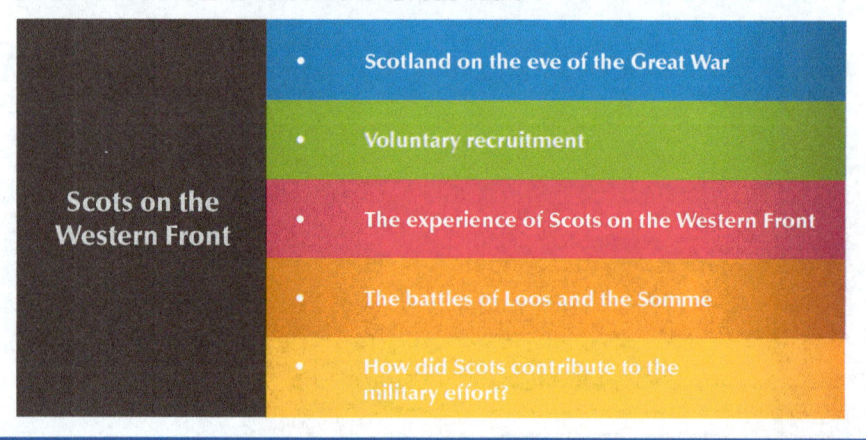

Scots on the Western Front
- Scotland on the eve of the Great War
- Voluntary recruitment
- The experience of Scots on the Western Front
- The battles of Loos and the Somme
- How did Scots contribute to the military effort?

Voluntary recruitment

When war broke out in August 1914 the British government expected a short war 'over by Christmas'. Lord Kitchener began a recruiting campaign and it was a huge success. More Scots volunteered in proportion to the size of the population than any other area of the UK. There are many different reasons why so many young Scottish men joined the army – self-sacrifice, honour and patriotism played a big part. Some young men thought they would look good in a kilt. Others wanted to escape the boredom and drudgery of their work and their lives. The attraction of adventure and excitement was strong. For men who were unemployed, the army offered a steady wage.

A feature of recruitment in Scotland was the territorial nature of each regiment. People who joined up did so together with their mates from the same area. In Glasgow, the 15th (City of Glasgow) Tramway Battalion was so called because most of the volunteers had worked in the city's transport department.

Another locally raised battalion in Glasgow was the 16th Battalion, known as the Boys' Brigade Battalion because most of the volunteers had been in the BBs. In Edinburgh, McCrae's Battalion was the most famous because of its connection with Hearts football club.

The Impact of the Great War, 1914–1928

> **Think point**
> What would happen if those battalions based on local friendships went into action and suffered heavy casualties? The effect on the communities they came from would be devastating.

The experience of Scots on the Western Front

As 1914 dragged into 1915, the Western Front was bogged down in trench warfare. Barbed wire and machine-gun fire made defence relatively easy and attack so much more difficult. For most of the next four years neither side managed a decisive breakthrough. Letters home from soldiers all report living with noise, itching, boredom and mud. Most letters do not describe the possibility of death at any moment from a mortar shell or sniper fire.

1. There is a difference between fighting on the western front and the experiences of trench life.

In fighting you must mention specific battles involving Scots such as Loos and the Somme. Mention of Piper Laidlaw at Loos and the Highland division on the Somme are examples of specific Scottish involvement. You could also mention how Scots had a reputation as fearsome fighters - 'Ladies from Hell' and were often used as first over the top shock troops. There are many other examples so build up a supply of specific, precise Scottish activity.

Likewise do not write generally about trench conditions - trench foot, rats, boredom etc. You MUST relate this to Scottish examples. For example the pleats in the kilts of Scottish soldiers were perfect for lice eggs to be laid and hatch out.

Loos

In September 1915, 35,000 Scots took part in the attack at Loos. Battalions from every Scottish regiment fought in the battle. Out of the 21,000 dead over 7,000 were Scottish soldiers. Almost every town and village in Scotland was affected by the losses at Loos. The battle was the first time Kitchener's armies of volunteers had been used in a major attack. It was also the first time the British army used poison gas as a weapon.

Scottish regiments charging and overwhelming German trenches during the Battle of Loos.

The battle of Loos is forever linked with one man – Piper Daniel Laidlaw of the King's Own Scottish Borders. Almost all Scottish troops were led into battle to the sound of bagpipes. At Loos the British plan to release gas backfired when the wind changed and the gas was blown back towards Scottish troops waiting in their trenches. The Scots were at first reluctant to advance into their own gas and the heavy German fire. When Laidlaw saw the situation he jumped over the top in full view of the enemy and marched up and down the front line parapet playing the pipes. Immediately the Scots in the trenches charged from their position encouraged by Laidlaw who kept playing throughout the attack even when wounded. For his bravery Laidlaw was awarded the Victoria Cross.

Question paper 2: Scottish History

The Somme

The battle of the Somme started on 1st July 1916. Three full Scottish divisions took part and many Scottish battalions also fought in other divisions.

General Douglas Haig (a Scot) planned to batter the enemy lines with a seven-day-long artillery barrage that would destroy the Germans' barbed wire, wreck their trenches and kill the German defenders. Haig argued that making the enemy fight and wearing them down, man by man and bullet by bullet, would make defeat for Germany inevitable. Haig's policy was called attrition. In reality, on the first day of the battle the British suffered their highest ever casualties – almost 60,000 dead, wounded or missing.

Scottish soldiers on the front line during the battle of the Somme.

The battle of the Somme has been described as the graveyard of Kitchener's armies and also of battalions raised from local communities. The 16th Battalion, Highland Light Infantry (the Boys' Brigade Battalion) suffered more than 500 casualties. The deaths of so many young men from the same background devastated the close-knit communities back home. The same could be said for Cranston's and McCrae's Battalions of the Royal Scots, which suffered 75% casualties.

At the end of the war the public were shocked by the huge casualty figures. Many grieving relatives blamed Haig for the slaughter on the Western Front. When reaching a conclusion about Haig's abilities as a military commander it is important to remember that Haig did encourage the use of new technology and tactics where available and appropriate. The technology available to generals in 1918 was not there in 1914 or even 1916. New thinking, new armies and new technology, all under the direction of Haig, led to the victory of 1918.

Why did the battles of Loos and the Somme have such an effect on Scotland?

So many Scottish battalions fought at Loos that it was said that every Scottish town and village was affected by the losses. Many men were recruited for the army with the promise they would fight with their mates and serve in regiments that recruited from the same city or area. The problem was that when those 'bands of brothers' were used in an attack then those men who joined together also died together.

Got it? ☐ ☐ ☐   **The Impact of the Great War, 1914–1928**

> ## Why did Scottish regiments become such a famous feature of the Western Front?
>
> Scots were very conspicuous with their bagpipes, kilts and often being quite small in height! Scots also had a reputation for being fearless, tough fighters. Germans were also reported as being very afraid of the 'Ladies from hell' – wee Scottish soldiers in kilts who fought fearlessly! It was also reported that Scottish soldiers were 'imported' to companies from other parts of the UK so as to raise morale. Scots were seen as 'superior soldiers' who could achieve victories.

Check Your Understanding

ESSENTIAL KNOWLEDGE

1. Suggest at least 5 different reasons why young men chose to volunteer for the army.
2. Why are the battles of Loos and the Somme remembered as 'Scottish battles'?

THEME QUESTION

1. In summary, why did so many young men choose to join up?
2. Does the old idea of lions led by donkeys really stand up to recent research?

TEST YOURSELF

Do you know the meaning of these key words?

Recruitment
Staple industries
Western Front
Attrition

Question paper 2: Scottish History

Key issue 2: Domestic impact of war: society and culture

What is this section all about?

The war affected the daily life of the Scottish people in many ways. DORA gave the government great powers to direct the war effort, perhaps most obviously when conscription was introduced in 1916. Another big social change was in the way women's lives were changed during the war. At the end of the war Scottish society was faced with the reality of the casualties, both in terms of the losses and also with the numbers of men who returned but would never be the same again.

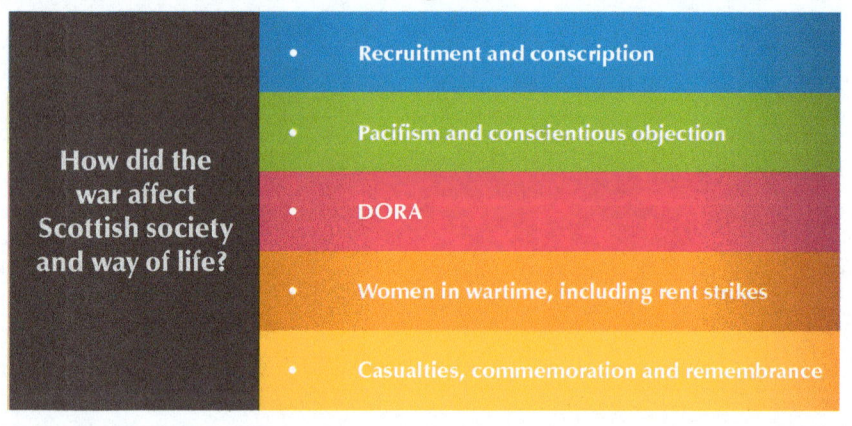

How did the war affect Scottish society and way of life?
- Recruitment and conscription
- Pacifism and conscientious objection
- DORA
- Women in wartime, including rent strikes
- Casualties, commemoration and remembrance

What was DORA?

DORA was the short name for the Defence of the Realm Act. It was a law that allowed the government to take action to protect the country during the war. For example, DORA increased censorship in newspapers.

At first, the public accepted the need for increased security and control over things that were seen to be vital for the war effort. However, as the war went on, the public became tired of restrictions. Critics of DORA felt the government was abusing its powers and silencing people who were against the war. DORA also gave the government the right to imprison people without trial and that was directly against the freedoms that British people had struggled to win over many years.

Overall, the public believed that DORA was necessary to win the war. The war required a huge effort from everyone to win it so DORA was seen as a way the government could direct and control the war effort necessary for victory.

The Impact of the Great War, 1914–1928

Conscription

In 1914, Britain was the only European country that did not use conscription. All Britain's soldiers and sailors were volunteers. Supporters of conscription argued that young men had a duty above all else to defend their country. When the voluntary recruitment rate seemed to fall after the initial rush in the late summer of 1914, the calls to introduce conscription became louder.

Why was conscription started in Britain?

By 1915, casualty figures were rising, the war was not over by Christmas and recruitment rates started to slow down. Conscription was needed to get more men for the army. There was also a feeling that young men who had not volunteered were 'shirking' their duty to their country.

In January 1916, the Military Service Act brought in conscription for single men from nineteen to forty years old. In May 1916, conscription was extended to married men and by 1918 men up to the age of fifty were being conscripted.

A poster threatens conscription if there are not enough volunteers for the forces during WWI.

The Military Service Act of 1916 made allowances for certain men to be exempt from military service. The first category exempted men involved in work of national importance to the war effort, the second category exempted men if their service in the armed forces would cause 'serious hardship to his family' owing to his exceptional financial or business obligations. The third category included young men who refused to fight on grounds of their conscience. These 'conscientious objectors' claimed exemption on the grounds of their political or religious beliefs.

Around 7,000 conscientious objectors agreed to perform non-combat duties, often as stretcher-bearers in the front line. However, more than 1,500 pacifists refused all military service. These 'absolutists' opposed undertaking any work whatsoever that helped Britain's war effort.

Women at war

As casualty rates increased on the battlefield, and as conscription was introduced, women were needed to fill the gaps in the workforce left by men who went off to fight. Industries that had previously excluded women now welcomed them. The biggest increase in female employment was in the engineering industry, especially the sector that made munitions. Before the war, fewer than 4,000 women worked in heavy industry in Scotland. By 1917, over 30,000 women were employed during the war making munitions in Scotland.

Women war workers feed charcoal kilns at a sugary refinery.

Question paper 2: Scottish History

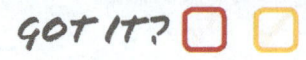

GOT IT? ☐ ☐ ☐

Radicalisation and rent strikes

The Great War is said to have made many Scots more politically aware. The rent strikes that started in and around Glasgow are perfect examples of people taking direct action to change or protect their way of life. Another word for the increasing awareness among ordinary people that taking direct action could have a big effect on their living and working conditions and even lead to political change is 'radicalisation'.

In February 1915, Helen Crawfurd, Mary Barbour, Agnes Dollan and Jessie Stephens helped to form the Glasgow Women's Housing Association to resist rent rises and threatened evictions. The rent strikes grew to the extent that they threatened wartime production of necessary machines and munitions. The answer was the Rent Restriction Act. Rents were frozen at 1914 levels unless improvements had been made to the property. The strikers' demands had been met, protests and profiteering now declined and wartime production was maintained without disruption. However, the strikers had learned an important lesson: that direct action could lead to positive results.

Casualties and commemoration

On the eleventh hour of the eleventh day of the eleventh month of 1918 the fighting stopped. Ever since then, 11th November 1918 has been called 'Armistice Day'.

Every community in Scotland was affected by the war. After four years of war, the Scottish population needed time to grieve, take stock of their losses and find some way to mark the sacrifice of their loved ones. In the years that followed the Great War, towns and villages across Scotland built their own memorials to remember and commemorate their own losses. To commemorate means to use a formal occasion to remember something or someone.

Scotland's sacrifice in the Great War is also remembered in the National War Memorial, which is in Edinburgh Castle. The opening ceremony took place on 14th July 1927.

Check Your Understanding

ESSENTIAL KNOWLEDGE

1. Why could conscientious objectors not exist without conscription?
2. Why were women so important to the war effort?
3. Why was conscription needed?

THEME QUESTION

1. How are Scottish losses commemorated locally, nationally and internationally?
2. How would you summarise the main ways that the war affected Scottish society?

TEST YOURSELF

Do you know the meaning of these key words?

Radicalisation
DORA
Commemoration
Voluntary recruitment
Shirking
Conscription
Conscientious objectors
Exemption
Non-combat
Absolutist
Munitions
Rent strikes

The Impact of the Great War, 1914–1928

Key issue 3: Domestic impact of war: industry and economy

What is this section all about?

This section deals with what happened to Scotland's industries, Scottish workers and the Scottish economy during and after the war. The war gave a huge boost to Scotland's industries such as coal mining and shipbuilding, but when the war ended so did the big wartime demand and many industries faced difficulties. Other industries were not so lucky to benefit from the war, such as fishing, but farming boomed to keep up with wartime demand when food was in short supply and rationing was introduced. In the Highlands the 'land question' was still an issue and from all over Scotland, many Scots saw emigration as an answer to their problems.

How did the war affect Scottish industry and economy?
- Wartime effects of war on industry, agriculture and fishing
- Price rises and rationing
- Post-war economic problems
- The land issue in the Highlands and Islands

Industry

In the short term, the war provided a temporary boost for Scotland's old traditional industries – coal, iron and steel-making and shipbuilding.

These industries had faced difficulties in the years before 1914 but the war years provided a big boost to their production. After the war, the slump in international trade, the fall in orders for new ships and the use of new production methods all combined to force unemployment upwards. Coal is used as the fuel for furnaces to make iron and steel. Iron and steel were used to make ships. When demand for ships fell with the collapse of international trade, so too did demand for the other traditional industries. The fact is these industries were in trouble before the war. The war made people forget about the problems during the artificial boom. The recession that followed the war was inevitable but unwelcome.

163

Question paper 2: Scottish History

In 1918, the fishing industry faced rising fuel costs and the need to repair and equip boats after war service. Although the fishing industry did recover after the war, revolution and post-war changes in Eastern Europe meant that traditional export markets for herring in Germany, Eastern Europe and Russia were lost.

During the war years, many men left farming to 'join up'. They were replaced by women, boys and older men. Even prisoners and conscientious objectors were used as farm workers during the war.

During the war, more machines were introduced to replace the horses taken away for the war effort.

In 1914, Britain bought much of its food from abroad. When Germany began to use submarines to sink ships carrying supplies to Britain, the government did two things:

1. It began a propaganda campaign to reduce waste and produce more food.
2. In January 1918, the government began a system of rationing.

The aim of rationing was to conserve food supplies, ensure fair distribution and control rising prices so everyone got fair shares of essential foodstuffs.

A poster advocating voluntary rationing in support of the war effort.

The jute industry

The jute industry was based in Dundee. It employed tens of thousands of people. There was no such thing as plastics around the time of the Great War, everything was loaded into or carried in sacks made from jute. Jute was course cloth made from the jute plant that grows in Bangladesh; at the time of the Great War, Bangladesh was part of India and so was part of the British Empire.

During the war, demand for jute soared as the need for sacks for sandbags and feed bags for horses increased.

After the war, the jute industry faced falling orders, worn-out machinery from round the clock working during the war and also increased foreign competition, which forced down prices and took away export markets.

Got it? ☐ ☐ ☐   The Impact of the Great War, 1914–1928

The Highland land question

The land question in the Highlands was about land ownership. When the war ended, many soldiers from the Highlands and Islands returned home believing that they would get land to farm as a reward for fighting for their country. When the ex-soldiers were not given the land they expected, many took the law into their own hands and began land raids, involving a number of men taking over land and setting up farms. The Land Settlement (Scotland) Act stated that land would be made available for men who had served in the war but for the Land Settlement Act to be successful, the government had to purchase land from the previous owners. Soon it became clear the government did not have enough money to buy the land. Land raids continued and by the end of the 1920s the problem of land ownership, overcrowding and poverty had still not been resolved in the Highlands.

Emigration

The war artificially boosted the economy and when the war ended there was an economic slump leading to people looking for fresh opportunities abroad. In the inter-war period Scotland had the highest rate of emigration of any European country. Many Scots saw emigration as an escape from unemployment and industrial decline. In the 1920s, three out of ten migrants to New Zealand came from Scotland and the migrants were not only from the Highlands but also from the depressed industrial areas of central Scotland. The Empire Settlement Act of 1922 created the first large-scale government-assisted migration programme. Emigration was also increased by the deliberate actions of Canadian government agents travelling around Scotland advertising the attractions of emigrating to Canada.

Check Your Understanding

ESSENTIAL KNOWLEDGE

1. Why was food rationing started in Britain?
2. What does it mean when Scottish staple industries are described as 'linked'?

THEME QUESTION

1. Did the war benefit Scotland's industries?
2. Why was emigration so high from Scotland after the war?

TEST YOURSELF

Do you know the meaning of these key words?

Emigration
Land raids
Rationing
Traditional export markets

Question paper 2: Scottish History

Key issue 4: Domestic impact of war: politics

What is this section all about?

This section is about how the war made people more politically aware, how people became more active in politics and what happened to the political parties. Before the war, the Liberal Party was the most powerful political party in Scotland. After 1918, the Liberal Party was split and after the mid-1920s they would never again be such a significant force in British politics, until the coalition government of 2010. The Labour Party became one of the big two parties alongside the Conservatives. The Independent Labour Party (ILP) was stronger in 1918 than it had been in 1914. The Conservative and Unionist Party (aka the Tories) began to attract new voters from the middle classes living in the cities.

How did the war affect Scottish politics?
- The growth of radicalism, the ILP and Red Clydeside
- Support for political unionism
- How the war affected Scottish identity

What does radicalisation mean? What effect did it have on post-war politics in Scotland?

The Great War made many Scots more politically aware. A word used to describe that increasing awareness and willingness to become politically involved is radicalisation. To become politically radicalised means to want fundamental changes in the way politics operates. During the war, the radicalisation of politics in Scotland at times meant people taking direct action to cause or prevent changes to their own lives. An example of this more direct action can be seen in the way that some women who became politically active in the rent strikes went on to become local councillors in Glasgow. In a similar way, the shop stewards of the Clyde Workers' Committee (CWC) went on to become MPs representing the ILP in the UK Parliament.

What was Red Clydeside?

Between 1915 and 1919, parts of Glasgow and its surrounding area became known as 'Red Clydeside' and this was a major cause of the radicalisation of Scottish politics. In reality there were two phases to 'Red Clydeside':

1. The first phase was a series of disputes in 1915 between the government and the workers in the factories and engineering works around the River Clyde.

The Impact of the Great War, 1914–1928

2. The second phase took place just after the war ended when strikes and conflict occurred between workers and police in George Square, Glasgow. This caused the government to worry that the strike leaders were preparing to start a revolution in Britain.

Why did the 'Red Clydeside' protests start?

Protests started in the engineering factories over the issue of dilution. Skilled men now saw their jobs under threat or, if they kept their jobs, it was certain their wages would be cut. The government was worried when engineers at shipbuilding and engineering factories went on strike as any action by workers could threaten wartime production. The rent strikes were also part of the tension and discontent that rumbled through Clydeside in 1915. When the Clyde Workers' Committee (CWC) was started, the government saw it as a nest of revolutionaries ready to upset the war effort and even lead revolution in Britain.

Did strikers on 'Red Clydeside' gain much public sympathy?

Most public opinion supported the government. Newspapers described the strikers as being greedy and selfish. Most public opinion saw the strikers as damaging the chances of winning the war and even endangering the lives of soldiers at the front by trying to limit the supply of munitions.

Why did more 'Red Clydeside' protests break out at the end of the war?

When the war ended, industrial workers across Britain began to fear for their jobs. As munitions factories closed, workers also faced competition for jobs from thousands of returning soldiers. Prime Minister Lloyd George had promised returning troops 'a land fit for heroes'. Instead, faced with bad housing and unemployment in Scotland after the war, workers and soldiers alike wanted improvements in their living and working conditions.

What was the George Square Riot?

At the end of January 1919 the CWC and other trade unions called a strike and then a large demonstration in George Square, Glasgow for Friday, 31st January 1919. As the crowds grew to almost 90,000 people, the authorities became concerned. The government had been advised that the crowd could easily become a revolutionary mob and the government's concern increased even more when some reports said a red flag was seen flying over the crowd. Fights broke out between demonstrators and police but within a week of the battle of George Square, the strike was over and a settlement was reached.

Did 'Red Clydeside' have much effect on Scottish politics after the war?

The events of 'Red Clydeside' gave hope to people who wanted change in Scottish society but had also scared the middle and upper classes who saw it as the possible start of revolution.

The war, rent strikes and 'Red Clydeside' seemed to have radicalised the voters in and around Glasgow. Immediately after the events in George Square, membership of the ILP increased. Support for the Labour Party grew while the Liberal support fell. The radicalisation of politics in Scotland greatly affected the main political parties. Many voters began to support the ILP or the Labour Party as a way of challenging the old ways of doing things. In the 1918 election, the Labour Party gained one-third of all votes cast in Scotland. The radicalisation of Scottish politics also had an effect on those who did not want change. The Conservative and Unionist Party became the party of choice for many who saw the party as the only way of stopping Scotland from sliding into 'Red revolution'.

Question paper 2: Scottish History

Why did the Liberal Party split?

The Liberal Party had certain core beliefs at its heart. One of these was that the state – or government – should intervene as little as possible in people's everyday lives. Clearly, as the war dragged on, everything from DORA to conscription and on to rationing ran against the beliefs of old-fashioned Liberals. The Liberal Party was also split by rivalry between Prime Minister Asquith and David Lloyd George, who eventually replaced Asquith as Prime Minister when the coalition government was formed in December 1916. When the war started Asquith's slogan had been 'business as usual' and he hoped for as little government intervention as possible. He was in that sense an old fashioned Liberal. On the other hand Lloyd George was a new breed of Liberal who believed in state, or government, intervention to manage and control the war effort.

The division between the Liberals led to election defeat for Asquith and his supporters. Meanwhile Lloyd George entered into a coalition, or alliance with the Conservatives.

Scottish politics had become polarised between left and right wings.

On the left wing side was the growing Labour Party with its more revolutionary off shoot in Scotland the Independent Labour Party while on the other side , the right wing, were the middle and upper classes who tended to support the Conservative and Unionist Party who represented stability and protection against any threat of communist revolution. By 1918 the Liberals has simply ceased to matter to voters.

Why did the Scottish Conservative and Unionist Party gain support after the Great War?

To the government and a worried middle class, the George Square riot provided proof that communist revolution was just around the corner. To the middle and upper classes, it was clear that only the Scottish Tories could protect their interests. In summary, the revival of the Tories after the war was the result of fear in the middle classes about what a Labour government might do and the collapse of the Liberals as an effective counterweight to the threat of socialism.

Scotland in the 1920s

Scotland was no longer the workshop of the empire. During the inter-war period, large-scale unemployment increased in traditional heavy industries such as shipbuilding, textiles and coal mining. Nevertheless, most Scots did not question the place of Scotland within the UK. In 1918, the Labour Party promised to fight for the 'Self-Determination of the Scottish People' but there was little public support. In May 1928, the National Party of Scotland was founded but it gained very few votes in the 1929 general election.

GOT IT? ☐ ☐ ☐ **The Impact of the Great War, 1914–1928**

> Be aware that any question that asks about UNIONISM is NOT asking about trade unionism. It IS asking about political unionism which means the desire to keep Scotland united within the United Kingdom. That's why the Conservatives were officially called the Conservative and Unionist party. They wanted to keep Scotland within the united kingdom.
>
> At the end of the war Scottish nationalism was not an important force but it grew in the 1920s.

Check Your Understanding

ESSENTIAL KNOWLEDGE

1. What was the connection between rent strikes and 'Red Clydeside'?
2. Was Red Clydeside a revolutionary threat?

THEME QUESTION

1. Why did Scottish politics become polarised?
2. What evidence is there that Scots became more radicalised by the war?

TEST YOURSELF

Do you know the meaning of these key words?

Radicalisation

Red

Polarised

Self-determination

Coalition

Unionism

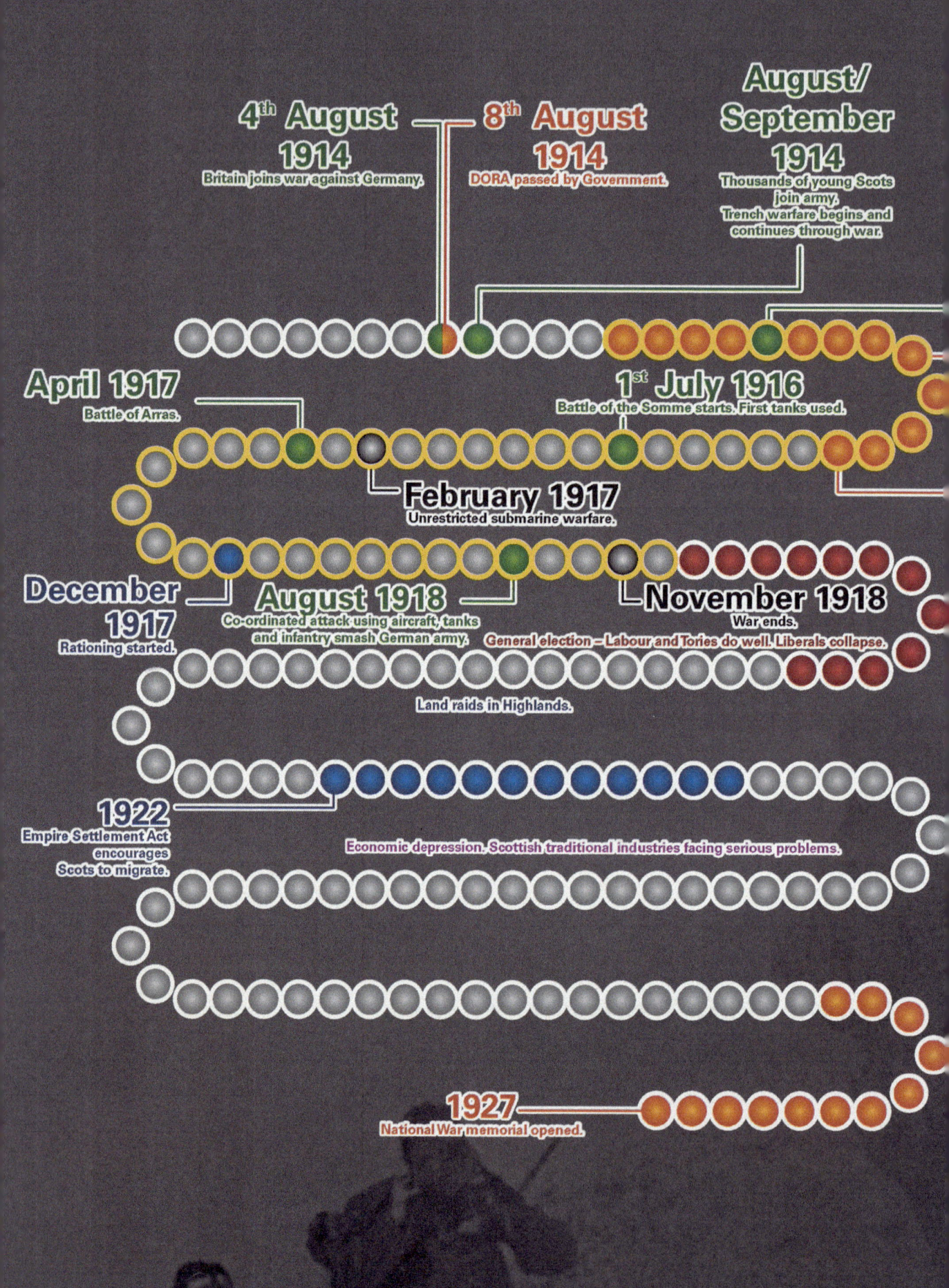

4th August 1914
Britain joins war against Germany.

8th August 1914
DORA passed by Government.

August/September 1914
Thousands of young Scots join army.
Trench warfare begins and continues through war.

April 1917
Battle of Arras.

1st July 1916
Battle of the Somme starts. First tanks used.

February 1917
Unrestricted submarine warfare.

December 1917
Rationing started.

August 1918
Co-ordinated attack using aircraft, tanks and infantry smash German army.

November 1918
War ends. General election – Labour and Tories do well. Liberals collapse.

Land raids in Highlands.

1922
Empire Settlement Act encourages Scots to migrate.

Economic depression. Scottish traditional industries facing serious problems.

1927
National War memorial opened.

Great War 1914–1927

May 1915
Battle of Loos. 20 Scottish regiments fought together. First time gas used by British.

1915
Rent strikes in Glasgow. Red Clydeside strikes.

1915–1918
Women working in men's jobs, especially munitions.

Jan 1916
Conscription started for first time in Britain.

1919
Red Clydeside – George Square riots.

Issue 1
Issue 2
Issue 3
Issue 4
Issues 2–4
Issues 3–4

Answers

Britain, 1851–1951

Key issue 1: An evaluation of the reasons why Britain became more democratic, 1851–1928 (page 23)

Test yourself

Franchise – the right to vote.

Electorate – people who could vote.

Constituency – an area of the country entitled to send one MP to parliament.

Pragmatic – doing something that will benefit you whether you agree with it or not.

Essential Knowledge

1. Urbanisation – this means the growth of towns, caused by changes in industry and population moving to find work. As towns and cities grew in size, rural areas became depopulated. Those changes were not reflected in political representation, so in some areas the people in busy towns had almost no political voice, whereas many MPs still represented areas of land on which very few people lived. That imbalance gave rise to demands for changes in political representation.

   Class consciousness – this means groups of people realising that by sharing the same sort of work and housing they shared a common identity. Individually they could change little but as they became aware of a collective identity called 'working class' then they would have more leverage as a united group. Earlier in history, the middle class who shared an interest in political stability and making money through business had already emerged. Some historians called Marxists argue that class conflict between working-class interests and middle-class interests led to change as one side struggled to resist change while the other wanted more change.

   Industrialisation – this means the spread of machine-based industries based in factories. These factories attracted workers and led to urbanisation. Factory-based workers also developed a class awareness or class consciousness, as described above.

   War – in the context of this area of study, the war that led to change was the Great War 1914–1918.

   The usual argument about this war is that it led to votes for women. That is partly true. The main argument is that women gained the vote as a 'thank you' for their war work. That is not really true. Women over 30 got the vote in 1918. Most of the war workers were below 30, so they got no vote.

   The war also gave many more men the right to vote. Previously, men had to have lived in the same house for a year. That was the residency qualification. Clearly that was upset by the war. How could a government tell men they had lost the right to vote? A decision was taken to give all men the right to vote based on age – 21. Another reason for this change was that men had been conscripted. Was it right for a government to order young men to fight and kill 'for their country' but not have the right to choose the government?

   Political pragmatism – this means doing something that is judged to be necessary or useful even if it is not genuinely believed in. By giving the vote to many working-class men in 1867, the Conservatives believed these new voters would be grateful to them in future elections. That did not mean the Conservatives genuinely believed in spreading democracy to the working class!

   Political pressure groups – these are groups of people such as women's campaign groups or trade unions who did things that put pressure on the government to grant more political changes.

Answers

Theme

1. Urbanisation means the growth of towns and industrialisation means the growth of machine-based factory work. Both of those developments brought working-class people together who lived and worked in similar circumstances. At the same time, the industrial revolution undermined the power of the old rulers – the landowners. The rise of industry and wealth in the middle classes and the attempt to keep the power of the older land-owning classes was shown in the Parliament Act when the House of Lords tried to hold back the forces for change.

2. They are groups of people who join together to campaign for one thing – in the case of this issue, then any group that campaigned for the right to vote qualifies as a pressure group. The National Reform Union and the reform League are two examples of pressure groups who were active in the 1860s. Two other pressure groups are the NUWSS (Suffragists) and the WSPU (Suffragettes), who both campaigned in the early 1900s for votes for women.

Key issue 2: An assessment of how democratic Britain became, 1867–1928 (page 26)

Test Your New Vocabulary

Veto – the right to cancel something or stop something happening.

Participation – taking part in something.

'The Commons' – the House of Commons, part of the Houses of Parliament where all elected MPs gather. In contrast to the Lords, MPs are commoners – people who have no title such as Duke or Earl or Lord.

Redistribution of seats – reorganising the areas of Britain, called constituencies, that have a right to elect an MP who then takes his seat in parliament. (Before 1918 it was always 'his' seat.)

Essential Knowledge

1. In terms of law making, the House of Lords was more powerful because it had the power to stop any new bills passed by the House of Commons.

2. In terms of greater democracy, the answer is the House of Commons because it represents the wishes of the voters of the country.

3. Because no one under 21 had the right to vote. Now, in Scotland the principle of voting at 16 has been made. There was still plural voting, the right of some people to have two votes. The House of Lords was still unelected and could delay bills for two years.

4. **The right to vote** – in a democracy, the voice of the people should be heard: democracy means people power.

    A fair system of voting – a vote is useless unless it really does represent the free choice of the voter.

    Choice – a fair system of voting is still not democratic if there is no choice about who to vote for.

    Information – to vote fairly, people must have information about the candidates and their policies.

Theme

1. The House of Lords is not elected and only represented the interests of a minority of the population. The House of Commons contains all MPs who are elected by the voters. As more people gained the vote between 1832 and 1928, the House of Commons became the more democratic House because it represented the choice of the majority of British voters.

Answers

Key issue 3: An evaluation of the reasons why women won greater political equality by 1928 (page 30)

Test Your New Vocabulary

Militant – prepared to use force to achieve a target.

Suffrage – the right to vote. Note the spelling - this word has nothing to do with suffering.

Representation of People Act – a law that allowed people to vote for a candidate to represent them in parliament.

Equal franchise – equal rules about who could vote.

Essential Knowledge

1. The SuffraGISTS used non-violent tactics to persuade people that women deserved the right to vote. The SuffraGETTES were prepared to use force and violence to gain publicity and force the government to give women the vote. Make the point that force was defined as attacking property and the Suffragettes did not intend to kill people.

2. In the later 19th century, women had greater access to education and the professions. Laws had also given women greater rights over their children and their property.

3. The Suffragettes had hoped to use hunger strikes as a way of keeping pressure on the government but when they were released under the new Act, there was no point in staying on hunger strike. The government had hoped that putting Suffragettes in prison and then force-feeding hunger strikers would stop their campaigns and avoid women dying in prison. The new law showed that neither aim was achieved and the government was getting a lot of negative publicity by force-feeding.

Theme

1. This topic focuses on the struggle by women to gain the right to vote and become MPs themselves. Ironically, the first woman elected to parliament was Countess Markievicz, an Irish member of Sinn Fein. She made a political point by not going to the Houses of Parliament because they were in London and as an Irish Sinn Feiner she wanted Ireland to be a free independent country, not ruled from London. If this issue had asked about women's rights, then the issue of social change, wage rates, sex discrimination and equal pay for equal work would have had to be covered.

Key issue 4: An evaluation of the reasons why the Liberals introduced social welfare reforms, 1906–1914 (page 33)

Test Your New Vocabulary

Laissez-faire – a French phrase literally meaning to leave alone. Until the early 20th century, government did not see it as their responsibility to become involved in social policy, which means people had a responsibility to look after themselves.

Intervention – becoming involved, changing things.

Municipal – to do with local town government.

Socialism – a political belief that wealth should be shared fairly across society and those who are better off should help those who are not.

Answers

Essential Knowledge

1. Most earlier reports on poverty were 'anecdotal', that is they relied on giving shocking tales of examples of poverty but could be dismissed as extreme examples probably caused by alcohol abuse, gambling or individual laziness. Booth's report gave hard statistical evidence about poverty and the conditions people lived in. His report on London life and poverty was in almost 20 volumes and had been researched over several years.

2. Booth's report on London poverty was shocking but London had always been extreme and people thought it was a London problem. Rowntree's report was based in York, a quiet, 'respectable' English town. When the Rowntree report showed that York had the same levels of poverty as London, it was realised that poverty was all over Britain and could not be ignored.

Theme

1. Laissez-faire ideas were based on the idea that individual people had a duty to look after themselves and their families. Victorian values supported the idea that hard work and saving for a rainy day were the main ways to prevent poverty. The reports of Booth and Rowntree provided hard factual evidence that poverty had real causes beyond the ability of any one person to do much about them, such as unemployment, sickness or old age.

Key issue 5: An assessment of the effectiveness of the Liberal social welfare reforms (page 36)

Test Your New Vocabulary

Contributory – involving the need to pay something towards (or contribute to) a benefit plan before any help is given.

Interventionist – the government believed it was their duty to intervene or get involved in social policy.

Transition – a point of change between an older system and a new system.

Borstals – a combination of prison and school for young offenders where they would be kept apart from adult prisoners.

Labour exchange – like Jobcentres today, where unemployed people can go to get help to find another job.

Essential Knowledge

1. He meant that he would help a swimmer in trouble to help themselves by encouraging them to try to swim ashore. What Churchill said he would not do is to pull the swimmer in trouble to the shore all by himself with no help from the swimmer.

2. The Liberal reforms did not provide something for nothing. Apart from children, who were not responsible for being born into poverty, every Liberal reform required the people who benefitted to do something to help themselves. Sometimes that was money paid into an insurance scheme – 9 pence for 4 pence – or, in the case of the elderly, to have led responsible lives and not have been in prison for drunkenness. That is why the Liberal reforms were a transition point – somewhere between government help and self help.

Theme

1. Probably yes. There was no Liberal promise for any social reform in the election of 1905. The Booth and Rowntree reforms were published five years before the Liberals came to power yet they did not rush to pass reforms. On the other hand, worries about national efficiency and security prompted reforms and if the Liberals had ignored social reforms would the Labour Party not have gained more votes from the working classes? Certainly the arrival of new Liberals into the government after 1908 combined both social conscience and more self-interested political reasons.

Answers

2. A Welfare State is a system where the government looks after the welfare of all people. The Liberal reforms certainly meant the government took steps to help some people if they also tried to help themselves. The Liberal reforms were never meant to provide benefits to everyone but they did help move government ideas towards giving a helping hand and the Labour government further developed their ideas after the Second World War.

Key issue 6: An assessment of the effectiveness of the Labour social welfare reforms, 1945–1951 (page 39)

Test Your New Vocabulary

Post war – after the war.

Cradle to grave – from birth to death.

The 5 giants – The Beveridge Report identified five giant problems facing Britain.

Welfare State – The government (state) looks after the welfare (wellbeing) of its people.

Essential Knowledge

1. The Beveridge Report provided a model of a better Britain and for many people that dream of something better coming out of six years of war was attractive. People had also become used to change so there would be less resistance to Labour's reforms.

2. Beveridge identified five giant social problems facing Britain. It was those five areas that Labour targeted in its social reforms between 1945 and 1951.

3. Want or poverty was tackled directly but the causes of poverty, as well as the consequences of poverty, were bad education, bad health, bad housing and unemployment. By trying to deal with all of those problems, Labour was trying to deal with all of the issues that kept people in poverty.

Theme

1. People had become used to government involvement in their lives as part of the war effort. Emergency hospital treatment for bomb casualties and evacuation are two examples of such involvement and control. The public also became used to paying high rates of income tax to pay for the services.

2. It was the first time a government had taken responsibility for all of its citizens and tried to create a safety net so that no one fell into poverty.

Answers

Germany, 1815–1939

Key issue 1: An evaluation of the reasons for the growth of nationalism in Germany, 1815–1850 (page 44)

Test Your New Vocabulary

Liberalism – a political idea that wants a government based on elections and a parliament similar to that in Britain.

Nationalism – wanting all people who share a common language and culture to be united as one independent country.

Identity – a sense of belonging to a group or nation that is different from others.

Zollverein – a group of German states, organised and led by Prussia, that got rid of customs barriers and rules that slowed down trade between states.

Napoleonic Wars – wars fought by Britain to defeat France. Between 1800 and 1815, most of mainland Europe was under the control of France, led by Emperor Napoleon.

Confederation – a union of states meeting together to decide on things that affect all of them but with each state remaining politically separate.

Essential Knowledge

1. Prussia was a big German state in the eastern part of the country. It was a main ally of Britain against Napoleon. In the treaty signed at the end of the Napoleonic Wars, Prussia was rewarded with land in western Germany known as the Rhineland. That area was rich in coal and iron; the river Rhine was like a 19th century trade motorway and so was born the industrial revolution in Prussia. Prussia went on to become the most powerful state in Germany and the centre of moves to unification.

2. In that year there were revolutions across Europe. It seemed that the old rulers would be overthrown, and liberals and nationalists thought there would be a united country with a German parliament. They were wrong. The revolutions fizzled out but laid the foundations for changes that would happen later.

Theme

1. The French Revolution and the American War of Independence sparked off a revolution in ideas and awoke the possibility of political change across Europe. Supporters of nationalism wanted the German states to be united into one country. When Napoleon invaded European states, he overthrew the old political systems. The French invasion also created a common enemy for different German states to realise what they had in common against a foreign invader. Although the old systems were put back in place when Napoleon was defeated in 1815, the idea of a united German nation had been kick-started.

2. A simple answer is that the German states made no real progress towards unity before 1848. By that date all the states were still separate and ruled by people who wanted no change. On the other hand, artists who developed the idea of German-ness through paintings, literature and, above all, music had encouraged the idea of nationalism. Beethoven in particular gave Germans a sense of national pride as he became popular across Europe. However, the most obvious move towards some form of unity between states was the Zollverein. States accepted the economic leadership of Prussia and started to drop the separate barriers to trade because with easier trade between the states, all the states would make more money.

Key issue 2: An assessment of the degree of growth of nationalism in Germany up to 1850 (page 47)

Test Your New Vocabulary

Metternich – the Chancellor (political leader of Austria) who represented complete opposition to any liberal or nationalist idea in Germany.

Answers

Grossdeutschland – the idea that a future united German state would **include** Austria within its borders, as Austria shared the German language and much of its culture.

Kleindeutschland – the idea that a future German state would **exclude** Austria.

Essential Knowledge

1. It was the fear of some states that, in a united Germany, Prussia would dominate and that, far from being a unification of equal states, Prussia would simply absorb the states under its control.

2. He was King of Prussia and a survivor. At first he encouraged the revolutionaries by accepting leadership of the new Germany that was to be created in 1848. If he had rejected that offer, he would have been overthrown. However, he changed his mind when Austria recovered. If he had resisted Austria, he would have been overthrown. His change of mind seriously weakened the supporters of the Frankfurt parliament.

Theme

1. Metternich was the Chancellor of Austria who was totally against the rise of nationalism and liberalism. When those political ideas grew in the years after 1815 he made new laws called the Karlsbad Decrees that led to strict censorship and the banning of political meetings to discuss new ideas.

2. In the short term, yes.

   - Too many different groups wanted different things to suit themselves.
   - The German princes only promised change as a short-term measure to guarantee their own survival.
   - The revolutions only gained momentum while Austria was distracted with problems in other parts of its Empire.
   - The revolutionaries had no military muscle or support to resist the power of Austria.
   - When Austria then threatened to move against the Frankfurt parliament, the revolutionaries faded away and the German princes changed back to supporting Austria.

   In the longer term, no.

   - The idea of a united Germany under the leadership of Prussia had been set alight by the Frankfurt parliament.
   - The failure of the revolution because of its military weakness when faced with Prussia was a lesson learnt by Bismarck. He would not repeat those mistakes.

Key issue 3: An evaluation of the obstacles to German unification up to 1850 (page 51)

Test Your New Vocabulary

German princes – before 1810 there had been over 400 separate German states, each ruled by its own prince. Those princes guarded their power jealously and were suspicious of any change that might threaten their position of being 'a big fish in a small pond'.

Constitutional government – one of the main threats to 'prince power' was constitutional government. A constitution is a set of rights and rules by which a country is governed and makes clear the rights and duties of people and leaders; the princes would no longer be able to do exactly what they liked.

Essential Knowledge

1. In the 16th century, Europe was split by the Reformation. The Catholic Church was challenged by people who wanted to change it. These protestors were called Protestants. The Reformation started in Germany, and afterwards the states in the northern part of Germany were Protestant and were very suspicious of the Catholic southern states. Prussia was a strongly Protestant state and that added to fears in some states about Prussianisation.

Answers

2. At a meeting at Erfurt, Frederick William IV of Prussia tried to increase his own power by suggesting a union of German states under his leadership. His plans of uniting German states under Prussian power were slapped down by Austria at a meeting at Olmutz where Frederick William was forced to abandon his ambitions.

Theme

1. The ideas of liberalism and nationalism released by the French Revolution could not be stopped by force or laws. The foundations of Prussian power were laid when Prussia gained territory on the Rhine. The Rhine was and still is a vital economic artery for Europe. In an age before railways and motorways all big trade went by river. In contrast, Austria controlled the Danube. This is a huge river but it flowed the wrong way – to the Black Sea, the Balkans and an economic dead end. Austria had no economically bright future to compete with the Zollverein.

2. The core of that argument involved the position of Austria, which did not want to be excluded from its power over the German states. The supporters of Austria feared that if Austria was excluded from the German states then there would be nothing to stop the increasing power of Prussia. In contrast, the supporters of Kleindeutschland argued that Germany would never be free if dominated by Austria.

Key issue 4: An evaluation of the reasons why unification was achieved in Germany by 1871 (page 54)

Test Your New Vocabulary

Landtag – the Prussian parliament.

Nationalverein – a nationalist group in the 1850s who promoted the idea of a united Germany under Prussian leadership.

Schleswig Holstein – German states on the border of Denmark that were the cause of the war in 1863.

Opportunist – someone who takes advantage of a situation and turns it to his or her advantage.

Essential Knowledge

1. To test his army and pose as a protector of the rights of the German Confederation. He then realised it could be used to 'corner' Austria.

2. Austria had been the block to unification and the resistance to Prussian power for a long time. Austria was also the 'big brother protector' of the south German Catholic states that feared the growing power of Prussia. Austria was the powerful threat to Prussian ambitions. It had to go!

3. The south German states were still wary of Prussia. By creating France under Napoleon III as a bogeyman threat to the southern states, Bismarck could pose as a protector of all German states. In removing France as a powerful neighbour, Bismarck also removed a potential supporter of Catholic states against Prussia.

Theme

1. You may answer either way. In support of 'the man':
   - He did not plan the army reforms but he created a situation that allowed them to happen.
   - The army was untested. He created a short, small war with Denmark to test his troops and also manoeuvre Austria into a difficult position at the end of the conflict.
   - He set up a war with Austria, made sure Italy was on side and France neutral and then ended the war when he had gained what he wanted. Austria was left as a friend but not a challenger.
   - He provoked the war with France by manipulating a slight difficulty over an issue in Spain into a cause of war that enraged France.

Answers

In support of 'catalyst':

- The issue of nationalism was important in the German states before Bismarck.
- A showdown between Prussia and Austria was inevitable before Bismarck.
- Prussia was already the dominant German state before Bismarck.
- The Prussian economy, spurred on by the Zollverein and railway development, was growing before Bismarck.
- The army reforms had been organised and were ready to go before Bismarck.

Key issue 5: An evaluation of the reasons why the Nazis achieved power in 1933 (page 57)

Test Your New Vocabulary

Weimar – a town in Germany where the constitution of the new republic was signed, far from the violence and street fighting in Berlin.

Spartacists – the name of the revolutionary group that tried to start a communist revolution in Germany in 1919. Later their name was changed to KPD, the German communist party.

Hindenburg – an old war hero who became president of the new republic from 1925 until his death in 1934.

Hugenberg – Alfred Hugenberg owned a national chain of cinemas and a network of local newspapers across Germany. His media empire was important in giving Hitler national publicity.

Hyperinflation – in 1923 an economic crisis hit Germany when France invaded the Ruhr area of Germany. As a result, the value of money collapsed dramatically, leaving many Germans desperate. That was hyperinflation.

Essential Knowledge

1. The new constitution of the Weimar Republic – its rules – tried to make the political and parliamentary system as fair as possible to everyone. The problem is the system was fair but confusing and by being fair to everyone, the Weimar Republic allowed its enemies to become more powerful. If something is good on paper, it means it is good in theory but not so good when it has to work for real.

2. Because he came to power legally, using the Weimar political system. The Nazis were elected and became the largest party in the Reichstag. Hitler was invited to become Chancellor. A few weeks later, Hitler engineered a crisis when the Reichstag caught fire. He claimed it was a communist plot and that he needed more powers to protect Germany in a time of crisis. Those powers grew into the Enabling Act, which enabled Hitler to destroy Weimar democracy.

Theme

1. The answer is a bit of both. Inside weaknesses:

    - The German public were confused by the new democratic political system. The people were unsure how to vote and were puzzled when so many parties joined together and prepared to rule.
    - Governments were made up of coalitions that only lasted a few weeks or months.
    - The Weimar Republic was blamed for starting the war and therefore responsible for the humiliating Versailles treaty.
    - Article 48 of the constitution allowed for the President to rule without approval from the Reichstag. That meant the President, or the person who controlled him, had the power to make new laws for Germany.

Answers

Events outside Germany:

- The victorious allies were always suspicious of Germany.
- The Communists hated the new Republic because Ebert, the President in 1919, used the regular army and some brutal ex-army soldiers called Freikorps to destroy the Communist Revolution.
- The inflation of 1923 was linked partly to events in Germany as well as the French and Belgian invasion.
- The Wall Street Crash in the USA caused banks to call in their loans. Germany had to pay back all its loans to the USA.

Key issue 6: An evaluation of the reasons why the Nazis were able to stay in power, 1933–1939 (page 61)

Test Your New Vocabulary

Totalitarian – having total control over everything.

Dictatorship – a political system where one person or one party is in charge. No opposition is allowed.

Anti-Semitism – prejudice against Jews.

Oath – a promise.

Appease – to give in to someone in the hope that they will cause no more trouble.

Acquiesce – to go with the flow. To accept something because it is the easiest thing to do.

Essential Knowledge

1. He could blame his main competitors – the Communists – for setting the fire. He could then claim that Weimar democracy was under threat and that he needed emergency powers to protect Germany.
2. By the summer of 1934, the regular German army was very suspicious of Hitler. It would not have taken much for the army generals to plot against him. By killing off the SA leadership, Hitler removed a challenge to himself from within his own party and also pleased the army who then swore an oath of personal loyalty to hium.
3. Because he gave them what they wanted. He removed the threat of Communism, gave people jobs and restored pride in Germany. For most Germans, what was there not to like?

Theme

1. Yes it is. The phrase 'carrot and stick' refers to an old way of making a donkey move. Tempt it with a carrot or hit it with a stick. Politically, the carrot methods are all the things that made life good for people who accepted Nazi control. The stick methods were the force, threats and violence the Nazis used against those who did not accept Nazi control.
2. The answer is August 1934. Until then President Hindenburg was still alive and technically the Weimar constitution still applied. When Hindenburg died, Hitler became Chancellor and President – and took complete power. He also had the support and the Oath of Loyalty from the Army. Until then, the army was suspicious of Hitler. Now he had them under his control.
3. That depends. You might like to think you would oppose the Nazis but what if your job, your comfortable home, your holidays, your car and your family's safety all depended on causing no trouble? Would you choose to see your family taken to a concentration camp? Would you choose to give up your comfortable life and be beaten, tortured and imprisoned or live in fear, hiding from the Nazis?

Answers

USA, 1918–1968

Key issue 1: An evaluation of the reasons for changing attitudes towards immigration in the 1920s (page 67)

Test Your New Vocabulary

Multi-ethnic – containing people from many different cultures and races.

Prohibition – a time in America when it was illegal to sell alcohol.

Nativism – small-town values, a suspicion of foreigners, a dislike of new ideas and the belief that people of WASP background were racially better than others.

Immigration – people from other countries coming to America to live.

Red – communist.

Isolationism – wanting nothing to do with other countries.

Mafia – an organised criminal gang that started in Sicily, Italy.

Essential Knowledge

1. Anyone could enter the USA, almost without restriction.

2. Yes, because the new laws made it easier for 'WASP' type people to get into America but much harder for non-WASPs.

3. The two men were accused of a crime. Whether they did the robbery and murder was almost irrelevant. What is important is that they 'fitted the frame'. Although Sacco and Vanzetti were not new immigrants, they had foreign names and looked 'olive skinned'. Vanzetti was also proud to say he was an anarchist, someone who wanted to overthrow the American government. The Sacco Vanzetti case therefore combined hatred of new immigrants, the idea that immigrants helped the spread of crime and their political beliefs that linked them to a fear of communism.

Theme

1. They would most probably claim that they came from a WASP background and it was people from such European backgrounds who had worked hard to make America a modern country. The 'new' immigrants were suspected of being lazy and criminal.

Key issue 2: An evaluation of the obstacles to the achievement of civil rights for black people up to 1941 (page 70)

Test Your New Vocabulary

Jim Crow laws – the name given to laws that segregated black people from white people.

Segregation – keeping black and white people apart.

Civil rights – all people in a society or country have equal rights regardless of gender or colour of skin.

Essential Knowledge

1. It was a legal decision made by the Supreme Court stating that Jim Crow laws and segregation across the USA were perfectly constitutional and legal.

2. As long as segregation was legal and accepted across the USA, why should any politician, either state or federal, try to change anything?

Answers

Theme

1. When black Americans were slaves they were property. When slavery was abolished, black Americans were free to do as they wished. Often, the local white population did not like the freedom given to black Americans so they invented new ways of control. Jim Crow laws are examples of control through law-making while the rise of the Ku Klux Klan is an example of control through fear.

2. Booker T. Washington believed that black Americans should work very hard until **some** of them were good enough to be accepted by white society. The NAACP believed that **all** black Americans had the right to fair and equal treatment by the law. Marcus Garvey and the UNIA wanted no help at all from white society and believed there should be **no** integration.

3. Because they struggled in their own ways to get better conditions for black Americans. Many in white society feared black communities that were prepared to fight for their rights and demand equality.

Key issue 3: An evaluation of the reasons for the economic crisis of 1929–1933 (page 73)

Test Your New Vocabulary

Hire purchase – paying for goods in instalments until the price plus interest is paid up. Only then is the item the property of the person who has paid the instalments.

Underconsumption – a situation that exists when there are not enough customers to buy the goods being made.

Overproduction – too much of anything being produced, resulting in prices falling.

Protection – in economic terms, a way of stopping foreign competition by using tariffs.

Tariffs – a type of tax put on foreign goods entering the country which therefore makes them more expensive.

Essential Knowledge

1. A boom means good times when people have jobs and confidence is high, whereas a crash is when confidence collapses, wages fall and unemployment rises.
2. When people have all they need of a certain item and no more of that item can be sold.
3. The Republican government believed in laissez-faire – no involvement in the economy. When the economy crashed in 1929, the government hoped or thought that things would get better by themselves. After two years, the economy had not recovered and America was deep in Depression. The government tried to help but they did not do enough and they had waited too long before helping – too little, too late.

Theme

1. The Wall Street Crash was for a long time seen as the start of the Depression and in a sense it was. However, the Wall Street Crash was like a starter's gun. It was the visible start of the Depression (the symptom) but its real causes (the disease) lay in other factors that had started earlier in the 1920s.
2. By doing nothing, the Republicans allowed banks to do what they wanted. Overproduction forced prices down. By ignoring poverty, the government limited the purchasing power of millions of Americans. By restricting foreign imports, the federal government artificially boosted home industries, which encouraged foreign countries to retaliate by not buying from America, thereby making the US economy even more of a disaster.

Key issue 4: An assessment of the effectiveness of the New Deal (page 77)

Test Your New Vocabulary

FDR – the nickname and initials of Franklin Delano Roosevelt, the new President.

Federal – central government, the government of the entire USA as opposed to the individual state governments that remained very suspicious of the power of federal government.

Answers

Rugged individualism – the belief that America was made great by ordinary people who headed west in the 19th century and, by their own hard work and without any help from government managed to turn a huge, underdeveloped land into a major world power.

Essential Knowledge

1. Relief to help things right away, Recovery to help businesses and people to get back on their feet and Reform to change things so that another crash did not happen.
2. The federal government passed a series of new laws to help the economy recover. The new laws needed government departments, or agencies, to run them. These agencies were known by their initial letters, hence, Alphabet Agencies.
3. The old laissez-faire idea meant no government intervention in the economy. The New Deal was the exact opposite, with federal government becoming directly involved in helping America recover from the Depression.
4. Individual states had their own governments and did not like outsiders such as federal authority telling them what to do.

Theme

1. The New Deal was an example of government intervention to help in a crisis. It was a deliberate federal government plan to build confidence in the USA. On the other hand, President Coolidge best summed up the Republican Party's policy – 'the business of America is business'. Republican policies followed laissez-faire – the least possible government involvement in the economy.

Key issue 5: An evaluation of the reasons for the development of the Civil Rights campaign, after 1945 (page 81)

Test Your New Vocabulary

Double V – stood for victory in the Second World War and victory against racism back home in America. It was the aim of black soldiers in the Second World War.

Boycott – to avoid using something or paying for a service in order to create pressure for change.

Desegregate – to stop segregation and integrate black and white people.

Integration – the mixing of races and the opposite of segregation. Integration would mean the end of separate facilities for black and white Americans.

Civil disobedience – deliberately disobeying the law.

The South – the southern states of the USA, which 100 years before had fought 'the North' in the American Civil War.

Essential Knowledge

1. TV spread into American homes in the 1940s and by the 1950s most homes had a television. For the first time Americans could see for themselves events that were happening across America. With the development of TV came TV news and news reporting, so Civil Rights campaigns and trials were shown in America's living rooms and people were shocked.
2. By remaining dignified and non-violent, the Civil Rights campaigners gained huge sympathy from the watching TV audience. In contrast, the violent racists who attacked the demonstrators looked like monsters. It was said at the time that the use of TV cameras was a masterpiece of showing complex problems in a simple way to the watching millions across America.
3. Sit-ins – freedom rides – bus boycott – Birmingham 1962.

Theme

1. It showed that change was possible. The door that had been locked since 1896 had now been opened and could be pushed further open. If segregation was wrong in schools, then surely it was wrong everywhere?

Answers

2. The answer lies in a build-up of frustration and also motivation. Thousands of American soldiers who had never been out of the South saw during the Second World War that life could be better. They also wondered why they were fighting against racism in Europe yet had to return to the same thing in America? The motivation of the 1954 Supreme Court decision that change was possible was also inspirational. When the Montgomery Bus Boycott happened, people then learned they could take direct action successfully. The rest followed on.

Key issue 6: An assessment of the effectiveness of the Civil Rights movement in meeting the needs of black Americans, up to 1968 (page 85)

Test Your New Vocabulary

Black Radical – Black Power, Nation of Islam (black Muslims) and Black Panthers are examples of Black Radical groups – groups that wanted extreme change in American society rather than integration within it.

Civil Rights Act – the 1964 law that made segregation and discrimination illegal.

Voting Rights Act – this 1965 law made it easier for black Americans to register for the vote without any threats, intimidation or obstruction.

Ghetto – an area of a city, usually run down, in which people of similar race live.

Kerner – Otto Kerner was asked by President Johnston to investigate the causes of the city riots across America in the mid-1960s. His report on the riots shocked white America.

Essential Knowledge

1. They are all examples of Black Radical groups who rejected the integration ideas of Martin Luther King.
2. The majority of white people thought that they were trouble-makers who should have been grateful for all that had been done for them by the Civil Rights Act of 1964 and the Voting Rights Act of 1965, and they were now more concerned with the Vietnam War.
3. Many black urban youths felt that the Civil Rights Act and Voting Rights Act were irrelevant to them and that Martin Luther King had done nothing to change their lives. Their concerns were unemployment, bad housing and the white police that harassed them. Many thought that they should fight back.
4. It reported that American society in 1968 was still racially divided, the black and white sides still separate and unequal. The report also blamed white society for creating the ghettos and doing nothing to get rid of them.

Theme Answers

1. For most white Americans, the Civil Rights campaigns of the 1950s and early 1960s ended with the Civil Rights Act of 1964 and the Voting Rights Act of 1965. As a result, white America felt the Black Radical groups were just ungrateful trouble-makers.
2. The earlier campaigns were located in the southern states and aimed at a very specific target – segregation. The later campaigns were located in the northern and western city ghettos and targeted wider social issues of bad housing, unemployment and poverty.
3. It was an official report from white authority that recognised that US society still had a very serious race problem.

Answers

Appeasement and the Road to War, to 1939

Key issue 1: An evaluation of the reasons for the aggressive nature of the foreign policies of Germany and Italy in the 1930s (page 88)

Test Your New Vocabulary

Fascism – an ideology that grew after the Great War. It was very nationalistic and aggressive. Fascist countries were totalitarian dictatorships led by dictators – Mussolini in Italy and Hitler in Germany.

League of Nations – an organisation set up after the First World War to keep peace.

Disarmament – reducing the amount of weapons a country has.

Lebensraum – a German word that literally means living space. For Hitler, Lebensraum meant expanding eastwards to take land and resources from Russia.

Essential Knowledge

1. Through the twin methods of disarmament and collective security.
2. Because France would not disarm. Other countries were also suspicious of their neighbours by the early 1930s but French refusal to disarm gave Hitler his justification to build up his own armies.
3. It was to avoid war, and to do that, appeasement was meant to remove any possible source of disagreement or dispute.
4. It had been hoped that the League of Nations would maintain the peace and that no countries would ever want to go to war again. Clearly, by the mid-1930s that was not the case, so appeasement was adopted as a way of keeping Britain out of any conflict.

Theme

1. After the Great War, surely no country would want to go to war again. It was assumed all countries would be peace loving and democratic, and would trust the League of Nations to look after them. By the early 1930s those ideas were in tatters and fascism – which rejected peace, democracy and the League – was on the rise.
2. Fascist ambitions talked about expansion. How could states expand into other territories without at least threatening aggression?

Key issue 2: An assessment of the methods used by Germany and Italy to pursue their foreign policies from 1933 (page 92)

Test Your New Vocabulary

Anglo, as in Anglo-German Treaty – refers to Britain (from the Angles, an ancient people who settled in England).

Remilitarisation – Moving military equipment and soldiers into an area where previously they had not been allowed to enter.

Diplomacy – trying to get what a politician wants through negotiations and agreements.

Pact – an agreement.

Justification – a reason or excuse for doing something.

Essential Knowledge

1.
   - He promised long-term peace to stop possible action against him – Rhineland, Sudetenland/Munich.
   - He destabilised countries to provide excuses for protecting Germans – Austria, Sudetenland.
   - He made treaties – Poland 1934, Russia 1939, Anglo-German Naval Treaty.

Answers

- He claimed to be justified in his actions – Rhineland.
- He lied – although part of the Non-intervention Committee, Hitler did intervene in the Spanish Civil War by sending his airforce and tanks and military personnel using the codename 'Condor Legion'.

2. The one that led immediately to war was the Nazi–Soviet agreement in August 1939. Hitler wanted Poland but did not want a war against Russia – yet! Stalin did not want a war and also hated Poland. The deal suited both leaders and Hitler could attack Poland knowing Russia would not get involved and there was no way Britain would support Poland – or so he thought!

Theme

1. Usually he would have a justification for his actions or he would offer 'sweeteners' before his actions. He would also destabilise or undermine his next targets such as in Austria or Czechoslovakia. Any country that might be concerned enough to try to stop him would stop and think if it would be better to accept what Hitler did and enjoy the deal that he offered. What that meant in military terms is that any action against Hitler would be delayed and he would gain the advantage. The more reasons he gave for his actions, of course, the more opinion would move towards appeasing his 'reasonable' demands.

2. Threats would anger his opponents and unite them against Hitler. By providing positive promises, opposition to Hitler would be divided or at least slow in reacting. Promises would need to be discussed and then the question would be asked – would it not be better to accept friendly promises than go to war? Most governments did not want war, so Hitler gave them a way out of the dilemma of what to do. And the threat was always in the background if countries did not appease.

Key issue 3: An evaluation of the reasons for the British policy of appeasement, 1936–1938 (page 96)

Test Your New Vocabulary

League of Nations – an organisation set up after the First World War to keep peace.

Disarmament – reducing the amount of weapons a country has.

Lebensraum – a German word that literally means living space. For Hitler, Lebensraum meant expanding eastwards to take land and resources from Russia.

Imperial – to do with the British Empire.

Pacifism – completely against going to war.

Isolationist – having nothing to do with any other country.

Hitlerism – a common term for Nazism or fascism in the 1930s.

Essential Knowledge

1. The Empire made Britain a world player. The Empire brought wealth to Britain and had provided the soldiers that had helped Britain win the First World War. The Empire also contained tens of thousands of people who had family ties to Britain. The Empire, quite simply, was British.

2. It had been hoped that the League of Nations would maintain the peace and that no countries would ever want to go to war again. Clearly, by the mid-1930s that was not the case, so appeasement was adopted as a way of keeping Britain out of any conflict.

3. In the mid-1930s, the British public watched newsreels of European towns being destroyed by planes dropping bombs. For the first time, they realised that they would all be in the front line of war, attacked from the air as they worked and their children played. A big movie of 1936 was 'Things to Come' which showed the world being destroyed by endless war involving planes dropping gas bombs. When a politician said in a careless moment that there was no defence against bombers and that 'the bomber will always get through' to drop bombs on its target, the public became desperate to avoid war.

Answers

Theme

1. In the years after the Second World War and up until the 1960s it was felt that politicians who had supported appeasement were 'Guilty Men' who had allowed Hitler to grow strong by not stopping him. These politicians were also called cowards. However, recent research and evidence shows that Chamberlain was well aware of the issues outlined in this area of study and therefore appeasement can be thought of as a pragmatic and practical response to the situation in Europe as it was then, not as Chamberlain would have liked it to be. Hitler could not be wished away.

Key issue 4: An assessment of the success of British foreign policy in containing fascist aggression, 1935–March 1938 (page 99)

Test Your New Vocabulary

Containment – limiting the effect of something.

Anschluss – Germany uniting with Austria.

Schuschnigg – the Chancellor of Austria in 1938.

Condor Legion – the name for all German military assistance sent to Spain during the Spanish Civil War.

Non-intervention – a policy of non-involvement in the Civil War.

Essential Knowledge

1. In the first and last examples, Hitler broke the Treaty of Versailles. If Britain had taken strong action against Germany it could have led to war. In Spain, the rebel side of the Civil War was supported by Germany. If Britain had got involved in supporting the official government of Spain it **might** have led to war between Germany and Britain. In all three cases, Britain did not get involved in a war, and the actions of Hitler did not lead to conflict, so the link is that possible crisis points were controlled and contained.

2. Everyone knew that the Condor Legion was just a cover name for German military involvement in Spain, but as long as Hitler denied all knowledge of it then Germany was not officially involved in Spain. Of course Britain could have proved it was the German military machine, but was it in Britain's interests to expose that? Britain would then have had to take action.

Theme

1. No, it means to stop it spreading. Imagine knocking over a tin of paint. If you contain the spill you do not remove it from the floor, you try to stop the puddle spreading and so limit the damage done by the paint.

2. In this section you are asked to judge how successfully Britain contained fascist aggression. Britain certainly did not stop fascist aggression but it did contain it in the sense that the aggression did not grow and lead to a major European war. Nor did Britain stop the spread of fascism, as fascist aggression took fascism into Austria and Spain. However, Britain did not get involved in a war over those countries, so as far as Britain was concerned it was a result!

Key issue 5: An assessment of the Munich Agreement (page 104)

Test Your New Vocabulary

Czechoslovakia – a country created in 1919 at the Paris Peace Settlements. Today it is two countries – the Czech Republic and Slovakia.

Sudetenland – an area around the western, southern and northern border of Czechoslovakia containing about 3 million German-speaking people. They had never been part of Germany because they were part of Austria-Hungary, but Hitler claimed them as his own!

Lebensraum – a German word that literally means living space – territory that Hitler wanted in Russia to supply Germany with land for his surplus population, food in the form of cereal crops from the Ukraine and oil from the Caucasus region of Russia.

Answers

Essential Knowledge

1. After Anschluss, German troops now stood on the northern, western and southern borders of the Sudetenland. At any moment Hitler could order an attack. Britain had shown during Anschluss that it was not going to defend central Europe.

2. Once Hitler had the Sudetenland, he also had almost all of Czechoslovakia's border defences. He also controlled the main railway lines. Hitler could move into the rest of Czechoslovakia any time he wanted and the next stop would be Poland.

3. It was a disaster because a democratic country was given away to Hitler. Czechoslovakia was not even invited to the Munich meeting. On the other hand, British foreign policy at the time was appeasement and the aim of appeasement was to prevent war. Czechoslovakia was not a vital British interest and Britain had not promised to support Czechoslovakia. As Chamberlain said, it was a faraway country about whom we knew nothing. It was also true that any war in support of Czechoslovakia would not have been supported by some countries in the British Empire so the Empire might have split up, leaving Britain even weaker.

4. Postponed is the more accurate phrase. War was not **prevented** but, rather than fight in October 1938, it was **postponed** by a year. Britain gained almost a year of preparation time.

Theme

1. Pragmatic means dealing with a situation in a sensible and practical way which will bring benefits regardless of the rights or wrongs of the situation. While politicians and people in Britain may have felt that Czechoslovakians had been betrayed, what was the choice? What could be done to stop Hitler? Most British people wanted to avoid war and the Munich settlement was a pragmatic solution which maintained peace in Europe and, if that peace collapsed, then at least the Munich agreement bought time for Britain to prepare for war.

Key issue 6: An evaluation of the reasons for the outbreak of war in 1939 (page 107)

Test Your New Vocabulary

Polish corridor – at the Treaty of Versailles the country of Poland was created from land taken from Germany and Russia. The new Poland had no coast, so to give it access to the sea, Poland was given a strip of land – the Polish Corridor – which cut through German territory. Clearly the population of the Polish Corridor were mostly German, but now they were part of Poland.

Bohemia and Moravia – the two states that made up western Czechoslovakia and that were taken over by Germany in March 1939.

Stalin – the leader of Russia.

Essential Knowledge

1. By invading either country, Hitler could attack Russia. There was no way of knowing which way Hitler would go.

2. The fascists and the Communists were sworn enemies. Hitler claimed he had 'saved' Germany from communism. Suddenly, those two enemies had now made an agreement not to fight each other. Clearly it was in the interests of Stalin and Hitler not to have to fight each other … at least not yet. When the policy of appeasement started it was a real attempt to sort out the problems that existed with the Paris Peace Treaties of 1919. Britain accepted that Germany and Italy had real problems with the peace treaty and even during the 1930s the policy of appeasement came to mean different things at different times. By the summer of 1939, appeasement was discredited. Hitler had broken his promises of peace. By 1939, Hitler was running out of excuses and justifications. Now appeasement seemed to mean desperately trying to avoid war by giving in to bullies, but also gaining time to become stronger.

Answers

> **Theme**
>
> 1. Politically it ended for Britain when Britain gave a promise of support to Poland and Romania. For the British public, it ended when western Czechoslovakia was invaded, thereby breaking the Munich Agreement and showing that Hitler would not keep his promises. For Hitler, appeasement probably ended at 11am on 3rd September 1939 when Britain declared war. Why should Hitler have expected Britain suddenly to stand and fight?
>
> 2. At first, in 1935, appeasement really was hoped to be the way to sort out arguments and discontent over land and boundaries that continued after the Treaty of Versailles. By 1938 that idealism of sorting out grievances had become a policy of avoiding war at any cost. By September 1938 appeasement had evolved into accepting war was likely but using the time bought with agreements like Munich to prepare for the coming Second World War.
>
> 3. This question is referring to Britain's failed attempts to reach an agreement with Stalin. Britain had a fear and hatred of reaching any agreement with Communist Russia. Britain and approached the whole idea of an alliance with Russia so slowly that Stalin knew that Britain was unlikely ever to reach an agreement. Stalin wondered if Britain would ever be prepared to fight for Russia. With Hitler growing stronger, Stalin needed time to build up his forces. That is what the Nazi–Soviet agreement was all about. Perhaps if Britain had made an alliance with Russia then the Second World War would not have happened.

The Wars of Independence, 1249–1328

Key issue 1: Alexander III and the succession problem 1286–92 (page 115)

Test Your New Vocabulary

Succession – the next in line to the throne.

Birgham – a village near the Scottish–English border where a treaty was made to marry young Princess Margaret to King Edward's son.

Guardians – six important people in Scotland who would look after Scotland until Margaret was old enough to rule as Queen of Scotland.

Overlord – the most important lord who demanded loyalty from the people to whom he had given land.

Homage – a ceremony in which people who had been given land by the overlord promised to support him and follow his orders.

Fealty – loyalty.

Essential knowledge

1. All of Alexander's children were dead so there was no adult to be the next ruler of Scotland. Only his granddaughter survived. Ambitious lords in Scotland and Edward of England saw their chance to grab power for themselves.

2. Edward of England was a qualified lawyer and a relative of Alexander III so it was not surprising he should be asked to help. At the time kings were not elected. 'Royalty' was a gift from God, so the Guardians believed they had no power to choose. Only another king could choose a king. It was also a way of avoiding Scots fighting amongst themselves for the throne.

3. If Edward became overlord it would mean any Scottish king would have to accept that Edward was his boss.

Answers

Theme

1. There was no obvious successor to Alexander apart from a young granddaughter in Norway. Scotland faced the danger of civil war as important nobles saw a chance to seize power and even take control of Margaret. The six Guardians would guide Scotland until Margaret was old enough to rule. The Guardians represented the powerful families and the Scottish church, so it was hoped that civil war could be avoided.

2. The Treaty of Birgham – Edward wanted his son to marry Margaret. That way Scotland would be merged with England.

   The Great Cause and demands for overlordship – Edward said he could not award Scotland to the person he chose as king unless Edward already owned it. Edward promised to give up his overlordship once a new king was chosen, but would he?

   Homage and overlordship – By demanding that the Claimants to the Scottish throne accepted Edward's overlordship, they would be accepting that Edward was more powerful than they were.

Key issue 2: John Balliol and Edward I, 1292–1296 (page 121)

Test Your New Vocablary

Feudal – the system of law and landownership at the time of the Scottish Wars of Independence. In all European countries the king owned all the land. He gave out large areas of land to people in exchange for their support. In feudal terms the king was the overlord and the supporters did homage for the land - they promised fealty to the overlord.

Royal Seal – this was a symbol that could be stamped on royal documents and represented Scottish independence and its separate identity.

Toom Tabard – Empty Jacket – the nickname given to John Balliol after his royal badges were ripped from his clothing.

Subjugation – taking over something completely and destroying its separate identity.

Essential Knowledge

1. Scotland had been without a king for some time and local lords did not accept his authority. At that time there was little contact between the royal centre of power around Edinburgh and the faraway parts of the country.

2. Edward ordered King John to do homage for his kingdom. This demonstrated that Edward was superior to John and that John must follow Edward's orders. As king, John Balliol should have had the final word in any law dispute. However, on several occasions people who had lost a court case appealed to Edward over the head of John Balliol and Edward chose to overrule John Balliol's decision. In other words, Edward could show he was the real boss of Scotland.

3. Balliol had done homage to Edward more than once. By doing so, Balliol was promising to be a loyal supporter of Edward and never to break his promise. So, once Edward had been accepted as feudal superior, then legally Edward could demand anything he wanted from Balliol and Balliol had no choice but to agree.

Theme

1. Balliol was seen as a puppet king, controlled by Edward. Balliol had enemies, especially the Bruce family. They lost no opportunity to make clear Balliol's weakness. Balliol was also trying to establish royal authority over territory that did not recognise either his royal authority or the power of the Comyns, Balliol's family.

2. Once Balliol accepted Edward's overlordship and did homage for the lands of Scotland, Balliol was bound by an oath of fealty to obey Edward in all things.

3. You could choose:

   The removal to London of the Stone of Destiny – an ancient symbol of Scotland's independence. Scots kings were crowned sitting on it, giving them a religious and magical importance.

191

Answers

All taxes taken south – Scottish money used to finance Edward's rule in England also left Balliol short of funds to rule Scotland.

Scotland became a land, not a kingdom – a land is controlled by someone but is not a separate country.

Crown jewels – the almost magical symbols of royalty and power used by kings and queens. Edward had taken Scotland's 'lucky charms'.

Ragman Rolls – all Scottish nobles accepted Edward's overlordship. They could not break their promise of fealty.

Key issue 3: William Wallace and Scottish Resistance (page 127)

Test Your New Vocabulary

Resistance – fighting back against control of Scotland by the English.

Schiltron – a military tactic of grouping many men together in a giant huddle, each holding very long spikes so that the group looked like a giant human hedgehog. It was a very good tactic against charging cavalry who could not break through, but the schiltron also provided an easy target for archers to pour arrows into it.

Ordinance – an order or command.

Allegiance – loyalty, like fealty.

Essential Knowledge

1. Edward tried to subjugate Scotland. He appointed English administrators to rule Scotland. Scots nobility were forced to sign the Ragman Rolls.

2. It was the first time in military history that a well-armed, mounted, organised army had been defeated in open battle by poorly armed ordinary people fighting mostly on foot.

    The victory at Stirling sent shock waves through England but gave a huge boost to Scottish confidence and allowed Wallace to became Guardian of Scotland.

3. Yes, he had joined with Wallace before Stirling Bridge and had led resistance in the north of Scotland. He was a trained and experienced knight and it is possible that he created the battle plan that led to victory at Stirling. He is now mainly forgotten because he was wounded and died at Stirling Bridge, leaving Wallace to be the central leader of resistance.

4. Defeat at Falkirk suggested that Wallace was not a good military leader or planner. He chose a bad position and left his schiltrons to be massacred by enemy archers. After Falkirk, Wallace escaped and was no longer a real threat to England. Wallace was popular as a war leader but only as long as he was a winner.

Theme

1. Wallace represented opposition and resistance to Edward and England. Edward had seen his army humiliated at Stirling Bridge. As long as Wallace remained free, Edward's authority in Scotland was weakened and the hopes of a free and independent Scotland could be kept alive. Wallace could perhaps once again become a later focus for resistance, or at least represent continuing defiance against English control.

Key issue 4: The rise and triumph of Robert Bruce (page 137)

Test Your New Vocabulary

Sacrilege – committing a sin in church.

Competitors – the people who claimed that they should be chosen as the next king of Scotland during the Great Cause. Robert the Bruce's grandfather had been 'Bruce the Competitor'.

Civil war – a war in one country between rival groups wanting to seize power.

Answers

Deploy – in military language, to move troops to gain an advantage.

Disinherit – to take away the right to own land.

Clergy – members of the Church such as bishops and priests. At this time the Church was entirely Catholic.

Celtic fringe alliance – an attempt to unite groups in Scotland, Ireland and Wales to fight against the English. Alliance means unite, fringe means edges and Celtic means the Irish, Scots and Welsh – all countries around the edge of England.

Papacy – the administration of the Church headed by the Pope. The support of the Papacy was vital for the people of a country. The Papacy was an international power at this time in selecting and approving kings and queens.

Essential Knowledge

1. Bruce had murdered Comyn in a church. That was sacrilege – a sin – and Bruce should have been excommunicated. Excommunication would mean that Bruce could not be crowned king. Bruce needed to be crowned before it was too late.

2. Castles were the biggest and best military bases of their time. They controlled the areas around them for many miles. As long as English forces could stay protected in their castles, Bruce could not take control of Scotland.

3. It was the defeat of the Comyns and their allies in the north-east of Scotland (an area still known as Buchan) and then the destruction of their resources so that the family could not recover its power. It was also a lesson of what would happen to anyone who might want to stand against Bruce.

4. This problem goes back to the Great Cause and the problems caused by homage and overlordship. Many Scottish nobles possessed land in Scotland **and** England. For the lands in England these nobles did homage to the English king. They promised to obey him. That would undermine Bruce's authority over his own nobles. Bruce gave his nobles a choice. If they wanted to keep their valuable lands in England they would lose their lands in Scotland. In other words, they would be disinherited. The decision to do this meant that the nobles who decided to keep their Scottish lands would no longer have split loyalties and Bruce could rely on their support.

Theme

1. Both families were related to the royal family of Scotland and both families thought they had the best claim to the throne after Alexander III died. John Balliol was a member of the Comyn family and the Bruces resented Edward's rejection of the claim of Robert Bruce. After King John was stripped of his power, Robert the Bruce was one of the two Guardians of Scotland, alongside John Comyn.

2. Soon after Bruce murdered Comyn, he was almost powerless, hiding from enemies. The Comyns had many friends and allies. As long as the Comyns remained strong there was no way Bruce would be accepted as King of all Scots. Nor could Bruce fight two wars at the same time – against his enemies in Scotland and the English. The death of Edward I gave Bruce breathing space to deal with his enemies in Scotland.

3. The 'secret war' would nowadays be called a guerrilla war involving 'hit-and-run' tactics in which small groups of armed men could attack quickly, ambush enemies and cause maximum nuisance while only taking small casualties. Meanwhile, Bruce's enemies would use up precious resources defending areas but not knowing where Bruce would strike next.

4. Bruce was annoyed when his brother made a deal with the governor of Stirling Castle. It meant the English had to relieve Stirling Castle by midsummer's day in June. That meant an army would march to Stirling and Bruce would have to face the English army or allow English forces to continue controlling central Scotland.

   However, in a way Bruce did not fully abandon guerrilla tactics.

   He used the terrain of Bannockburn to his advantage to limit the options and the actions of the English forces.

   He kept his options open and even considered abandoning the battle after day one.

   He kept his troops hidden in forests.

   He might have used 'the wee folk' as a trick to demoralise the English.

Answers

Migration and Empire, 1830–1939

Key issue 1: The migration of Scots (page 142)

Test Your New Vocabulary

Overpopulation – too many people living in an area for the available resources to support them.

Emigration – leaving the home area to settle elsewhere.

Internal migration – moving from one area of Scotland to another to settle.

Depopulation – areas left relatively empty by people moving away.

Crofters – farmers in the Highlands who looked after small farms.

Coercion – force.

Opportunity – a chance for a better life.

Essential Knowledge

1. Those areas were part of the British Empire. The people spoke the same language, friends and family were already there and the institutions were familiar, ranging from schools to place names and to churches.

2. There are three main points to this answer: firstly, it was the nearest part of the British Empire to Scotland so travelling times were shortest and costs were lowest. Secondly, it minimised the time that an emigrant traveller would be out of work, and therefore not being paid. Thirdly, once into Canada many Scots took the opportunity to cross the border into the USA.

3. A push reason is anything that makes someone do something they would rather not due to a lack of alternatives. A pull reason is something that attracts and makes a person want to do something.

Theme

1. Coercion could be the use of roof burnings during the Highland Clearances. Sometimes the timbers holding up the roof would be burned making it impossible for evicted crofters to return to their homes. Opportunity could be, for example, the offer of free land to settle on and farm in Canada. The possibility of owning land and the security it gave was very important to people who had lived in fear of being evicted by their landlord.

2. Emigration means leaving the home country and settling overseas. Internal migration means moving to another part of the same country, for example crofters in Highland glens moving to the coast or farm workers in the Scottish Borders moving to find work in the cities of Edinburgh or Glasgow – or even in England!

Key issue 2: The experience of immigrants in Scotland (page 145)

Test Your New Vocabulary

Lithuanians – immigrants from the Baltic country of Lithuania, then part of Russia.

Assimilated – mixed in, joining together.

Integrated – almost the same as assimilated, when distinct and separate groups live together.

Industrialisation – changes in the way people worked caused by an increase in heavy industry-based work.

Urbanisation – the growth of cities to house the new factory and office-based working and middle classes.

Synagogues – Jewish places of worship.

Catholic Irish – immigrants from Ireland who were Roman Catholic, a part of the Christian religion who worshipped God in different ways from Protestants.

Answers

Protestant Irish – immigrants from Ireland who were Protestant, therefore more welcomed by Scots because they shared the same religious customs and beliefs.

Sectarian – differences between groups of people of different religions often resulting in dislike, distrust and violence.

Essential Knowledge

1. One reason was religion and the other fear of what they were said to bring with them. Catholic Irish kept themselves to themselves, remaining bound to their Catholic identity with the Church at its heart. Scots blamed the Irish for all the problems of urbanisation and industrialisation such as disease, poverty and unemployment. The Catholic Irish were a tribe with a different identity, meaning Scots could use them as a target for their resentment and anger.

2. The two main reasons were religious and economic. The two reasons often combined, e.g. the Catholic Irish and Lithuanians were seen as competitors for jobs who were prepared to work longer for less money. They were also used as strike-breakers so they were accused of keeping poor working conditions for Scots in place. Most Irish immigrants and Lithuanians were Catholic and many Scots saw them as a threat to their Protestant identity.

3. Many Scottish ice cream and fish and chip shops still bear Italian names. Scottish artists such as Nicola Benedetti and Paolo Nutini reveal their Italian ancestry in their names. Jewish synagogues still serve a Jewish community in Scotland. Probably the most famous image that links Scottish culture with its Irish roots is the Irish flag that flies over Celtic football club's stadium at Parkhead, Glasgow.

4. Irish immigration continued from the 1840s until well into the 20th century. Irish workers competed for jobs with local Scots, and Catholic Irish were disliked by the majority Protestant population of Scotland. Italian, Jewish and Lithuanian immigration involved much fewer people and took place over a shorter period of time. Italian and Jewish immigrants also kept themselves to themselves and were not seen by local Scots as competition for jobs.

Key issue 3: The impact of Scots emigrants on the Empire (page 149)

Test Your New Vocabulary

Métis – children born in 19th century Canada to a white immigrant father and local-born mother.

First Peoples – the name used for Aboriginal people in Canada rather than 'Indians'.

Aboriginal people – the original people in a country, although most people think it refers only to Australia.

Maori – the Aboriginal people of New Zealand.

Mutiny – a refusal by soldiers to obey legitimate orders. In 1857, Indian soldiers (sepoys) refused to follow orders from their British officers, and this triggered a wider Indian mutiny/rebellion.

Essential Knowledge

1. Many Scots emigrated because they were forced off land they farmed by landowners who wanted to make their estates more profitable. When Scots emigrants developed farms and sheep runs in Australia and New Zealand they too took land, often by force, from local Aboriginal people who found their way of life destroyed.

Theme

1. To answer this you must look at social, economic and political influence. Concentrate on Canada, Australasia and India. It really is impossible to say that Scots influenced one aspect of Empire development more than any other. Scots were important in the development of the whole Empire and in all three main ways – economic, social and political. You should have examples ready to support any point you want to make.

2. This is a difficult question, the answer to which has changed with the rise of political correctness.

    In the 19th and early 20th centuries there was no doubt in the minds of British people that the Empire was a force for good. It civilised and modernised many counties that were called at the time undeveloped, barbaric or 'backward'.

Answers

> In more recent times there has been an acceptance that Scots played an important part in the economic and political development of relatively empty areas such as Australasia or Canada but even here there is now an awareness of the bad things that happened to local people.
>
> India is a more difficult country to make a decision about. India had a large population with very definite cultures and customs. India was also a very religious continent. When Britain tried to destroy these customs and religious beliefs, local people quite rightly resisted. Britain used force to keep control. Thousands of Indians did benefit from the development of India but others saw the development as one-way traffic aimed at profiting Britain by exploiting India.

Key issue 4: The effects of migration and Empire on Scotland, to 1939 (page 152)

Test Your New Vocabulary

The British Empire/The Empire – by the end of the 19th century the British empire was the greatest Empire the world had ever seen. Over a quarter of the world's population was under British rule. It was said that the sun never set on the Empire, it stretched around the world's time zones and so there was always an area of the Empire where it was daytime.

Constituencies – an area of the country that elects one MP.

Jute – a plant grown in India/Bangladesh that produces a fibre used to make sacks and bags. Dundee was the main British production centre for jute.

Identity – what gives a sense of belonging to a group or nation.

Investments – money spent on projects overseas with the aim of making a profit for the investor.

Essential Knowledge

1. Large areas of the Empire developed because of Scottish emigrant expertise and Scottish investment so it was natural the economic ties with the Empire brought wealth back to Scotland. In an age before air transport, all trade with the Empire went by ship – mostly built on the Clyde - and most foodstuffs were brought to the UK in sacks made from jute – made in Scotland.

   Put simply, any trade with, or investment in, the Empire linked to Scotland made a profit for Scottish businesses.

2. The answer is simply to do with numbers and time. Irish immigration was high for almost a hundred years. Lithuanians, Italians and Jews mainly arrived in Scotland between 1880 and 1910. Immigrant Irish populations settled mainly in the west of Scotland. The other groups were more scattered.

Theme

1. This is almost impossible to answer. Scots had a huge effect on the development of the British Empire, disproportionate to the size of the country. But so did other countries, especially England.

   The effect of the Empire on Scotland was also immense, for a long time bringing great wealth. However, by the 1920s, as the Empire became more developed (thanks to Scots!), Scotland faced a fall in its earnings from the Empire.

2. This depends on your point of view. In the 19th century many social reforms (Dalhousie's reforms in India for example) were thought by British people to bring 'civilisation' to 'barbaric' people. On the other hand, many Indians saw the reforms as ways of increasing control over India so that India's wealth could more easily be developed for British interests. In the Empire generally, native peoples suffered loss of land and their culture as the Scots immigrants 'developed' the new lands to their own advantage.

Answers

3. The answer is economic. Push reasons to emigrate are always because people cannot get enough money to survive so they must move to find jobs, land or places to live. Pull reasons are similar in that people move where they can find work, better wages or land. Social reasons such as friends and family or joining a community that feels right will always be secondary considerations after the basic needs of enough money and food to live on are met. Political reasons for emigration mean that people are under threat because of their political beliefs and in some countries people did have to move or die. That was not the case in 19th century Britain, so political reasons were not a cause of Scottish emigration.

The Impact of the Great War, 1914–1928

Key issue 1: Scots on the Western Front (page 159)

Test Your New Vocabulary

Recruitment – volunteering to join the army.

Staple industries – the basic industries of coal mining, iron and steel-making and shipbuilding that were the biggest employers in Scotland at the time.

Western Front – a line of unbroken trench defences stretching from the English Channel coast to the Swiss border.

Attrition – accepting high casualties and calculating that Britain could replace the losses more easily than Germany.

Essential Knowledge

1. Unemployment – the army offered jobs.

    Patriotism – the desire to help one's country.

    Friendship – to do what their mates were doing.

    Anger at Germany – horror stories of what German soldiers did as they invaded Belgium (most of them invented to boost recruitment) caused people to join up.

    Guilt and worry – posters were deliberately designed to make young men who had not volunteered feel bad about themselves.

    Excitement – volunteers wanted to look good in front of their friends and families and if they did not join up quickly then they would miss the adventure, as they believed that the war would be over by Christmas.

2. So many Scottish regiments were involved in those battles and casualty rates affected almost every Scottish town and village.

Theme

1. There were many reasons why Scots were persuaded to join up but at the back of most minds was the firm belief that it would be a short war, Britain would win it and the young men wanted to be part of the action.

2. Many people believe an old idea that the immense casualty rate in the First World War was caused by old fashioned and out of touch generals (the donkeys) ordering brave young men (lions) to their deaths without reason and without caring.

    Recent research takes a more balanced view. When war broke out nobody expected it to be as destructive and last as long as it did. The young men who joined were civilians. They had to be trained quickly and often sent into battle 'raw'. As a result, the tactics used could not be too difficult to follow under extreme fire.

    Towards the end of the war, the army had learned a lot, recruits or conscripts were better trained and it was an old 'donkey' – Field Marshal Douglas Haig – who created a civilian army that defeated the German army.

Answers

Key issue 2: Domestic impact of war: society and culture (page 162)

Test Your New Vocabulary

Radicalisation – becoming politically aware that by your own actions you can make things change.

DORA – a government law that stood for 'Defence of the Realm Act'.

Commemoration – doing something that helps people remember the sacrifice that others made during the war.

Voluntary recruitment – choosing to join up.

Shirking – dodging or avoiding something.

Conscription – being forced to join up.

Conscientious objectors – people who resisted joining the armed forces.

Exemption – being excused form having to join up.

Non-combat – being part of the army but not involved in the fighting or in a combat role; for example, a stretcher bearer.

Absolutist – someone who absolutely refused to be conscripted and do any job in the army – non-combat or not.

Munitions – the bullets and explosive shells fired by rifles and artillery.

Rent strikes – a campaign organised by women to resist rent rises, especially in the Glasgow area during the war.

Essential Knowledge

1. Conscription forced people to join the armed forces. Conscientious objectors did not agree with this and opposed it. If there was no conscription then the objectors would have nothing to object to!

2. As the war continued, two things became clear: (i) the lack of men in the workforce as the armed forces signed up more and more recruits; (ii) British industry needed to become much faster and bigger in its production of war essentials. Women helped in both of these areas by increasing the workforce in every area from munition workers making explosive shells to 'lumber jills' working in forestry.

3. The short answer is to replace the casualties. A second common reason is because the rates of volunteering were dropping as people became aware that war was no exciting adventure. However, the real reason was the realisation that there was no end in sight for the war. By the end of 1915 it was clear that the war would not be over as quickly as originally thought. More battles with high casualties would have to be fought and if Britain did not introduce conscription and the war went on for much longer, then Britain would simply run out of trained soldiers.

Theme

1. Locally – almost every village has a war memorial or a list of names in the local church or some other way to remember the losses of the Great War. Each year there is still a remembrance ceremony and poppy wreaths are laid at those memorials.

   Nationally – the National War Memorial stands within Edinburgh Castle. Opened in 1927, it commemorates all the Scottish war dead.

   Internationally – the Commonwealth War Graves Commission tends the cemeteries across the world where Scottish soldiers are buried. For soldiers whose remains were never found, vast lists of names are on monuments across the Western Front, for example on the Menin Gate, Ypres.

2. The answer could be summed up as (i) civil liberties and (ii) the effect on women.

   In terms of civil liberties, conscription was an example of government control that was largely welcomed. Most people accepted that the government took responsibility for looking after its citizens to an extent – the Liberal social reforms showed that and people felt that they had a duty to serve in the army if asked. Conscientious objectors did resist but they were a very small minority of those who were ordered to fight.

Answers

Women were needed for the war effort and suddenly jobs were opened up that had once been closed. After the war, those jobs disappeared but having raised the possibility of change it was hard to remove it again.

DORA caused most upset as the war went on. Check this sub-section to see how and why.

Key issue 3: Domestic impact of war: industry and economy (page 165)

Test Your New Vocabulary

Emigration – leaving one country to go and settle in another.

Land raids – the occupation of land by Highland farmers who believed they had a right to farm it.

Rationing – restricting the amount of food that people could buy so that scarce supplies could be shared out more fairly.

Traditional export markets – the places abroad to which British industry (including fishing) sold their produce.

Essential Knowledge

1. The short answer is because there was not enough food to go round. Germany had deliberately tried to starve Britain out of the war by sinking as many supply ships coming to Britain as it could. As food supplies decreased, the government was faced with the possibility of food prices rising very quickly so that many people would not be able to afford to eat. That would not have helped the war effort, so the government used rationing to make sure everyone got a fair share.

2. The staple industries were also known as the heavy industries – coal mining, iron and steel-making and shipbuilding. All of them depended on the others. Coal was needed in furnaces to make iron and steel and the metals were used to make ships. When demand fell for shipping after the war, so did demand for the other industries.

Theme

1. There are two answers to this.
    a. In the short term, the war did benefit Scottish industry because more people were employed, production increased and wartime orders meant production was at full pace. There was no unemployment.
    b. The second answer is that in the long term, the war did not help Scotland's industries. Before the war, Scottish industry was facing problems with old production methods, falling demand and also foreign competition. The wartime boom disguised those problems and the increase in demand for things made by Scottish industry was only ever going to last until the war ended. When the war ended, the slump seemed worse than before.

2. People were told that Britain would have 'homes fit for heroes to live in' after the war but that promise seemed to have been broken. Unemployment increased and Scots saw no future in Scotland. Add that feeling of discontent to Scotland's 19th century tradition of emigration and it seems clear that Canada, Australia and other places in the Empire offered a fresh start and a new life.

Key issue 4: Domestic impact of war: politics (page 169)

Test Your New Vocabulary

Radicalisation – the realisation by ordinary people that they could take action to change their living and working conditions and make politicians pay attention to them.

Red – a colour associated with revolution. Around 1919 the word Red was also used to mean a Communist.

Polarised – opinion divided between two extremes.

Self-determination – a form of devolution where people decide their own political futures.

Coalition – different political parties working together as one government for a period of time.

Unionism – support for the Union of Scotland and England.

199

Answers

Essential Knowledge

1. In 1915, some women in Glasgow began rent strikes in protest at rent rises by landlords hoping to exploit women while their men were away fighting. Workers in several Clydeside factories went on strike to support the women and the image of wartime strikes disrupting production along with large street demonstrations in support of the women created the image of an unsettled and troublesome area – possibly revolutionary – that became known as 'Red Clydeside'.

2. That depends on your point of view in terms of time and political ideology. The George Square demonstration of January 1919 was just a few months after strikes in Russia had led to a revolution. In January 1919, revolution was causing fierce fighting in Berlin. At the time it was not unreasonable to see the mass demonstration in Glasgow as potentially dangerous. From the strikers' point of view, they wanted better working conditions but their demand for a shorter working week was really an attempt to provide jobs for returning ex-soldiers. They were not preparing for a revolution. In hindsight, the fear of 'Red Clydeside' was really a product of the political polarisation that had taken place in Scotland.

Theme

1. During the war, the Labour Party increased its influence, the Independent Labour Party took an anti-war, socialist position and the Liberal Party collapsed as a united and attractive political party. All that was left for those who feared the rise of Labour was the Scottish Conservative and Unionist Party.

2. The Liberals dominated Scottish politics before the war and in a general way the Scottish people were politically passive. They voted and then allowed the elected government to govern them. During the war and shortly afterwards, many Scots felt that the only way to deal with the issues facing them was to take radical action. In the shipyards of Clydebank, workers went on strike against the threat to their liberties posed by DORA. Women took action against landlords trying to raise rents. Men disillusioned by the war and empty promises of homes fit for heroes took to the streets of George Square in Glasgow, while in the Highlands returning soldiers turned to land raids to take what they felt they deserved. Even migration could be seen as a radical act, with people deciding to leave the country and take action themselves to forge a better future.

Leckie
the education publisher
for Scotland

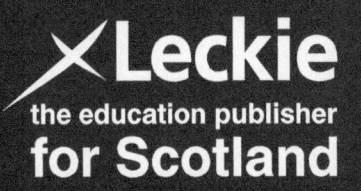

Higher
HISTORY
For SQA 2019 and beyond

Practice Papers

John Kerr and
Holly Robertson

Introduction

The Higher History course is made up of two exam papers, each one 1 hour and 30 minutes long. This book is going to prepare you for that exam and give you advice, guidance and practice papers to help you gain the mark you deserve. It will also show you how the source-based questions differ and how the essay structure and approach has slightly changed.

There are always three topics covered in the Higher History course. The British and European and World topics are examined by one essay per topic. The Scottish topic is examined mostly in source-based questions.

Higher History source-based questions – Scottish topic

You will study a Scottish topic, which will be used to complete four questions in total, three source-based questions: and an 'explain' question that is not source based.

- 'How much do sources … reveal about differing interpretations of …"

The 'Evaluate the usefulness' question

This is worth 8 marks in the final exam and asks you to establish how useful a primary source is in relation to a historical event that you have studied in your Scottish topic.

When answering this question at Higher level you need to always consider the following:

- The origin and possible purpose of the source
- The content of the source
- Your own knowledge

The origin and possible purpose of the source

Author – who produced the source?

Ask yourself the following questions:

- Is the author an eyewitness to the event in question? (Remember to say what the event is.)
- Could they be showing an element of bias?
- Is the source only showing one person's view of the event?
- Could they be writing it for some form of financial gain?
- Could they be exaggerating to make it more sensational?
- Is the author an expert on the event in question? (Remember to say what the event is.)
- Using the advantage of hindsight, will the author be neutral/balanced in their viewpoint?
- Will the author have researched the topic well?

TOP TIP
Make a judgement on the author and state whether that makes the source more or less useful.

Purpose – why is the source being written?

Consider the following:

- If the source is an extract from a newspaper, it could contain bias and exaggeration.
- If the source is from a personal memoir, it is more likely to be the documentation of the event and therefore unbiased.
- If the source is an extract from a politician's speech, it could show an element of bias.
- If the source is a piece of propaganda, it may be biased.

TOP TIP
Make a judgement on the purpose of the source and whether that makes it more or less useful.

Timing – when was the source written?

Ask yourself the following questions:

- Was it written at the time in question? (You must state exactly what the event in question is.)
- Why would it be useful to have a source from the time of the event in question?
- Was it written a long time after the event?
- Why would it be better to have a source from years after the event happened with the benefit of hindsight?

TOP TIP
Make a judgement on the date of the source and whether it makes the source more or less useful.

Type of source – what is the source and does that affect its usefulness?

Different types of source:

- Speech – would this be biased?
- Diary – would a personal account give an honest viewpoint (but only one)?
- Government document – would this have to be factual and unbiased?
- Newspaper article – would this show bias and possible exaggeration?

> **TOP TIP**
> Make a comment on the type of source and how this could affect its usefulness.

The content of the source

What does the source say and how does that help you to answer the question?

- What has helped you identify that the source is or isn't useful?
- What information from the source has helped you answer the question and state whether the source is useful or not?
- What information from the source tells you more about what the question is asking?

Give two valid points from the source.

> **TOP TIP**
> Take two points from the source content to gain 2 marks.

Your own knowledge

What omissions are there? (What crucial information about the event is being left out?)

- Does the source only give you one viewpoint and limit the amount of information on the event in question?
- Is the source telling the whole story or only selecting certain information about the event in question?

Ensure you give three knowledge points that are missing from the source.

The 'How fully' question

This is worth 10 marks in the final exam and allows you to identify relevant information from the source given, as well as provide relevant recalled knowledge to describe and explain the question/issue being highlighted within the Scottish topic you have studied.

When answering this question at Higher level you need to always consider the following:

- Your opening statement should make it clear how fully the source describes or explains the issue at the centre of the question. Generally, you can state that the source describes/explains the issue to an extent. To what extent is up to your judgement; You MUST MAKE YOUR JUDGEMENT IN TERMS OF THE QUESTION CLEAR. If you do not have at least something such as 'the source partly ...' or 'quite fully' then you will only get 2 marks out of 10, regardless of how correct the rest of your answer is.

- You should then go on to find four points from the source that help answer the question.

- The final stage is to provide up to seven points that are not present in the source from your recalled knowledge on the issue.

TOP TIP
This question relies upon a detailed knowledge of the Scottish topic, so ensure that you are confident on the four issues before the exam.

The two-source question, which always asks, 'How much do sources ... reveal about differing attitudes towards ...

This is worth 10 marks and uses two sources. You will be given two sources. Both sources will be about the same subject but will contain different points of view.

Your first task is to identify the points of view in each source and second, to explain what the views are and why they differ. Use your own background knowledge of the topic. Try also to explain why the common issue to both sources causes such different opinions.

- To Bruce and his supporters, the action to stop the problem of divided loyalties made good political sense. Bruce had to be sure of his nobles' loyalty. Bruce rewarded those who now sided with him with land taken from the disinherited nobles and from Bruce's enemies who had died at Bannockburn.

The 'Explain' question

It is worth 8 marks and is NOT based on any of the sources.

Beware your answer does not just become a description of events liked to the question topic. This question requires you to give reasons why something happened, not just descriptions.

The main point about this question is to be clear about what you are being asked to explain and to not just read the topic of the question.

A good way to answer this question and keep it relevant is to write "There are many reasons why … (insert the core of the question here).

The first reason why … is because …..

The next reason why …is because… and so on until you have written at least 8 reasons.

The word 'because' is always useful because you cannot write 'because' without giving a reason and that is what the question wants you to do.

Higher History essay – British topic and European and World topic

The essay structure for Higher History has only changed slightly, but these changes are important ones. The essay is worth 22 marks and the marks are broken up as shown below:

- Introduction **(I)** = 3 marks
- Knowledge and Understanding **(KU)** = 6 marks
- Analysis **(A)** = 6 marks
- Evaluation **(E)** = 4 marks
- Conclusion **(C)** = 3 marks

Structure

Introduction

- Start by setting the question in context using at least two different points of relevant information. What was going on just before the event in question?

- Using the wording of the question, establish a line of argument. It is likely that a factor is mentioned in the question. The factor in the title is certainly an important reason but there were other factors that were also important.

- Outline the factors you are going to discuss to answer the question. You could write 'Other important factors include …'. **(I)**

Main part of your essay

- You should start with the factor mentioned in the question that you will use to create your line of argument.

- Ensure you provide at least two or three pieces of evidence in each paragraph, demonstrating developed knowledge relevant to the issue in the question to support the factor and its importance. **(KU)**

- Explain how each piece of evidence helps to answer the question. After a developed point you should state how that piece of evidence helps support the importance of the factor. You can gain up to 4 marks for this.

- You can gain a further 2 marks for linking important pieces of evidence back to the question. This can also help build your line of argument. **(A)**

- Evaluation marks can come in the form of a judgement, e.g. historical importance, counter argument or historical debate. 1–2 marks are given for isolated evaluation but 3–4 evaluation marks are awarded where the candidate connects their evaluation to a line of argument established throughout the essay. **(E)**

Conclusion

- Start by summarising the points made in your answer linked to your line of argument. You should also make a relative overall judgement about the importance of the various factors in terms of the question asked. Make a direct answer to the question that is based clearly on the arguments you have presented throughout your essay.

Higher History topics

This book is aimed at improving Higher History source-based and essay skills. There are 20 topics to choose from for the Higher History course. In this book, original source-based and essay questions have been provided for the eight most popular topics:

Scottish

- The Wars of Independence, 1249–1328
- The Treaty of Union, 1689–1740
- Migration and Empire, 1830–1939
- The Impact of the Great War, 1914–1928

There are four questions for each of these topics, one each of 'Evaluate the usefulness', 'How fully', 'Explain' and 'How much do the sources reveal about differing interpretations of' along with complete marking instructions.

Britain

- Britain, 1851–1951

There are three essay questions and one fully worked model answer for this topic, along with complete marking instructions.

European and World

- Germany, 1815–1939
- USA, 1918–1968
- Appeasement and the Road to War, to 1939

There are three essay questions and one fully worked model answer for each of these topics, along with complete marking instructions.

H

HISTORY
BRITISH, EUROPEAN AND WORLD HISTORY

Duration - 1 hour 30 minutes

Total marks — 44

SECTION 1 — BRITISH — 22 marks

Attempt ONE question from the part you have chosen.

SECTION 2 — EUROPEAN AND WORLD — 22 marks

Attempt ONE question from the part you have chosen.

Write your answers clearly in the answer booklet provided. In the answer booklet you must clearly identify the question number you are attempting.

Use **blue** or **black** ink.

Before leaving the examination room you must give your answer booklet to the Invigilator; if you do not, you may lose all the marks for this paper.

×Leckie
the education publisher
for Scotland

PAPER 1 – HISTORY, BRITISH, EUROPEAN AND WORLD HISTORY

Part D: The Making of Modern Britain, 1851–1951

PAPER 1 – BRITISH – 22 marks

Part D: Britain, 1851–1951

Attempt one question.

1. To what extent were the Suffragettes the main reason that some women gained the vote by 1918? **22**

2. How important were the reports on poverty in Britain by Booth and Rowntree and to what extent could they have been responsible for the Liberal Government's decision to introduce social reforms, 1906–1914? **22**

3. The social reforms of the Labour Government of 1945–1951 failed to deal effectively with the needs of the people. How valid is this view? **22**

PAPER 1 - HISTORY, BRITISH, EUROPEAN AND WORLD HISTORY

Part D: Germany, 1815–1939

PAPER 1 – EUROPEAN AND WORLD – 22 marks

Part D: Germany, 1815–1939

Attempt one question.

1. By 1850, political nationalism had made little progress in Germany. How valid is this view? **22**

2. To what extent were the Weimar's economic difficulties the main reason why the Nazis achieved power in 1933? **22**

3. To what extent were fear and terror the main reasons why the Nazis were able to stay in power during 1933–1939? **22**

PAPER 1 - HISTORY, BRITISH, EUROPEAN AND WORLD HISTORY

Part G: USA, 1918-1968

PAPER 1 – EUROPEAN AND WORLD – 22 marks

Part G: USA, 1918–1968

Attempt one question.

1. To what extent were divisions in the black community the main obstacle to the achievement of civil rights for black people up to 1941? **22**

2. 'The Wall Street Crash was the main cause of the Great Depression in the 1930s.' How valid is this view? **22**

3. Improvements in the lives of black Americans by 1968 were mainly due to changes in federal policy. How valid is this view? **22**

PAPER 1 – HISTORY, BRITISH, EUROPEAN AND WORLD HISTORY

Part H: Appeasement and the Road to War, to 1939

PAPER 1 – EUROPEAN AND WORLD – 22 marks

Part H: Appeasement and the Road to War, to 1939

Attempt one question.

1. To what extent were pacts and alliances the main methods used by Germany and Italy to pursue their foreign policies from 1933? **22**

2. 'British foreign policy was successful in containing fascist aggression up to March 1938.' How valid is this view? **22**

3. To what extent was the invasion of Poland the main reason for the decision to abandon the policy of appeasement and for the outbreak of war in 1939? **22**

H

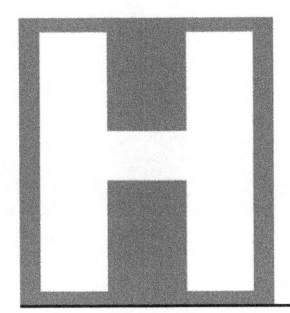

HISTORY
SCOTTISH HISTORY

Duration - 1 hour 30 minutes

Total marks — 36

SCOTTISH HISTORY — 36 marks

Attempt ONE Part.

Write your answers clearly in the answer booklet provided. In the answer booklet you must clearly identify the question number you are attempting.

Use **blue** or **black** ink.

Before leaving the examination room you must give your answer booklet to the Invigilator; if you do not, you may lose all the marks for this paper.

×Leckie
the education publisher
for Scotland

PAPER 2 – HISTORY, SCOTTISH HISTORY

Part A: The Wars of Independence, 1249–1328

PAPER 2 – SCOTTISH HISTORY – 36 marks

Part A: The Wars of Independence, 1249–1328

Study the sources below and attempt the questions which follow.

Source A: from the *Chronicle of John of Fordoun*, 1350.

> In March 1296, the King of England, being strongly stirred up, marched in person, with a large force, on Scotland. Upon the town of Berwick, sparing neither sex nor age, the aforesaid King of England, put to the sword some 7500 souls. On 27 April, in the same year, was fought the battle of Dunbar, where Patrick of Graham and many Scottish nobles fell wounded in defeat, while a great many other knights fled to Dunbar Castle. However, up to 70 of them, including William, Earl of Ross, were betrayed by the warden of the castle and handed over to the King of England, like sheep offered to the slaughter. In this, Balliol's war, all the supporters of Bruce's party were generally considered traitors to their King and country.

Source B: from the *Chronicle of Walter of Guisborough*, around 1300.

> Meanwhile two friars were sent to the army of the Scots, to William Wallace, to see if they wanted to embrace the peace which the English offered. Wallace replied, "Tell your men that we have not come for peace but are ready for the fight, to vindicate ourselves and to free our kingdom." There was not a more suitable place to put the English into the hands of the Scots. When the Scots saw that they could win, they came down from the hill. Sending men with pikes, they seized the end of the bridge so that no Englishman could cross or return. Among the English nobles cut down by the Scottish pikemen was Lord Hugh de Cressingham. The Scots hated him and cut his hide into little bits. They called him not the King's "treasurer" but his "treacherer".

Source C: from Ronald McNair Scott, *Robert the Bruce, King of Scots* (1993).

> Robert Bruce had no wish to prolong the war. He saw his victory, above all, as an opportunity for reconciliation and peace. Soon after Bannockburn many Scottish barons and knights who had served under the two Edwards offered to him their allegiance and were received into his peace. In November 1314 Bruce with increased confidence, convened a Parliament at Cambuskenneth. The Parliament adjudged that all Scottish landowners who had failed to offer allegiance by that date should be disinherited. His sole aim was that those who wished to regain their Scottish lands must do homage to him alone. They could no longer be feudatories in two countries and serve two kings. They must choose their nationality once and for all.

Source D: from Richard Oram, *The Kings and Queens of Scotland* (2006).

> Robert was quick to capitalise on Bannockburn. Not only was he able to recover his queen and daughter from captivity in exchange for English prisoners, but this also gave him extensive resources with which to reward his supporters and subjects in order to secure their loyalty. A Parliament at Cambuskenneth was possible for Bruce due to favourable circumstances. At the Parliament in November he overcame his remaining Scottish opponents and took their lands in Scotland. Robert also intensified his attacks on northern England both in search for cash and to force Edward II to recognise Bruce's kingship of a free Scotland. By 1323 Bruce attempted to secure peace for war-weary Scotland, even negotiating a peace. Yet faced with the English King's refusal to give up Scotland, Robert had to settle for a long uneasy truce in 1323.

Attempt all of the following questions.

1. Explain why the death of Alexander III led to the succession problem 1286–1292. **8**

2. Evaluate the usefulness of **Source A** as evidence of the subjugation of Scotland by Edward I. **8**

    In reaching a conclusion you should refer to:
    - the origin and possible purpose of the source
    - the content of the source
    - recalled knowledge

3. How fully does **Source B** explain the reasons for the growth of William Wallace and Scottish resistance? **10**

    Use the source and recalled knowledge.

4. How much do **Sources C and D** reveal about differing interpretations about the ambitions and ultimate success of Robert Bruce. **10**

    Use the sources and recallled knowledge.

PAPER 2 – HISTORY, SCOTTISH HISTORY

Part D: Migration and Empire, 1830–1939

PAPER 2 – SCOTTISH – 36 marks

Part D: Migration and Empire, 1830–1939

Study the sources below and attempt the questions which follow.

Source A: from Angus Nicholson, Canada's Special Immigration Agent in the Highlands of Scotland, 1875.

> All the competing Emigration Agencies formerly reported on, are still at work as actively as ever. The New Zealand and Australian authorities are particularly alert, the streets of every town and village displaying their bills and posters offering opportunities for emigrants to gain employment and wealth. Not only so, but nearly all newspapers' advertisements are doing their full share to help. It has to be noted that a considerable number of potential recruits have been diverted from Canada to New Zealand as a result of the latter's offer of free passages. It is extremely difficult for us to attract emigrants when these territories are offering free passages while we expect the emigrants to pay their own fares to Canada. Yet land and a new life can easily be found in Canada and should not be ignored by Scottish emigrants.

Source B: from a letter by an Italian immigrant to Glasgow in 1921.

> School was a nightmare for me but my oldest brother Giacomo, a name that was quickly shortened to Jack, revelled in school life. He was a quick learner and always able to take care of himself. A few times I found myself surrounded by classmates chanting at me because I was a foreigner. Jack scattered them and they stopped bothering me completely. Our family moved house a few times in an effort to improve our life. Domenico took a job in the largely Italian trade of terrazzo tile workers and most of my brothers followed him into the trade. Meanwhile my grasp of the Glasgow dialect improved. Within a couple of years I lost all trace of my mother tongue and developed a strong, guttural Glasgow accent. In no time at all I was a complete Glaswegian.

Source C: from a report by the Immigration Agent for Victoria, Australia, 1853.

> I do not consider that the inhabitants of the islands of Scotland are well suited to the wants and needs of Australia. Their total ignorance of the English language has made it difficult for them to mix with many English people already here. Their laziness and extremely filthy habits have made it difficult for them to prosper. It would be better if such immigration was restricted at least, since these wretches have little of worth to offer this society. They have made no effective contribution to the many business opportunities to be found in Australia. Indeed, it cannot be argued other than that their arrival is having a most unwelcome and detrimental effect on the inhabitants of this colony, making little or no contribution to the economic life in this colony.

Source D: from Ian Donnachie, *Success in the "Lucky" Country* (1988).

> There were many examples of Scottish achievement in Australia. Scots were early and successful pioneers in sheep farming and the wool trade, centred in places such as Melbourne and Adelaide. Scots also invested heavily in mining, at first in coal and later in copper, silver and gold. The Gold Rush of the 1850s brought to Australia a considerable number of Scottish miners, many of whom stayed after the initial gold fever died down and prospered. Shipping and trade were other areas of enterprise in which Scots excelled. Two later shipping firms were both fiercely Scottish, McIllwraith McEachan and Burns Philp. Their profits were built on the Queensland boom of the 1880s in which Scots played a large part in creating the profitable business. It should be noted that Scots made a sustained financial contribution to life in Australia.

Attempt all of the following questions.

1. Evaluate the usefulness of **Source A** as evidence of the reasons why Scots migrated. **8**

   In reaching a conclusion you should refer to:
   - *the origin and possible purpose of the source*
   - *the content of the source*
   - *recalled knowledge*

2. How fully does **Source B** describe the experience of immigrants in Scotland? **10**

   Use the source and recalled knowledge.

3. How much do **Sources C and D** reveal about differing interpretations on the contribution of Scots to the economic development of the Empire? **10**

   Use the sources and recallled knowledge.

4. Explain the effects of migration and Empire on Scotland before 1939. **8**

PAPER 2 – HISTORY, SCOTTISH HISTORY

Part E: The Impact of the Great War, 1914–1928

PAPER 2 – SCOTTISH – 36 marks

Part E: The Impact of the Great War, 1914–1928

Study the sources below and attempt the questions which follow.

Source A: from a diary entry from Private Moir of the Queen's Own Cameron Highlanders: Loos, 29th September 1915.

> We were relieved on Sunday, after holding our own against the Germans' repeated counter attacks, but we were not out an hour when the lot that came in lost one of the trenches that we had taken. On Monday we had another charge and got the trench back before coming out of the trenches yesterday with about 70 or 80 of us surviving, out of the 1100 originals, "the pride of Scotland".
>
> Sir John French came along just as we were leaving our old billets and gave us a few words of praise. He told us he was proud to meet us, and congratulated us on our fine work. He told us we had done what Camerons liked to do, and what they always did; he never knew the Camerons to fail in anything they had ever put their hands to.

Source B: from Clive H. Lee, *The Scottish Economy and the First World War* (1999).

> Many of the changes caused by the war were temporary such as the readjustment of agricultural production to improve self-sufficiency and the boom in the jute industry. When normal trade was resumed in the 1920s, the massively weakened position of British manufacturers in export markets became apparent. As a consequence of the war, Scottish and British industry lost its international competitiveness. The war certainly shifted the balance of international trade against Scottish shipbuilders by increasing world-wide capacity which hit the industry after the war. Also, Scottish textile manufacturers were never able to regain the Asian markets, especially India, as the war allowed competitors to move in. But the war also demonstrated the fragility of the Scottish heavy industry base and the growing need for imported raw materials.

Source C: from W. Hamish Fraser, *Scottish Popular Politics From Radicalism to Labour* (2000).

> The war years also showed that support for Scottish Home Rule had not really declined. The policy of the Scottish Trade Union Congress was to call on the Parliamentary Labour Party to support "the enactment of a Scottish Home Rule Bill". The same spirit of nationalism forced Arthur Henderson and the Labour leadership in London, much against their better judgement, to allow a separate Scottish Council of Labour with a considerable amount of self-government. At the same time, the war undermined even further the organisation of Scottish Liberalism, but also much of its moral authority. The more radical elements were disenchanted by Lloyd George's political tactics and his attitude towards strikers. Liberalism was thrown into disarray while the ILP was able to emerge as the natural successor to advanced liberal radicalism.

Source D: from T. M. Devine, *The Scottish Nation 1700–2007* (2006).

> The emergence of Red Clydeside and the Labour breakthrough was only one part of the change in Scottish politics after the war. The most decisive feature was the complete collapse of Liberalism as an effective electoral force. At the end of 1916 Lloyd George had split the party and by the election of 1918 Liberalism was in disarray. Among the working classes the Labour Party was most likely to benefit from Liberal misfortunes. The Liberal government denounced strikers as unpatriotic and lost support. The ILP supported the workers' grievances over prices and rents and therefore Labour gained new support after WWI. The reward came in 1924 when Labour became the biggest party in Scotland, sending 29 MPs to parliament.

Attempt all of the following questions.

1. Evaluate the usefulness of **Source A** as evidence of the involvement of Scots on the Western Front. **8**

   In reaching a conclusion you should refer to:
   - *the origin and possible purpose of the source*
   - *the content of the source*
   - *recalled knowledge*

2. Explain the reasons why the First World War had such a big effect on Scottish society and culture. **8**

3. How fully does **Source B** explain the economic difficulties Scotland faced after 1918? **10**

   Use the source and recalled knowledge.

4. How much do sources C and D reveal about differing interpretations of the impact of the war on political development in Scotland. **10**

   Use the sources and recalled knowledge.